Palgrave Studies in Oral History

Series Editors
David P. Cline
SDSU Center for Public and Oral History
San Diego State University
San Diego, CA, USA

Natalie Fousekis
California State University
Fullerton, USA

'A premier publisher of oral history.' - CHOICE

The world's leading English-language oral history book series, *Palgrave Studies in Oral History* brings together engaging work from scholars, activists, and other practitioners. Books in the series are aimed at a broad community of readers; they employ edited oral history interviews to explore a wide variety of topics and themes in all areas of history, placing first-person accounts in broad historical context and engaging issues of historical memory and narrative construction. Fresh approaches to the use and analysis of oral history, as well as to the organization of text, are a particular strength of the series, as are projects that use oral accounts to illuminate human rights issues. Submissions are welcomed for projects from any geographical region, as well as cross-cultural and comparative work.

More information about this series at
http://link.springer.com/series/14606

Jesse Adams Stein

Industrial Craft in Australia

Oral Histories of Creativity and Survival

Jesse Adams Stein
University of Technology Sydney
Sydney, NSW, Australia

ISSN 2731-5673 ISSN 2731-5681 (electronic)
Palgrave Studies in Oral History
ISBN 978-3-030-87242-7 ISBN 978-3-030-87243-4 (eBook)
https://doi.org/10.1007/978-3-030-87243-4

© The Editor(s) (if applicable) and The Author(s), under exclusive licence to Springer Nature Switzerland AG 2021
This work is subject to copyright. All rights are solely and exclusively licensed by the Publisher, whether the whole or part of the material is concerned, specifically the rights of translation, reprinting, reuse of illustrations, recitation, broadcasting, reproduction on microfilms or in any other physical way, and transmission or information storage and retrieval, electronic adaptation, computer software, or by similar or dissimilar methodology now known or hereafter developed.
The use of general descriptive names, registered names, trademarks, service marks, etc. in this publication does not imply, even in the absence of a specific statement, that such names are exempt from the relevant protective laws and regulations and therefore free for general use.
The publisher, the authors and the editors are safe to assume that the advice and information in this book are believed to be true and accurate at the date of publication. Neither the publisher nor the authors or the editors give a warranty, expressed or implied, with respect to the material contained herein or for any errors or omissions that may have been made. The publisher remains neutral with regard to jurisdictional claims in published maps and institutional affiliations.

Cover image: Stephen Smith, Discarded patterns, 2019. Courtesy of Stephen Smith, reproduced with permission

This Palgrave Macmillan imprint is published by the registered company Springer Nature Switzerland AG.
The registered company address is: Gewerbestrasse 11, 6330 Cham, Switzerland

Acknowledgements

This book would not exist without the willingness of the industrial crafts-people who shared their stories with me. I owe special gratitude to the engineering patternmakers, industrial modelmakers and woodworkers (and their families), who shared their time and memories with me, through both formal interviews and informal communications along the way. Thank you to Alan Cooke, Anthony Freemantle, Serge Haidutschyk, Anthony Hood, Paul Kay, John Looker, Stuart McCorkelle, Scott Murrells, Bruce Phipps, Peter Phipps, Bryan Poynton, Jon-Michael Rubinich, Debra Schuckar, Stephen Smith, Deborah Tyrrell, Greg Tyrrell, Joe Vecchio, Jim Walker, Peter Watts, Peter White, Tim Wighton, Eric Wilenski and Peter Williams.

Within the University of Technology Sydney (UTS), a significant group of researchers supported me through what ended up being a six-year project. Warm thanks extend to Distinguished Professor Peter McNeil, Associate Professor Kate Sweetapple, Associate Professor Jacqueline Lorber-Kasunic, Associate Professor Alexandra Crosby and Professor Cameron Tonkinwise from the UTS School of Design. Thank you also to the UTS Business School's Associate Professor Antoine Hermens, Dr Marco Berti and Dr Ace Volkmann Simpson (now at Brunel University). The Australian Centre for Public History at UTS has been an incredibly supportive environment in which to share research in progress, with special thanks to Associate Professor Tamson Pietsch, Emeritus Professor Paula Hamilton and Associate Professor Anna Clark. In 2019, Pietsch and the marvellous audio producer Olivia Rosenman transformed my research into a sharp and engaging *History Lab* podcast about patternmakers. The

vi ACKNOWLEDGEMENTS

podcast is called *Invisible Hands* (episode 2, season 2 of *History Lab*) and can be accessed here: https://historylab.net/s2ep2-invisible-hands/.

I received assistance and encouragement from a number of international experts in oral history, deindustrialisation studies, design history and modern craft studies, most notably: Glenn Adamson, Professor Steven High, Professor Tim Strangleman, Marilyn Zapf, Professor Alistair Thomson, Dr Stephen Knott, Professor Kjetil Fallan, Professor Ezra Shales and Professor Kim Christian Priemel. Warm thanks also extend to Marni Williams, Alice Grundy, Dr Chantel Carr, Dr Tracey Cernak Chee-Quee, Damian Butler, Dr Hannah Forsyth, Dr Cathy Lockhart, Dr Frances Flanagan, Dr Susan Stewart, Enya Moore, Associate Professor Clare Monagle, Dr Rebecca Sheehan, Dr Anisa Puri and Dr Livia Lazzaro Rezende. I also acknowledge the anonymous reviewers, whose insights were precise and highly relevant.

Editorial and transcript assistance was provided by Liz Brownlee and Hazel Baker, with research assistance from Dr Evelyn Kwok, Dr Alyssa Critchley and Dr Liam Kane. Acknowledgement extends to Paul Murrin from the Australian Bureau of Statistics and Brett Ambrosio from GO TAFE Victoria. Thank you also to the Palgrave Macmillan/Springer editorial team, including Tikoji Rao Mega Rao, Meagan Simpson, Anisha Rajavikraman and Megan Laddusaw, among others.

After the sad passing of artisanal woodworker and patternmaker Bryan Poynton in 2020, it was humbling to have had a role in facilitating the acquisition of Poynton's toolbox, hand tools and bespoke workbench to the collection of Museums Victoria. For that I thank Museums Victoria curator Matilda Vaughan, as well as Museum of Applied Arts & Sciences curators Matthew Connell and Angelique Hutchison. I also extend thanks to Poynton's family, particularly Edie, Barrie and Soleil Poynton, as well as Alastair Boell and Jacqueline Boell from the Melbourne Guild of Fine Woodworking, and to Linda Nathan from the *Australian Wood Review*.

The National Library of Australia (NLA) has remained a significant and ongoing part of my oral history work. Gratitude extends to (former NLA) Margy Burn and Shelly Grant and to the NLA's current oral history team, including but not limited to Dr Shirleene Robinson, Mark Piva and Dave Blanken.

On a personal note, this book has been enriched and improved significantly by its most constructive unofficial reviewer, Eugene Schofield-Georgeson. And all this would not have been possible without the endless love, support, dinners and time spent childcaring provided by Eugene, as well as Barbara Adams, Paul Stein, Toni Schofield, Arthur Georgeson and Madeleine Spielman. Together, we make an incredible village for Archie and Renzo.

Funding Acknowledgement
This research was made possible through funding from

- National Library of Australia, Canberra
- University of Technology Sydney's Chancellor's Postdoctoral Research Fellowship
- University of Technology Sydney's Faculty of Design, Architecture & Building

Acknowledgement of Country
This book was written on the ancestral country of the Gadigal People of the Eora nation. I pay my respects to Elders, past and present, acknowledging them as the traditional custodians of knowledge for this land. Their ancestors' skilled hands held knowledge about Australian timbers long before engineering patternmakers' hands ever did.

Praise for *Industrial Craft in Australia*

"Stein's *Industrial Craft in Australia* is an incredibly important and timely book. In listening to the voices of a vital group of skilled workers she highlights how necessary their skills are for any country that wants to make things and how fragile the manufacturing base is. This is a book that should be required reading for any politician serious about the future of manufacturing industry and a national skills base."

—Tim Strangleman, *University of Kent, UK*

"Yes, there are still toolmakers. So writes Stein in her important new book—the first to provide a finely detailed account of the experiences and methods of industrial artisans. Drawing on extensive interviews, and benefitting from Stein's deep technical understanding and writerly skill, this is a major addition to craft studies, and will serve as a model for scholars in other geographies to follow."

—Glenn Adamson, author of *The Invention of Craft* (2013) and *Craft: An American History* (2021)

"This fascinating book opens our eyes to a world of highly skilled industrial work, grounded in traditional knowledge and creativity, that extends into the 'postindustrial' world of digital fabrication, 3D printing, maker-culture, and artistic practice. Deindustrialization is not just about loss. This book represents a remarkable original contribution to the global study of deindustrialization and oral history more generally."

—Steven High, *Concordia University, Canada*

"The global pandemic has reminded us, just in time, that no country can afford to 'offshore' manufacturing and lose the ability to make things. Stein's extraordinary book takes readers inside the 'black box' of contemporary manufacturing. Through sensitive analysis of vivid oral histories, it shows us how highly-skilled crafts men and women, combining old skills and new technologies, are behind the manufactured objects that we all use every moment of our lives."

—Alistair Thomson, *Monash University, Australia*

CONTENTS

1 Introduction: Re-evaluating Industrial Craft Through the Lives of Engineering Patternmakers   1

2 Navigating Class and Populist Politics in Contemporary Oral History Practice   33

3 The Patternmaker's Toolbox: Making Things on the Side in Industrial Craft Apprenticeship   63

4 Industrial Craft as Design Knowledge: Hidden Intermediaries of Design and Production   95

5 'Just Finishing': From Manual Patternmaking to CNC Machine Milling   121

6 Not Fitting the Pattern: Women in Industrial Craft   159

7 Patternmaker-Artists: Creative Pathways for Industrial Craftspeople in the Context of Australian Deindustrialisation   191

xii CONTENTS

8 Conclusion: Industrial Craft and Alternative Futures for Australian Manufacturing 225

Glossary 239

Index 243

About the Author

Jesse Adams Stein is an interdisciplinary design researcher and oral historian. She is a senior lecturer and an ARC DECRA Fellow (Australian Research Council Discovery Early Career Research Award) at the School of Design, University of Technology Sydney (UTS). She is the author of *Hot Metal: Material Culture & Tangible Labour* (2016). She has led a number of oral history projects, including *Makers, Manufacturers and Designers: Connecting Histories* (2021–ongoing), *Reshaping Australian Manufacturing* (2017–2019) and *Precarious Printers* (2011–2014).

LIST OF FIGURES

Fig. 1.1   A dead lever brake bracket pattern in process, by Tim Wighton, c. 2009. (Photograph by Wighton, reproduced with permission)   7

Fig. 1.2   Gear pattern (with resultant casting) by Peter White, Dolman Pattern and Model Makers, South Australia, 2008. (Photograph by White, reproduced with permission)   9

Fig. 1.3   Master pattern for a bearing cover by Peter White, Dolman Pattern and Model Makers, 2006, Jelutong timber, 400 mm diameter, later moulded in Epoxy resin for production. (Photograph by White, reproduced with permission)   10

Fig. 3.1   Bryan Poynton, photograph by the author, 2018   64

Fig. 3.2   Bryan Poynton's first toolbox, c. mid-1950s. Photograph by the author, 2018. Toolbox and hand tools now held with Museums Victoria, Melbourne   65

Fig. 3.3   Stephen Smith's toolbox, 1990s. Photograph courtesy of Stephen Smith   71

Fig. 3.4   Paul Kay and his toolbox, under his workbench. Photograph by the author, 2018   75

Fig. 3.5   Debra Schuckar's toolbox. Photograph by the author, 2018   76

Fig. 3.6   Serge Haidutschyk's handmade tools. Photograph by the author, 2018   81

Fig. 3.7   Tim Wighton's workbench and red metal toolbox after 5S standardisation, foundry patternshop, Victoria. Photograph by Wighton, c. 2007   87

Fig. 4.1   Patternmaking process for a dead lever brake bracket, including layout, pattern, corebox and casting, 2009. Pattern and photographs by Tim Wighton   102

xvi LIST OF FIGURES

Fig. 4.2   E. Preston & Sons brass contraction rule. Photograph by Peter Williams, reproduced with permission   107

Fig. 5.1   Thermwood CNC machine nicknamed 'Woody', with patternmakers, Victorian patternshop, 2017. (Photograph by the author)   126

Fig. 5.2   Scott Murrells. (Photograph by the author, 2017)   132

Fig. 5.3   Haas CNC machining centre, access granted by Deborah and Greg Tyrrell, Kimbeny Pty. Ltd., Sydney. (Photograph by the author, 2018)   144

Fig. 5.4   Paul Kay in his home workshop, W.G. Kay & Co. (Photograph by the author, 2018)   151

Fig. 6.1   Debra Schuckar as an apprentice patternmaker, 1982, State Electricity Commission of Victoria, Melbourne. (Courtesy of Debra Schuckar, reproduced with permission)   168

Fig. 6.2   Debra Schuckar as an apprentice in the patternstore, 1982, State Electricity Commission of Victoria, Melbourne. (Courtesy of Debra Schuckar, reproduced with permission)   169

Fig. 6.3   Debra Schuckar's patternmaking class, George Thompson School of Foundry Technology, RMIT, Melbourne, c. early 1980s. (Courtesy of Debra Schuckar, reproduced with permission)   171

Fig. 7.1   Glucose lollies such as Swedish Fish, Gummi Bears and Gummi Worms. (Courtesy of ChildofMidnight, Creative Commons licence)   196

Fig. 7.2   Paul Kay's jube patterns for food manufacturing, 2018. (Photograph by the author)   197

Fig. 7.3   Paul Kay, *Contemplation of an Uncertain Future*, 2017, Queensland White Beech, 37.5 cm × 37.5 cm × 5 cm. (Courtesy of the artist)   199

Fig. 7.4   Serge Haidutschyk. (Photograph by the author, 2018)   201

Fig. 7.5   Serge Haidutschyk, Makita 8" Circular Saw, 1992–1994, 13 Australian recycled timbers. (Courtesy of Haidutschyk, reproduced with permission)   203

Fig. 7.6   Bryan Poynton, *Self-portrait with Pigeon Hole*, 2001, Blackwood, Myrtle, Huon Pine, Brass and Copper, created for 'Box Forms', an exhibition curated by the Victorian Woodworkers' Association. (Courtesy of the Poynton family, reproduced with permission)   208

Fig. 7.7   Peter Watts, *Creek Sculpture*, 2003, Castlemaine Steiner School, ferro cement, 12 m (length). (Courtesy of the artist)   215

Fig. 7.8   Installation view of *Assembled: The Art of Robert Klippel*, TarraWarra Museum of Art, 2019–2020. (Courtesy of the Robert Klippel Estate, represented by Annette Larkin Fine Art, Sydney, and Galerie Gmurzynska, Zurich. Copyright Agency 2019. Photo: Andrew Curtis)   216

CHAPTER 1

Introduction: Re-evaluating Industrial Craft Through the Lives of Engineering Patternmakers

INDUSTRIAL CRAFT IS DEAD, LONG LIVE INDUSTRIAL CRAFT

The craftsman, as is normally understood, has far from disappeared. He has found a number of very important niches within the structure of manufacturing industry. We do not get his products directly, but nevertheless we do get his products.[1]
—Reyner Banham, 1973 lecture at the Victoria and Albert Museum, London

It's a bit of a black art. An integral part of the manufacturing process—but no one knows it's there. They think that the design is made, and then all of a sudden out comes a part. And you just can't explain it. It's impossible to explain what I did for a living.[2]
—Scott Murrells, former engineering patternmaker

In the refurbished industrial warehouses of inner-city Sydney and Melbourne, fashionable cafes and venues feature crumbling paint and remnant cast-iron machinery, and have names such as Blacksmiths, Brickfields, Tramsheds and Industry Beans. The nostalgic aestheticisation of industrial heritage is widespread in gentrified urban centres across Australia, North America and Europe. Manifest in such trends is an indifference to working-class history: the workers themselves are usually absent from these palatable traces of industrial production.[3] So what has

© The Author(s), under exclusive license to Springer Nature Switzerland AG 2021
J. A. Stein, *Industrial Craft in Australia*, Palgrave Studies in Oral History, https://doi.org/10.1007/978-3-030-87243-4_1

1

2   J. A. STEIN

happened to that specialist of twentieth-century manufacturing, the industrial craftsperson? *Industrial craft*, in the manner I use it in this book, is the confluence of refined manual skill and specialist production knowledge in manufacturing processes. It includes, but is not limited to, manual processes undertaken in the pre-production stage of manufacturing, and in the hand-finishing stages, after machine production.

Today in the Global North, industrial craftspeople are almost invisible. If we come across them at all, they tend to be consigned to museum demonstrations, 'Lost Trades' fairs, obscure hobby societies or 'Men's Sheds'. In such contexts, industrial craftspeople are understood as entertaining anachronisms, as 'living heritage'. We love to watch them work and marvel at their skill. It's thrilling, it feels like time travel. But the general consensus is that industrial craft is a thing of the past and that this is a result of inexorable industrial decline.

The conventional explanation for deindustrialisation is that all this loss—of jobs, of workplace cultures and of trade knowledge—has been inevitable. The widely accepted narrative is that 'developed' capitalist economies have merely followed the logic of the globalised market.[4] From this view, skilled tradespeople in manufacturing are nostalgically framed as noble but tragic figures, as heroic crafts*men* that belong to a former golden age of industry in the Global North. Less charitably, they might be disparaged as dinosaurs, clinging to their craft tradition in the face of seemingly inescapable 'disruption'. Most of their prospects for secure employment in their original trade appear to have disappeared. Business, governments and society at large have advised them to 'move on', to retrain for a new service economy and to 'keep up' with technology (or to retire).

Concurrently, manufacturing today—both as an imagined phenomenon and as a set of networked practices—is opaque. Mass-production is now bound up with algorithmically driven global supply chains, so complex that even manufacturers themselves cannot always trace their parts and materials.[5] Australians, for example, readily accept that most mass-production is now conducted in 'cheaper' locations somewhere else, in exploitative environments we can only hazily imagine. To those in affluent capitalist economies, it is as if products just arrive, fully formed and packaged, and if we think about their manufacture at all, we might assume they have spun off a highly automated production line. From this worldview, it tends to be assumed that the industrial craftsperson's work has been eliminated. We might imagine that skilled hands have been replaced by high-precision robotic arms and sophisticated software. Or, we might guiltily consider the conditions of the low-paid workers that may well have been involved in that product's assembly, and make a flimsy pledge to consume as ethically as we can.

Like all clichés, the picture above has elements of truth, but it simplifies and distorts. It is undeniable that manufacturing employment in the Global North has contracted enormously over the past four decades, largely as a result of economic policies leading to deindustrialisation, with devastating consequences that have been well documented.[6] But deindustrialisation is not a finished process. Remnants of industrial craft linger with us and within those remnants may be the potential for more sustainable and equitable futures of work and production.

*   *   *

This book is a reassertion of the significance of industrial craft, both in its historical and in its contemporary forms. Here I explore how industrial craft is about more than the rudimentary production of everyday objects; it is also about people and the material knowledge and skills they carry. Industrial craft is investigated here through a detailed engagement with an intriguing and little-known trade: *engineering patternmaking*. (The reader need not be concerned if this trade is unfamiliar; the following section will outline the essential details.) Rather than being a book strictly about pattern*making*, this book is about pattern*makers*: their training, the role of class and gender as a structuring force in their working lives, their creative practices and their evolving relationship to technology and the labour market.

A great deal has been said about deindustrialisation and its impacts, in mainstream culture, in the media and in academic writing. A more specific understanding of industrial craft, however, is essentially missing from public recognition, as well as being largely absent from political discussions about work, production and skills. In addressing industrial craft, craft theorist Glenn Adamson observed that

> craft operations were crucial for the industrial revolution in ways historians often miss. ... Patterns and prototypes, which could be replicated through casting or other processes, are an understudied but vital instance of industrial craft.

He later added,

4 J. A. STEIN

> In these areas of industrial craft—finishing, prototyping and tooling—there is a thorough interdependence of hand and automated processes. ... Among the greatest failings of modern craft historians has been their neglect of this vast terrain of second-order workmanship.[7]

In part, this book is a response to Adamson's call. It is my hope that *Industrial Craft in Australia* will change the way you see the manufactured world around you and will open eyes to all those invisible hands involved in industrial production.

A core concept in this book is that industrial craft *is* historical, but it is also continuous and evolving, and these tensions are ever-present in craft practices, workplaces and human lives. As noted by historian and deindustrialisation scholar Steven High, "industrial labour is still part of our present".[8] This book presents an alternative to the nostalgic construct of the tragic, lost 'craftsman': through a nuanced lens that understands industrial craftspeople as dynamic, creative, diverse and extremely valuable to a sustainable, functional society. Through the use of detailed human stories— as relayed through oral history—I provide an historically informed interpretation of how digital fabrication technologies and globalisation may modify or transform, but should not completely destroy, industrial craft. What I relay are experiences growing up, of skill accrual, of adaptability and precarious employment, of childcare challenges, of retraining and, particularly, of creative practice in unexpected places. These subjects are developed alongside reflexive methodological insights into the tensions that implicate both class and gender in the oral history process.

To clarify, industrial craft in the Australian context is associated with those who have completed a formal apprenticeship in a specific industrial trade. Examples of industrial trades include fitting and turning, toolmaking, boilermaking and engineering patternmaking. Elsewhere in the world, industrial craft skills may be recognised through other measures, formal or informal. When I speak of a 'tradesperson' here, I am referring to someone who has completed a trade apprenticeship, someone who defines themselves by their trade: "I'm a toolmaker", for example. (Yes, there are still toolmakers.) Even for those who leave their trade and retrain in other industries, they carry the legacy of their apprenticeship, and all that followed, with them. Patternmakers are, in a sense, always patternmakers. Their background in industrial craft continues to inform how they live, work, educate and create, well beyond the factory walls.[9]

This work picks up where my previous book left off. *Hot Metal* focused on the dramatic labour and technology transitions experienced in the printing industry in the second-half of the twentieth century. In its concluding sentence I noted that

> [t]he design and labour histories of the future will have to account for the increasingly ephemeral and slippery concepts associated with digital labour, digital design and the material culture of post-industrial work.[10]

Industrial Craft in Australia takes the next steps in this broader project of analysing how digitisation has impacted labour and skill in design and production. In so doing, it moves us further along in time, examining the social and cultural impacts of late twentieth-century and early twenty-first-century technologies, such as computer numerically controlled (CNC) milling machines, additive manufacturing (3D Printing) and CAD/CAM software (Computer Aided Design/Computer Aided Manufacturing). While topics related to technological unemployment appear regularly in the media, as I noted above, they are often framed deterministically in terms of innovation and the unavoidability of technological change. Throughout this book I continue to question that assumption, putting forward a claim for the possibility of a generative linkage between older and newer ways of working.

Digital fabrication technologies are undeniably ever-present and disruptive, but they are not all-consuming. There are *still* industrial craftspeople at work, using their hands, adapting tools and technologies, applying their specialist manufacturing knowledge. In this text I move beyond a straightforward story of labour's replacement by technology, instead revealing the creative, artistic and critical capacities of industrial craftspeople. To be sure, industrial craft is fragile. But it survives, it is evolving technologically and materially, and it remains essential for quality manufacturing. In some industries, for example the Australian foundry sector, skilled industrial craftspeople are in high demand and in short supply.[11] (This is further discussed in Chap. 8.)

Australia is a particularly useful example for considering the fate of the industrial craftsperson, in part because of the continuation of the traditional apprenticeship system, albeit now in a more impoverished, underfunded form has previously been the case. Apprenticeship allows for strong continuities of skill and practice, across generations. The other reason Australia is intriguing is that this country often suffers from something of

6   J. A. STEIN

a 'time-lag' in technological uptake, due in part to the relatively small size of its industries and markets. This means, for example, that today it is still possible to find patternmakers in Australia who are still making wooden patterns manually, not by CNC machine, in limited cases. Skilled manual practices continue, unacknowledged, on the fringes. I expand further on the specificities of Australian deindustrialisation later in this Introduction.

The following section outlines and explains engineering patternmaking as a practice and then contextualises this trade specifically in relation to Australia's history of deindustrialisation. From there, I situate this book's engagement with industrial craft in relation to relevant academic disciplines such as design history, modern craft studies and oral histories of deindustrialisation. The Introduction also provides stark statistical data indicating just how small the engineering patternmaking trade has become, in terms of sheer numbers. The final part of this Introduction outlines the book's chapter structure: from handmade toolboxes to CNC machines, and beyond.

ENGINEERING PATTERNMAKING: AN INTRODUCTION

At the core of that was patternmaking, where an idea grew legs, *literally* grew legs. An idea from, y'know, an engineer's or a designer's mind, made it onto paper in two dimensions, and then, through the skill of the patternmaker, it gained a third dimension and became real. And that *really* had me, I mean I *wanted* to be a part of that.[12]
—Peter Williams, former engineering patternmaker

Speaking to patternmakers enables us to step inside the 'black box' of industrial manufacturing, to uncover the industrial craft labour involved in producing the one-off originals required for mass-production. From the tiny shape of a confectionery jube, to a railway brake bracket, to a large cast-steel 'bucket' on the end of an excavator—quotidian objects such as these all required a three-dimensional original, a *pattern*, before the final production process (Fig. 1.1). Patterns are necessary to make moulds and tooling for a variety of plastic and metal production processes, for example, metal casting and plastic injection moulding. While patterns themselves are generally discarded when no longer required, the legacy of this industrial craft can still be gleaned from patternmakers' stories, as relayed through oral history.

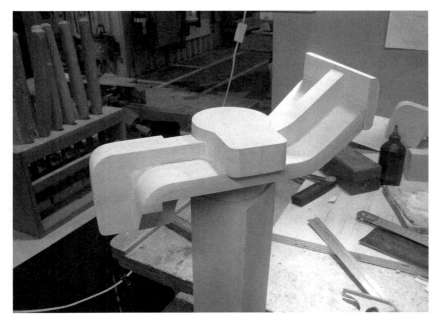

Fig. 1.1 A dead lever brake bracket pattern in process, by Tim Wighton, c. 2009. (Photograph by Wighton, reproduced with permission)

Metal casting—the pouring of molten metal into a mould to produce a form—has been practiced since 3200 BCE in Mesopotamia, and iron casting has been traced to around 700 BCE in China. The specific trade of engineering patternmaking, however, is a specifically modern phenomenon. During the industrial revolution the patternmaker emerged as a distinct role in response to the growth of metal foundries, with their demarcation focused on the production of the pattern (and affiliated parts), after which the pattern was handed to another tradesperson, a moulder, to continue the metal casting process. Patternmakers therefore operate in the pre-production phase of the manufacturing supply chain, using engineering or design drawings to construct a three-dimensional form (a pattern) with great precision, so that it can effectively produce a mould. Patternmakers are not designers, since in their industrial roles they do not generate the original idea for the form to be manufactured. But nor are they production-line workers: their hands do not touch the finished product, and their work is rarely repetitive. While the trade began in metal casting, throughout the twentieth century patternmakers have also worked in the service of the plastics industry, alongside toolmakers and industrial modelmakers.

A simple explanation of the patternmaking process is as follows: patternmakers transform a designer's or an engineer's two-dimensional plans into a positive three-dimensional form (pattern). This pattern is generally used to make a negative mould. The mould is filled with molten metal, or melted plastic, to produce a positive form. Sometimes this positive form is the final product (in the case of metal casting in sand). In other cases patterns produce tooling for processes such as plastic injection moulding or vacuum moulding, among other techniques. Patternmakers also generate the associated cores, coreboxes and plates that encase the pattern, enabling the mould to work effectively. A particularly technical part of their work is planning how these elements will function together. Patternmakers also plan for how the pattern will be removed without damaging the mould (through features such as a pattern's taper), and accounting for how the metal will shrink as it cools. An example of a pattern and pattern collaterals, alongside its cast final product, can be seen in Fig. 1.2. (Chapter 5 describes this process in more detail.)

Alongside toolmakers and industrial modelmakers, patternmakers once handmade the 'original' forms for everything that was cast or moulded: from large earth-moving equipment, to Tupperware containers, to die-cast toy cars, to a car's rear-vision mirror. Having said this, it must be acknowledged that recent technological changes in CAD/CAM, CNC and globalised supply chains have transformed the way in which many patterns are brought into being. For a great deal of what is produced today (particularly plastics), creators of positive one-offs for production in high-intensity manufacturing economies are not necessarily called 'patternmakers' and 'toolmakers', any more. This designation is dependent upon location-specific occupational structures. In the case of Australia, at the time of writing (2021) a small number of engineering patternmakers are still working as patternmakers, for foundries, in standalone patternshops or in niche manufacturing areas.

Traditionally, patterns were made out of timber, and patternmakers were renowned for the precision of their woodworking capacities: they could produce forms with extreme degrees of dimensional accuracy (Fig. 1.3). The significance of timber craftsmanship should not be underplayed here. More than carpenters or cabinetmakers, craft mastery in

1 INTRODUCTION: RE-EVALUATING INDUSTRIAL CRAFT… 9

Fig. 1.2 Gear pattern (with resultant casting) by Peter White, Dolman Pattern and Model Makers, South Australia, 2008. (Photograph by White, reproduced with permission)

wood was traditionally what really *made* a patternmaker. Patternmakers made patterns out of dimensionally stable timbers such as Sugar Pine, King Billy Pine, Mahogany or Jelutong. In foundries, large-scale patterns were used to cast mining and agricultural equipment, as well as metal parts for railways, shipping and other industrial machinery. Beyond this, patterns could be made for anything that required casting: iron 'lace' fencing, belt buckles, cast metal hand tools, iron signage, cast metal cemetery plaques, and so on. Patternmakers—being the intermediaries between the planned thing and the final form in metal—had to develop expertise in everything from technical drawing to metallurgy, as well as fine woodwork, as described by former patternmaker Serge Haidutschyk:

> Learning the trade was just magnificent. … I did trade theory and trade practice in patternmaking, but also the emphasis on moulding and how

Fig. 1.3 Master pattern for a bearing cover by Peter White, Dolman Pattern and Model Makers, 2006, Jelutong timber, 400 mm diameter, later moulded in Epoxy resin for production. (Photograph by White, reproduced with permission)

molten metal works, and metallurgy, was just as important. So, to be quite honest, I sort of feel like I've done two trades … working with wood and being skillful at creating things in wood, and also working as a moulder.[13]

From the nineteenth century onwards, Australian patternmakers tended to work within metal foundries or in discrete small businesses known as 'patternshops'. With the growth of plastics manufacturing in the twentieth century, patternmakers also adapted to embrace more precise, smaller forms of patternmaking, in the service of toolmaking for plastics production. Prior to the decline of car manufacturing in Australia, patternmakers also had a strong employment base in that sector, where they tended to work in industrial modelmaking and clay modelling for car design.

At first glance, the connection between plastics production and highly refined woodwork might seem obscure, but throughout much of the

1 INTRODUCTION: RE-EVALUATING INDUSTRIAL CRAFT... 11

twentieth century, dimensionally stable timbers such as Huon Pine were used a great deal in plastics pre-production and seen as ideal materials for making intricate industrial models. Former patternmaker and artisanal woodworker Bryan Poynton reflected,

> The range of different articles we made was amazing. Sometimes we'd be making a model of a Donald Duck, or a catcher off the side of a motor mower, or a cosmetic bottle, or a drink bottle. It all had to be terribly accurate. You think, oh, it's just a drink bottle, but it has to hold a certain capacity, and be designed in a certain way to do that. I know one time I had to make, out of Huon Pine, a very fine cup and saucer which was a model to be approved of for Ansett Airways.[14]

(This, too, had its price, however, and Tasmania's extraordinary Huon Pine species has borne the brunt of an unsustainable nineteenth- and twentieth-century forestry industry.)

In the latter half of the twentieth century, patternmakers expanded their materials repertoire, working with Epoxy resins, silicone, polyester filler (known in Australia as 'bog filler'), high-density polyurethane board (such as Ureol), fibreglass, polystyrene and aluminium, among other materials. In this sense, patternmakers were the initial beneficiaries of technological change in the twentieth century, as booming plastics production led to further demand for their services. This also resulted in the emergence of specialisations within the patternmaking trade, with some patternmakers, for example, collaborating with toolmakers, using a pantographic machine to reproduce patterns in metal. Other patternmakers focused on resin patterns and mouldings for food manufacturing, or patterns for vacuum formed plastics. In the twentieth-century Australian context, another major employer for patternmakers was large publicly owned industrial organisations, such as for state-run railways, electricity generation and shipyards. These organisations sometimes had their own foundries, so as to produce parts required locally, on their own terms. Wherever there are foundries, patternmakers are needed—if not on-site at the foundry, then in a local patternshop.

Fast-paced commercial 'jobbing shops' also existed: this is where patternmakers were exposed to a wide range of manufacturing industries, taking on whatever work was thrown their way. As described by currently practicing patternmaker, Stuart McCorkelle, jobbing shop patternmakers highly value the diversity of their tasks at work:

As a patternmaker everything in life relates to the job, you can't go to the supermarket without being fascinated by the way products are packaged and you spend more time looking at the cast iron gates at a botanical garden than you do looking at the flowers. Patternmaking isn't a job, it's a way of life. ... I was extremely fortunate to have been trained in a fantastic jobbing patternshop that saw me learn a wide range of traditional skills and be able to produce tooling for some incredibly large and accurate castings. As I've spent my career in various jobbing shops this has meant I have made tooling for castings up to 60 tonne right down to carving intricate models for soap moulds. Every day brings another challenge, which is why patternmaking is such a fantastic job.[15]

McCorkelle's quote points to the hidden ubiquity of patterns in everyday objects.

Patternmakers have always felt somewhat under-appreciated or unrecognised, even historically. In 1904, an unnamed British patternmaker complained in *The Socialist* that it is "seldom that we hear very much about" patternmakers, despite the fact that they are

necessary for the production of ordinary lamp posts, piano frames, fire grates, any kind of brackets, all sorts of machinery, locomotive, turbine and marine engines, or any other article which must be moulded and cast in brass, iron, steel or other metal.[16]

The lesser-known status of patternmaking can be partly explained by the very nature of industrial moulding and casting processes: patternmaking occurs after the design and prototyping stages, but before the final product comes into fruition. In this sense, patternmakers are intermediaries, working in the shadows of design and engineering. While their labour is crucial for the actualisation of objects requiring moulding and/or casting, as noted above, patternmakers' hands tend not to touch the final produced object. This disconnection from the 'real thing' is one of the reasons—according to the patternmaker quoted above—that patternmakers were regularly underpaid, undervalued and misunderstood.[6]

Patternmakers and Australian Deindustrialisation

From the late twentieth century onwards, Australian patternmakers faced dual, interrelated threats: politically driven economic restructuring and technological change (this applies both in Australia and in other deindustrialising economies in the Global North). Australian manufacturing suffered the human and industrial consequences of the opening of trade to global markets, particularly from the 1980s onwards, resulting in widespread manufacturing decline. As a consequence of the Australian Labor Government's Accord with Australian Council of Trade Unions (ACTU) between 1983 and 1997, the country retained a centralised wage fixing system, but floated the Australian dollar and gradually dismantled the tariff protection system in favour of 'free trade', among other policy shifts.[17] As a result, Australian manufacturing firms—many of which were typically small to medium size businesses—were thrust into global competition. Their overseas competitors, particularly in Asia, often had access to looser regulatory structures, lower wages, larger markets, geographical advantages and cheaper supplies. What followed was a now familiar pattern of plant closings and 'offshoring', as well as a concurrent devaluation of industrial trades education, through the gradual defunding of Australia's public vocational training body, TAFE (Technical and Further Education). Manufacturing went from being one of the biggest employers in Australia between the 1950s and the 1980s, to making up only 6.9 per cent of Australian employment (in 2021).[18] Patternmakers' reliance on other manufacturing industries made them particularly vulnerable to these shifts.

The diminishing political support for manufacturing in Australia was further entrenched in the first two decades of the twenty-first century, both by Liberal-National and by Labor governments. During this period, local manufacturers faced the challenges of a high Australian dollar, the 2007–2008 Global Financial Crisis, and a political preference for subsidising minerals extraction and fossil-fuel industries over manufacturing (among other sectors). Ultimately, this lack of support for manufacturing led to the aforementioned exit of all large-scale automotive manufacturing from Australia in 2017 (which has had cascading impacts in many other sectors, including patternmaking).[19]

The other major challenge for patternmakers has been technological change. Since the late twentieth century, patternmakers' tasks have been transformed—and arguably alienated and deskilled—by the increasing uptake of digital fabrication technologies. This includes the widespread uptake of CNC milling machines, CAD/CAM software and, to a lesser extent, 3D printing. Digital fabrication technologies such as these have been deployed in ways that reduce patternmakers' labour to machine set-up and the hand-finishing of computer-generated patterns. More recently, 3D sand printing presents an even bigger challenge for patternmakers.

It is now theoretically possible to 3D print complex sand moulds, producing a mould without the need for a pattern; however, the expense of such printing technologies has precluded their widespread use.[20] In countries such as Japan and the United States, the digitisation of pattern production occurred relatively early, from the 1970s onwards. In Australia, the uptake of CNC was not strongly felt by patternmakers until the 1990s, and more particularly the early 2000s. CNC has made the patternmaking trade less attractive as a source of satisfying work, and it contributes to the perception that the trade is unnecessary. But, as we have seen above, patternmaking is about more than just the rudimentary making of the pattern, it is about all of the manufacturing process planning and specialist knowledge that patternmakers possess about a variety of production processes.

For decades now, mainstream political forces (on both sides of Australia's political spectrum) have been happy to don a 'high-vis' vest and use local manufacturing for publicity opportunities. But in terms of genuinely supportive policy measures, both major parties (the Australian Labor Party and the Liberal/National Coalition) have largely turned their backs on local manufacturing. Instead, the economic winners have been minerals extraction and carbon-based energy production, with complete disregard for the changing climate, and other environmental consequences. Despite this lack of political support, manufacturing in Australia continues. To be sure, it is not thriving, but it struggles on, hovering at around 5.5 per cent of Australian GDP in 2020 (down from a high of just under 30 per cent of GDP in the late 1950s).[21]

Australia's recent trade difficulties and supply chain challenges—as a result of the Covid-19 pandemic and strained diplomatic tensions with China—have only served to increase the significance of local production. In Australia, local industries from textiles to steel-making report that the pandemic has resulted in increased demand for locally produced products, and there is great potential for expansion if the skilled workers can be found.[22] Tradespeople and business owners continue to produce specialist parts and products within urban and regional industrial estates across the country. However, the widespread devaluation of trade skills has resulted in an ageing workforce and a generational risk of knowledge loss, which will be very difficult to recover once those with industrial craft knowledge are gone. What is at stake is a wider problem for countries such as Australia: if we lose the capacity to *make things*, there is a sovereign risk of a fundamental lack of national self-sufficiency. I return to this issue in Chap. 8.

Patternmakers: A Statistical Picture

Patternmaking is a particularly intriguing litmus test for the status of industrial craft, as it is one of the smallest industrial craft specialisations still in existence. In this way, it operates as a discrete microcosm, a white rhinoceros of industrial craft. At the time of writing, patternmaking is not a dead trade, but it is one of the smallest occupations in the United States, for example. The US Bureau of Labor Statistics lists "Patternmakers (Wood)" as being the smallest occupation recorded working in the United States in 2020, with 190 recorded patternmakers.[23] I must provide a caveat however: there is another occupational category in the United States, that of "Patternmaker (Plastics and Metal)". (In Australia both categories would be collected under the title "Engineering Patternmaker".) In 2020 in the United States, there were 2400 "Patternmakers (Metal and Plastic)" recorded as working.[24] So the figure is somewhat higher, but still right at the bottom of the occupational spectrum, alongside "watch and clock repairers" at 2340 employed in 2020.

In Australia the basic numbers are even smaller, due to the comparative population and industry sizes. The Australian Bureau of Statistics, using the Australian Census 2016 and Australian Labour Force data, suggests that in 2016 there were 270 engineering patternmakers recorded as working in Australia.[25] At the time of writing, the 2021 Australian Census is due to be conducted in a few months, so the most recent Census data I have is from 2016. My best guess, based on years of observing this sector, is that there may be as few as 180 people currently working as engineering patternmakers in Australia. The patternmakers I have interacted with are even more pessimistic in their predictions, such as this currently working Australian patternmaker, quoted from a Patternmakers' Facebook group:

> I reckon there'd be less than 100 that do it to earn a full-time living, without relying on other (non-pattern) work. Of those left doing it, check out the average age of them, that's the really worrying bit. A recent phone call from a foundry in [Western Australia] said there are no patternmakers in the west under 55. Our foundries have never been busier since Covid, yet they have nowhere to get patterns. Going to be an interesting 5–10 years in the trade.[26]

This quote above again points to the unresolved tension between industry demand and the lack of local skilled labour to supply that demand.

16   J. A. STEIN

Historical data from the Australian Census can give us some sense of the decline of patternmakers over time, but it also shows us that the trade was *always* relatively small, largely due to its place in the supply chain (you only need one pattern to produce thousands of products). It is difficult to provide clear, time-comparable data on the Australian situation, due to the constant changes of job classifications across the twentieth century. For example, in 1911 there were 139 tradespeople known as 'millwrights' recorded working in Australia. By 1933 there were 1186 people recorded under the broader occupational category 'patternmaker, engraver and designer'. The delightfully detailed post-war Census of 1947 records 1647 patternmakers, and of these, eight are female, presumably an outcome of war-time need for skilled workers, placing women in traditionally 'male' roles. By 1961, there were 1927 patternmakers recorded, all of which were male. By 1981, there were 669 patternmakers recorded in Australia. That number drops to 440 in 2011 and 270 by 2016.[27]

In my research, I estimate that I interacted with around 30 currently practicing patternmakers and formally interviewed 12 (both currently working and retired). While the lack of consistent, time-comparable categories impedes me from producing a neat graph with a single line, it can be said that these statistics indicate that patternmaking in Australia has always been a relatively small trade. It expanded significantly during the post-World War II reconstruction phase, in accordance with concurrent expansion in other manufacturing industries. It then contracted markedly from the 1980s onwards, again following the pattern of larger manufacturing sectors. At the time of writing (2021), there are six patternmaking apprentices currently training in Australia: four at TAFE Queensland and two at GO TAFE Victoria. (Marvellously, one of those six current apprentices is female.) As the older group of patternmakers near retirement age, there is a serious lack of younger, fully trained patternmakers to learn from them and ultimately take their place.

Industrial Craft in Academic Analysis

Despite the fact that design history and modern craft studies are academic disciplines that are specifically concerned with making, makers, production and human-made things, industrial craft is not a popular topic. In recent decades, design history has tended to gloss over the messy work of production, focusing more on designers' activities, and on the processes of consumption and meaning-making.[28] In its earlier years design history did admittedly attend to what it called 'production'; however, this focus was often restricted to a concern for designers designing and not to manufacturing processes or industrial labour.[29] Recent years, however, have seen the emergence of a small number of studies focused on industrial craft training and on the broader value of artisanal practice for industry.[30] Indeed, some of the best work in this area is yet to be formally published, but has emerged in thorough and innovative PhD and Master's research projects.[31] The field is ripe for further work, particularly in considering how industrial craft may evolve very differently from one geographical context to another.

Indeed, the relationship between design, industrial trades and working life is where my own research has been situated for the past decade. I locate my work loosely within the field of design history, but frequently and deliberately make connections to other disciplines such as oral history, modern craft studies, human geography and labour history. This interdisciplinary approach emerges from an understanding (initially developed in my first book and extended here) that the material and embodied experience of work is indivisibly bound up with social understandings of skill, technology, class and gender. This makes an interdisciplinary engagement not only desirable but entirely necessary.

Labour history and oral history have a strong and interrelated legacy of unearthing accounts from working-class people, providing platforms for histories that would have been inaccessible through printed records. Within this, the industrial crafts*man* looms large, particularly in accounts from the mid- to late twentieth century. However, the notion of the industrial artisan still remains relatively one-dimensional: often imagined as a lost, tragic male figure of the early to mid-twentieth century.[32] In the early years of my research into engineering patternmaking, I assumed that my focus on industrial craft simply made my research somewhat old fashioned, a bit 'daggy', or not in sync with the zeitgeist. I recall discussing this problem with oral historian Paula Hamilton in 2019. She was adamant that oral histories with Australian tradespeople are lacking and that I should not be dissuaded. Hamilton urged me to continue analysing the experience of working in a trade, moving past the rose-tinted glorification stories, bringing in an early twenty-first-century perspective.

Internationally, more nuanced accounts of workers and deindustrialisation are emergent across humanities and social sciences disciplines. Broadly speaking, the discourse has moved from studies of plant closures in the 1980s to the early 2000s, towards analyses of the wider social, economic, urban and cultural impacts of deindustrialisation in cities and regional areas.[33] It is no accident that oral history is deeply interconnected with deindustrialisation studies—oral histories offer some of the most detailed and insightful ways in which to comprehend the emotional toll of deindustrialisation and its long-term impacts.[34] Influentially, working-class studies scholar Sherry Lee Linkon identified how deindustrialisation has a 'half life' that continues to be felt for generations, a concept that other analysts have expanded.[35] Recent work by North American and European scholars affiliated with DéPOT (Deindustrialization and the Politics of Our Time) has connected oral history, working-class studies, sociology, urban policy and analysis of populist politics.[36] DéPOT scholars continue to challenge the widespread deterministic assumption that deindustrialisation is an inevitable by-product of linear economic and technological 'progress'.

It is important to note that there is no lack of recent academic attention to *craft*, per se. For example, in the recent reinvigoration of craft analysis in the social sciences, we have seen strong interest in craft's place in the cultural industries and in craft's relationship to urban gentrification and regional culture.[37] Alternative histories of making and DIY practice are gaining momentum.[38] Craft has returned as a category worthy of serious analysis. But even within this critical resurgence, the *industrial* craftsperson is relatively absent, perhaps in favour of more fashionable and aesthetically appealing forms of craft practice. There are of course exceptions, and human geographers such as Chantel Carr, Chris Gibson and Andrew Warren, among others, have come some way to tracing the place-based significance of economic restructuring on people's lives, work and cultural landscapes, within which industrial craft often has an articulated presence.[39] Academic studies of craft are discussed further in Chap. 4.

The Reshaping Australian Manufacturing Oral History Project

This book springs from a funded oral history project that I initiated in 2017, the *Reshaping Australian Manufacturing Oral History Project*, collected with National Library of Australia's Oral History and Folklore Collection.[40] This project features twelve interviews with engineering patternmakers and patternmaking business owners (ten men and two women), ranging in age from their early 30s to their late 80s, from the Australian states of Victoria and New South Wales. (See Table 1.1 for a full list of interviewees and their biographical details.) Interview participants included currently working patternmakers, retired patternmakers, business owners and former patternmakers now working in other industries. These other industries included school teaching, retail, hospitality, accountancy and visual art practice. As I discuss in detail in Chap. 7, it was an initial surprise to me that 9 of the 12 patternmakers I interviewed had some kind of visual art or creative practice that they conducted from their home workshops, and more specifically, six of them would comfortably be defined as *artists*. The connection between creative practice and industrial craft is rarely acknowledged, and it is my hope that this text goes some way to addressing this gap in our assessment of what sort of people might be defined as 'creative'.

There is long-established analysis about the use of oral history to understand working life and working-class experience. Verbal accounts provide insights into socially inscribed labour relations, tacit knowledge, unofficial practices and sensory experiences. It is now broadly accepted that oral histories do not, generally speaking, uncover 'what happened' on a purely factual basis. Rather, oral testimony helps us understand how people construct narratives about the past. In this sense, the content generated conveys nuances of meaning, memory, perception and politics. Oral histories also provide a way to understand material culture, changing practices and perceptions of skill in social context, opening up paths to understanding the embodied experience of work. As Linkon notes, "if we want to understand the cultural influence of economic restructuring, we must attend to its emotional, intimate, everyday effects".[41] The detailed human stories afforded by oral histories are one such way to examine the cultural and social impacts of industrial transformation. In a similar manner to Giovanni Contini's interviews with Italian miners and quarry workers, my interviews with patternmakers demonstrate how craftworkers understand and situate their own knowledge and skill, how they articulate their material engagement and how they perceive their role in bringing things into being.[42] But beyond this, the interviews present the patternmakers as *more than* patternmakers: as complex humans in a continual process of redefining their skills, identities and relationships to community, place and making.

The interviews, conducted between 2017 and 2019, tended to be lengthy: up to 5.5 hours' duration. They followed the National Library of Australia's preferred 'whole of life' approach. The life history form of oral

20   J. A. STEIN

Table 1.1 List of interviews—reshaping Australian Manufacturing Oral History Project

Reshaping Australian Manufacturing Oral History Project: interviews

Interviewee	Biographical details	Date of interview
Serge Haidutschyk (b. 1950)	Engineering patternmaker, aged care maintenance worker, artisanal woodworker, Melbourne (Retired.)	4 December 2018, Altona Meadows, Victoria
Paul Kay (b. 1954)	Third-generation engineering patternmaker, patternmaking business owner, W.G. Kay & Co. Pty. Ltd., artist, Sydney.	30 April 2018, Mona Vale, New South Wales
Scott Murrells (b. 1964)	Engineering patternmaker, automotive clay modeller, artisanal woodworker, artist, hardware retail worker, regional Victoria.	25 November 2017, Freeburgh, Victoria
Bruce Phipps (b. 1933)	Second-generation engineering patternmaker, patternmaking business owner, H. Phipps Patternmakers Pty. Ltd., Sydney (Retired.)	31 May 2018, Caringbah South, New South Wales
Peter Phipps (b. 1965)	Third-generation engineering patternmaker, patternmaking business owner, H. Phipps Patternmakers Pty. Ltd., Sydney.	11 May 2018, Bulli, New South Wales
Bryan Poynton (1939–2020)	Engineering patternmaker, artisanal woodworker, poet, artist, regional Victoria.	22 February 2018, Allenvale, Victoria
Debra Schuckar (b. 1966)	Engineering patternmaker, book-keeper, textiles maker, artist, singer, Melbourne.	23 February 2018, Kingsville, Victoria
Deborah Tyrrell (b. 1962)	Patternmaking business owner, Kimbeny Pty. Ltd., Sydney.	19 October 2018, Beacon Hill, New South Wales
Jim Walker (b. 1930)	Engineering patternmaker, apprentice educator and head of Patternmaking at George Thompson School of Foundry Technology, Royal Melbourne Institute of Technology (RMIT), artisanal woodworker, Melbourne (Retired.)	7 December 2018, Aspendale, Victoria
Peter Watts (b. 1955)	Engineering patternmaker, set design worker, design and art educator, artist, regional Victoria.	11 July 2019, Ultimo, New South Wales
Tim Wighton (b. 1985)	Engineering patternmaker (foundry sector), artisanal woodworker, laser cast maker, regional Victoria.	27 November 2017, Bendigo, Victoria
Peter Williams (b. 1961)	Engineering patternmaker, apprentice educator, secondary school teacher (current), artist, regional Victoria.	26 November 2017, Baranduda, Victoria

Interviewer: Jesse Adams Stein. Held in the National Library of Australia's Oral History and Folklore Collection

history offers opportunities for slow, contextualised reflection and allows the interviewees something of a 'warm up'. This biographical mode of interviewing also enables continuities and differences about working experience to emerge through the interview process.[43] For instance, I asked each interviewee if they could recall the first day, and the first year, of their apprenticeship. The resultant responses demonstrated distinct continuities over many decades, as I discuss in more detail in Chap. 3. The interviewees introduced their parents' backgrounds, and their grandparents, as well describing the area where they grew up, and their educational experiences. In this way, engineering patternmaking—and industrial craft more generally—was not always at the centre of our interview. This approach provided a rich contextual background in order to more deeply understand their experiences as workers and as family members, as tradespeople and educators, both past and present. The issue of family dynamics and child-caring came up relatively frequently, and as a result those elements also form a thread throughout this book. It is important to normalise the notion that tradespeople and tradesmen in particular have family and childcare responsibilities.

Evidently, my quotation of these interviews will reveal only a partial picture of these patternmakers' lives and experiences. As oral historian Alessandro Portelli has so evocatively described, within oral history there are many layers of interpretation and narrativisation occurring.[44] Oral history interviews are a moment in time where memory is reformulated through a relation between the interviewer and interviewee. Further, the (re)construction of meaning continues, through the stages of transcription, quote selection, historical writing, publication and, hopefully, being read. In this process, the historian has a fair degree of control and agency, and they must use this power carefully. There are always limits on what we think we can know about people's lives, as shared through oral history writing. Nonetheless, I hope my quotation selections hint at the contextual richness that this type of interview can provide. Historians must also guard against the tendency to find quotations to support our arguments. I began this research without much clear understanding of industrial craft or engineering patternmaking at all, and it is only through over six years of close engagement with the interview content (and the interviewees themselves) that I have pulled together threads, themes and ideas that have eventually become academic arguments. Beyond the recorded interview, I regularly contacted interviewees with follow-up questions, a process that is ongoing.

Most of the interviews were undertaken at the interviewees' homes, when accessible. There were stressful parts to this process. The recordings I was making were not just for my own research purposes—they were to be collected with the National Library of Australia, and accordingly, sound quality was important. The National Library had emphasised sound quality to me so strongly that I went about politely asking people to turn their houses upside down by switching off their refrigerators and all other humming electronic equipment. As oral historians often find—notwithstanding our best efforts—the audio quality of the interviews was invariably punctuated by things outside of my control: a poodle snoring, the neighbour mowing the lawn or some kid practising drumming, a few doors up the street. On one memorable occasion, I had asked the interviewee Tim Wighton to meet me at a studio at Bendigo Community Radio Station, given his house was filled with exuberant children. As it turned out, the radio station was literally at a *station*. By this I mean, the radio station occupied an old railway station building and was therefore next to a train line. Probably like all community radio venues, this one certainly had character. The appointed 'studio' (I use the term loosely) was filled with whirring clocks and other noisy twentieth-century machinery, and we abandoned the location entirely.

Conducting the interviews in people's homes often allowed me the opportunity to visit many of the patternmakers' home workshops, which added a valuable dimension to the interview. The introduction of objects—tools, machinery and photographs—into the interview provided the patternmakers with another way of speaking: lending meaning where they could not always find the words. In some ways, this literally opened up another level of dialogue, featuring material objects, practice, skill and space. There are, however, challenges to dealing with objects and photographs during interviews: the conversation does not always adequately produce the spoken words to describe the visuality, physicality and designed nature of what is being discussed. When possible, I documented the objects we discussed through photographs.

In addition to oral history sources, my research also made use of sources as diverse as ethnographic fieldwork, object collections and ephemera. I also conducted informal phone interviews and online communications with other patternmakers, for example the former patternmaker and patternmaking educator Anthony Freemantle from TAFE Queensland, who is quoted throughout this text. I estimate that in total I have communicated with around 30 patternmakers in Australia, as well as a small handful from New Zealand, Canada, the United Kingdom and the United States. Observational fieldwork was conducted in 2015 and 2017, in a steel foundry with a dedicated patternshop, a 3D printing facility, an industrial design consultancy and at a patternmaking 'jobbing shop'. The ephemera and objects I engaged with included patternmaking educational manuals, hand tools, discarded patterns and materials from trade societies such as the Hand Tool Preservation Association of Australia.

Throughout this research, I also regularly followed a 'Patternmakers' social media group on Facebook, which began as an Australian group, but now includes members from the United Kingdom, India and the United States.[45] Observation of interactions in this group has provided valuable contemporary insights into international patternmakers' attitudes, industry jargon, a place to test my own particular hunches or thoughts, as well as a source for interviewee recruitment. As always, the observations in this book should be seen as a provisional, an opening up of conversation with industrial craftspeople and others, not as a final or definitive statement of knowledge.

In the oral history quotations used throughout this book, I apply ellipses to indicate where parts have been excised. These sections were edited so as to be comprehended more clearly by the reader, or because of repetition. I encourage interested readers to supplement their experience of reading by listening to the original recorded interviews, which can be accessed via the National Library of Australia.[46] At the time of writing, some interviews are easily accessible online, via the Library's Audio Management and Delivery System, while other uploads are still in process.[47] All interviews have rights agreements with open, unrestricted access, and the digital audio and text-based 'timed summaries' can be ordered through the Library. The written transcript is no substitute for hearing the spoken voice, and although I have attempted to provide an

24   J. A. STEIN

evocative and informed picture of the lives and experiences of a number of my interviewees, deeper contextualisation can be gleaned from listening to the interviews.[48]

OVERVIEW OF THIS BOOK

While oral history has a long background of engaging with working-class narratives and questions of power and representation, the twenty-first century has brought a fresh set of challenges and tensions regarding social class, power and politics. Chapter 2 is a personal and reflective chapter, in which I engage with the question of what it means to be conducting interviews with manufacturing workers in the twenty-first century. More specifically, I ask what it means to be interviewing such subjects in the context of divisive populist politics, precarious employment and deeply embedded social resentment. Here I draw particularly on the work of economist Michael Zweig, and historian Steven High, to explore deindustrialisation and working-class issues in the context of contemporary oral history practice. This chapter charts my (not always successful) attempts to articulate generative connections across entrenched divisions, particularly in relation to social class. The chapter journeys through a failed attempt to interview a Trump-supporting craftsman—an axe-sharpener—towards more productive connections with the engineering patternmakers I interviewed in this project. In this chapter I also situate the patternmakers in class context, a process that is complex due to the nature of patternmaking as a highly skilled and very small trade. Accordingly, this chapter engages with unionised and non-unionised workers, as well as small-business owners, and with class-stratification issues pertinent to the Australian context.

Importantly, this book moves beyond only considering the paid labour process, to also encompass unsanctioned creative practices undertaken by patternmakers, both within and beyond the workplace: the other things they make. In this way, this book contributes to a small but emerging critical discourse in design history and modern craft studies, which seeks to decentre the designer in design history writing, and to revisit the class biases inherent in assumptions about *who* is seen as 'creative'. Chapter 3 specifically considers the educational and social significance of the practice of handmaking toolboxes, and customised tools, during an engineering patternmaking apprenticeship, in the pedagogical context of twentieth-century Australian trades training. This practice is contextualised within the broader customary practice of making 'foreigners'. A 'foreigner' is an Australian colloquial term referring to a practice whereby workers produce personal objects at work, with the tacit support of colleagues. Foreigner-making is also known as *homers, government jobs* and *la perruque*, and has been examined extensively elsewhere.[49] This chapter finds that this type of 'semi-legitimate' production was a pedagogical strategy and held particular social significance in the moral economy of industrial workplaces. I explore how this process has transformed, and eventually disappeared, following the recent business trend towards standardisation and factory uniformity.

The middle section of this book engages with patternmaking practice and knowledge on two levels: in Chap. 4, I articulate patternmaking practice in its non-alienated (manual) form, with a focus on knowledge, before examining transformed technological relations in Chap. 5. Chapter 4 makes a claim about a particular kind of design knowledge that is possessed by engineering patternmakers. With close reference to oral history material, I argue that patternmakers possess and enact a form of expertise and design knowledge that has thus far been undervalued. Drawing on Nigel Cross' influential theorisation of 'designerly ways of knowing', this chapter explores the connections and divergences between design and patternmaking knowledge sets, reminding us that the making of manufactured objects is deeply collaborative across professional and class formations. In this way, I draw our attention to existing design knowledge and skill within manufacturing, rather than simply arguing that 'creatives' such as designers should be imported into the manufacturing process, so as to revive it. This example has broader historical implications for how we frame and value the knowledge, skills and influence of those engaged in industrial production.

Chapter 5 then challenges the deterministic notion (described at the beginning of this Introduction) that manufacturing is now a fully automated arena without need for industrial craft. This chapter engages with the experiences of patternmakers who have experienced the relatively recent transition from manual patternmaking to CNC machine milling and CAD/CAM software. I explore a variety of responses to this technological change, from leaving the trade, to experiences of (self-funded) retraining and technological adaptation. I maintain that CNC milling continues to dehumanise and alienate industrial craft workers, and yet other pathways could be taken, approaches which incorporate a mix of newer and older technologies and extant knowledge sets. My approach challenges the widespread belief that manufacturing workers must simply retrain and be 'flexible' to ensure employability. Operating at a detailed and personal level, I uncover stories about complex individuals as they retrain and reinvent themselves, at some personal cost.

It is worth mentioning that very little has ever been written about engineering patternmakers specifically and most particularly about their experience of technological change in the late twentieth century. While invisibility alone is not a sufficient reason to undertake such a study, the patternmakers' experience points to broader, important questions facing manufacturing and trades education: What are the risks, and what might be lost, when industrial craft practices are absorbed into proprietary digital software? How else can such a diverse and significant skillset (as patternmakers have) be applied? What can we reclaim, reimagine and salvage? How did Australian patternmakers go from being among the world's best—on par with the United Kingdom and Germany—to having only six remaining apprentices in 2021? And what does it mean to be in a country that is losing its capacity make things?[50] I return to these themes in the book's Conclusion.

At this stage in the book, gender comes more into focus. Chapter 6 engages with the stories of two women in patternmaking, demonstrating how their experiences of work, deindustrialisation and retraining are set at a very different tenor to the dominant group of patternmakers, that is trades*men*. This chapter parallels Australian tradeswomen's experiences in the 1970s and 1980s to the contemporary context, and finds that for working-class women, anti-discrimination legislation and equal employment opportunity measures have done very little to transform gender-labour segregation and patriarchal culture in industrial and manufacturing sectors. While such reforms may have improved upper middle-class women's representation in white-collar managerial and leadership roles, the status quo is almost completely unchanged for working-class women. Through tracing the stories of an engineering patternmaker and a pattern-making business owner, I find that women in industrial craft have had to traverse demanding expectations as parents and breadwinners, all the while finding their skills in industrial craft remain under-recognised and disparaged by (some) tradesmen and employers. This chapter also engages with existing methodological and theoretical discussions concerning the gendered nature of the oral history interview itself.

Chapter 7 engages again with creative practice, but this time it tends to focus on patternmakers *after* they have left the trade: the creative legacies of deindustrialisation. This chapter examines the motivations of engineering patternmakers who have also become artists, as a way of investigating the significance of Australian class context in relation to an artist's occupational pathway and their critical reception. I reveal how, for some patternmakers, their art practice can be seen as an assertion of mastery in the face of technological and economic change that has made their professional skills seem redundant. For others, moving from patternmaking to art answered creative aspirations never fulfilled by their paid labour. Further, this chapter discusses how the social constructions surrounding craft masculinity have served to shape and limit engineering patternmakers' trajectories and self-image. Ultimately, this chapter surfaces tensions between Australian manufacturing, industrial craft, various art world/s and perceptions of social class. This tension is made explicit through reference to patternmakers' responses to the work of twentieth-century modernist Australian sculptor Robert Klippel.

The book's conclusion (Chap. 8) addresses the present state of Australian manufacturing more directly. I argue that there are concrete measures that can be taken to shift the current pattern of declining manufacturing and devaluation of trade skills. Particular industries could be targeted for support, producing high-quality outcomes utilising sustainable systems and developing employees' skills. The chapter emphasises that engineering patternmakers offer a body of knowledge of manufacturing processes, materials and design, and there is the risk that such skills and knowledge will disappear entirely. The fundamental basis of industrial craft knowledge need not be made redundant by technological change, but can in fact complement it, if technologies are introduced in a way that respects existing craft knowledge and human dignity in labour. Arguing for a revitalisation of state involvement in manufacturing, I reason that such a policy change would provide a secure base from which to expand local technical, production and design capacity, in a manner that sensitively responds to impending environmental and social challenges. In the uncertain years to come—most likely featuring resource scarcity, environmental depletion and natural disasters of an unprecedented scale—the manual and mental ability to *make* and *repair* will come to have more urgent significance. Industrial craft can, and should, be part of this process of care, maintenance and local sustainment.

NOTES

1. Reyner Banham, "Sparks from a Plastic Anvil: The Craftsman in Technology", *Journal of Modern Craft* 1, no. 1 (2008): 137–45. Republication of a 1973 lecture Banham gave at the Victoria and Albert Museum, London.
2. Scott Murrells, interview with author, *Reshaping Australian Manufacturing*, 25 November 2017 (Canberra: National Library of Australia [NLA]), https://nla.gov.au/nla.cat-vn7540149.
3. For nuanced discussions of this issue, see Jefferson Cowie and Joseph Heathcott (eds) *Beyond the Ruins: The Meanings of Deindustrialization* (Ithaca: Cornell University Press, 2003); Tim Strangleman, "'Smokestack Nostalgia,' 'Ruin Porn' or Working-Class Obituary: The Role and Meaning of Deindustrial Representation", *International Labor and Working-Class History* 84, no. 1 (2013): 23–37; Lucy Taksa, "Machines and Ghosts: Politics, Industrial Heritage, and the History of Working Life at Eveleigh Workshops", *Labour History* 85 (2003): 65–88.
4. Tracy Neumann, *Remaking the Rust Belt: The Postindustrial Transformation of North America* (Philadelphia: University of Pennsylvania Press, 2019).
5. Miriam Posner, "The Software that Shapes Workers' Lives", *The New Yorker* (12 March 2019), online: www.newyorker.com/science/elements/the-software-that-shapes-workers-lives, accessed 21 April 2021.
6. The discipline/area of deindustrialisation studies has been charted in detail in Steven High, "'The Wounds of Class': A Historiographical Reflection on the Study of Deindustrialization, 1973–2013", *History Compass* 11, no. 11 (2013): 994–1007. See also: Cowie and Heathcott, *Beyond the Ruins;* Sherry Lee Linkon, *The Half-Life of Deindustrialization: Working-Class Writing about Economic Restructuring* (Ann Arbour: University of Michigan Press, 2018); Steven High, Lachlan MacKinnon, and Andrew Perchard (eds), *The Deindustrialized World: Confronting Ruination in Postindustrial Places* (Vancouver and Toronto: UBC Press, 2017); Michele Fazio, Christie Launius and Tim Strangleman (eds) *Routledge International Handbook of Working-Class Studies* (London and New York: Routledge, 2020). For an Australian perspective, see, for example, Julianne Schultz. *Steel City Blues: The Human Cost of Industrial Crisis* (London, New York and Melbourne: Penguin Books, 1985).
7. Glenn Adamson, *The Invention of Craft* (London and New York: Bloomsbury, 2013), 145–7.
8. Steven High, "Deindustrialization and its Consequences", in *Routledge International Handbook of Working-Class Studies*, 179.
9. Linkon, *The Half-Life of Deindustrialization;* Chantel Carr, "Maintenance and Repair beyond the Perimeter of the Plant: Linking Industrial Labour and the Home", *Transactions of the Institute of British Geographers* 42, no. 4 (2017): 642–54.

1 INTRODUCTION: RE-EVALUATING INDUSTRIAL CRAFT... 29

10. Jesse Adams Stein, *Hot Metal: Material Culture & Tangible Labour* (Manchester: Manchester University Press, 2016), 194.
11. Larissa Romensky, "Hard, Dirty Foundry Work Copes with Digital Disruption and Lack of Apprenticeship Courses", *ABC News* (30 September 2018), online: www.abc.net.au/news/2018-09-30/hard-dirty-foundry-work-coping-with-digital-disruption/10303254, accessed 21 May 2021.
12. Peter Williams, interview with author, *Reshaping Australian Manufacturing*, 26 November 2017 (Canberra: NLA), https://nla.gov.au/nla.cat-vn7540153. Italics indicate speaker's emphasis.
13. Haidutschyk, interview with author.
14. Bryan Poynton, interview with author, *Reshaping Australian Manufacturing Oral History Project*, 22 February 2018 (Canberra: NLA), https://nla.gov.au/nla.cat-vn7580610.
15. Stuart McCorkelle, quotation from Patternmakers' Facebook group, online: www.facebook.com/groups/502920693172756/search/?q=stuart%20mccorkelle, accessed 1 March 2021.
16. Anon., "Patternmaking and Capitalism", *The Socialist* (November 1904): 7.
17. Elizabeth Humphrys, *How Labour Built Neoliberalism: Australia's Accord, the Labour Movement and the Neoliberal Project* (Leiden: Brill, 2019).
18. "Manufacturing", in *Labour Market Information Portal* (Canberra: Australian Government, 2021), online: https://lmip.gov.au/default.aspx?LMIP/GainInsights/IndustryInformation/Manufacturing, accessed 21 May 2021.
19. Tom Barnes et al., "Employment, Spillovers and 'Decent Work': Challenging the Productivity Commission's Auto Industry Narrative", *The Economic and Labour Relations Review* 27, no. 2 (2016): 215–30.
20. "Voxeljet Sand Printer", *CSIRO* (Canberra: 2021), online: https://research.csiro.au/metals/add-manufacturing/aus-innovation/voxeljet-sand-3d-printer/, accessed 20 May 2021.
21. "Australia—Manufacturing, Value Added (% Of GDP)", in *Trading Economics*, online: https://tradingeconomics.com/australia/manufacturing-value-added-percent-of-gdp-wb-data.html, accessed 1 May 2021; Rachel Pupazzoni, "Australian Manufacturing has been in Terminal Decline but Coronavirus Might Revive It", *ABC News* (23 July 2020), online: https://www.abc.net.au/news/2020-07-23/coronavirus-pandemic-leads-to-australian-manufacturing-revival/12481568, accessed 23 May 2021.
22. Saskia Mabin, "Demand for Australian-made Products Soars as Consumer Attitudes Change During Pandemic", *ABC News* (11 May 2021), online: www.abc.net.au/news/2021-05-11/aussie-made-products-flying-off-shelves/100128812, accessed 11 May 2021.

23. US Bureau of Labor Statistics, *Occupation Profiles* (2020), online: www.bls.gov/oes/current/oes_stru.htm, accessed 21 May 2021.
24. US Bureau of Labor Statistics.
25. "Engineering Patternmakers ANZSCO ID 323411", *Job Outlook*, using statistics from the Australian Bureau of Statistics and Australian Labour Force sample data, online: https://joboutlook.gov.au/occupations/engineering-patternmakers?occupationCode=323411, accessed 21 May 2021.
26. Anonymous, Patternmakers' Facebook Group, May 2021.
27. Australian Bureau of Statistics, Historical Australian Census data. Generally online (with some exceptions) at www.abs.gov.au/census/find-census-data/historical, accessed 21 May 2021.
28. Grace Lees-Maffei, "The Production-Consumption-Mediation Paradigm", *Journal of Design History* 22, no. 4 (2009): 351–76.
29. Lees-Maffei, "The Production-Consumption-Mediation Paradigm"; see also Marilyn Zapf, *The Making of Industrial Artisans, Training Engineers in Britain*, MA dissertation (London: V&A, RCA, 2012). One early exception is Tony Fry, *Design History Australia* (Sydney: Hale & Iremonger & the Power Institute, 1988), which called for a focus on the labour of production and economic patterns when shaping design histories.
30. See, for example, Ezra Shales, *The Shape of Craft* (London: Reaktion Books, 2017); Ezra Shales, "A 'Little Journey' to Empathize with (and Complicate) the Factory", *Design and Culture* 4, no. 2 (2012): 215–20; Sarah Fayen Scarlett, "The Craft of Industrial Patternmaking", *Journal of Modern Craft* 4, no. 1 (2011): 27–48; Tom Fisher and Julie Botticello, "Machine-Made Lace, the Spaces of Skilled Practices and the Paradoxes of Contemporary Craft Production", *Cultural Geographies* 25, no. 1 (2018): 49–69; Marco Bettiol and Stefano Micelli, "The Hidden Side of Design: The Relevance of Artisanship", *Design Issues* 30, no. 1 (2014): 7–18; Richard K. Blundel and David J. Smith, "Reinventing Artisanal Knowledge and Practice: A Critical Review of Innovation in a Craft-Based Industry", *Prometheus* 31, no. 1 (2013): 55–73.
31. Zapf, *The Making of Industrial Artisans*; Elise Hodson, *Design in Motion: The Everyday Object and the Global Division of Design Labour*, PhD thesis (Toronto: York University, 2019); John Charles Wren, *Skilled Trades' Work and Apprentice Training in the Manufacturing Industry with a Primary Focus on the Millwright Trade: An Inter-Generational Study*, PhD thesis (Toronto: Ontario Institute for the Studies in Education, University of Toronto, 2008; Simon Lloyd, *The Designer—Artisan Dialogue: Establishing the Conditions for an Expanded Design Practice*, PhD thesis (Melbourne: RMIT 2021).

32. See, for example, John Shields (ed), *All Our Labours: Oral Histories of Working Life in Twentieth Century Sydney* (New South Wales University Press, 1992).
33. For a thorough overview of publications related to deindustrialisation (from a North American and European perspective), see DéPOT's publication list: https://deindustrialization.org/outcomes/publications/, accessed 21 May 2021.
34. See, for example, Tracy E. K'Meyer and Joy L. Hart, *I Saw It Coming: Worker Narratives of Plant Closings* (New York: Palgrave Macmillan, 2009); Allesandro Portelli, *Biography of an Industrial Town Terni, Italy, 1831–2014* (New York: Palgrave Macmillan, 2017).
35. Linkon, *The Half-Life of Deindustrialization*; Tim Strangleman, "Deindustrialisation and the Historical Sociological Imagination: Making Sense of Work and Industrial Change", *Sociology* 51, no. 2 (2017): 466–82; Alistair Fraser and Andy Clark, "Damaged Hardmen: Organized Crime and the Half-life of Deindustrialization", *British Journal of Sociology*, early release online (2021), https://doi-org.ezproxy.lib.uts.edu.au/10.1111/1468-4446.12828.
36. See https://deindustrialization.org/ for the DéPOT project overview.
37. See, for example, Susan Luckman, *Craft and the Creative Economy* (London: Palgrave Macmillan, 2015); Richard Sennett, *The Craftsman* (London and New York: Penguin, 2008); Glenn Adamson (ed.), *The Craft Reader* (New York, Oxford: Berg Publishers, 2010); Adamson, *The Invention of Craft*; Richard E. Ocejo, *Masters of Craft: Old Jobs in the New Economy* (Princeton: Princeton University Press, 2017); Merle Patchett, "Historical Geographies of Apprenticeship: Rethinking and Retracing Craft Conveyance over Time and Place", *Journal of Historical Geography* 55 (2017): 30–43; Clare M. Wilkinson-Weber and Alicia Ory DeNicola (eds), *Critical Craft: Technology, Globalization and Capitalism* (London and New York: Bloomsbury, 2016); Mark Banks, "Craft Labour and Creative Industries", *International Journal of Cultural Policy* 16, no. 3 (2010): 305–21.
38. See, for example, the recent special issue and editorial: Cindy Kohtala, Yana Boeva and Peter Troxler (eds), "Introduction: Alternative Histories in DIY Cultures and Maker Utopias", *Digital Culture & Society* 6, no. 1 (2020): 5–36.
39. Chantel Carr and Chris Gibson, "Geographies of Making: Rethinking Materials and Skills for Volatile Futures", *Progress in Human Geography* 40, no. 3 (2015), 1–19; Andrew Warren and Chris Gibson, *Surfing Places, Surfboard Makers: Craft, Creativity and Cultural Heritage in Hawai'I, California and Australia* (Honolulu: University of Hawai'i Press, 2014); Chris Gibson and Andrew Warren, *The Guitar: Tracing the Grain Back to the Tree* (Chicago: University of Chicago Press, 2021).

40. *The Reshaping Australian Manufacturing Oral History Project*, National Library of Australia (NLA), Canberra. See: https://catalogue.nla.gov.au/Search/Home?lookfor=my_parent%3A%22(AuCNL)7540760%22&iknowwhatimean=1. UTS (University of Technology Sydney) Human Research Ethics Committee (HREC) approval no. ETH17-1385. Uses the NLA's oral history interview Rights Agreement.
41. Linkon, *The Half-Life of Deindustrialization*, 9.
42. Giovanni Contini, "Creativity at Work: Miners and Quarrymen in Tuscany", *Oral History* 37, no. 2 (2009): 64–70.
43. See further discussion of the biographical form in Ben Rogaly, *Stories from a Migrant City: Living and Working Together in the Shadow of Brexit* (Manchester: Manchester University Press, 2020); Daniel James, *Dona Maria's Story: Life History, Memory, and Political Identity* (Durham: Duke University Press, 2001).
44. Alessandro Portelli, "The Peculiarities of Oral History", *History Workshop Journal* 12, no. 1 (1981): 96–107. See also: Linda Shopes, "Editing Oral History for Publication", *Oral History Forum/d'histoire Orale* 31 (2011): 1–24.
45. Research ethics approved, see details in note 40.
46. To listen to online material or to order material not yet available online, this link is a good place to start: https://catalogue.nla.gov.au/Search/Home?lookfor=my_parent%3A%22(AuCNL)7540760%22&iknowwhatimean=1.
47. Kevin Bradley, "Built on Sound Principles: Audio Management and Delivery at the National Library of Australia", *IFLA Journal* 40, no. 3 (2014): 186–94.
48. Kevin Bradley and Anisa Puri, "Creating an Oral History Archive: Digital Opportunities and Ethical Issues", *Australian Historical Studies* 47, no. 1 (2016): 75–91.
49. Michel Anteby, *Moral Gray Zones: Side Productions, Identity, and Regulation in an Aeronautic Plant* (Princeton: Princeton University Press, 2008); Jennifer Harris, (ed.) *Foreigners: Secret Artefacts of Industrialism* (Perth: Black Swan Press, 2009).
50. Also addressed in Chris Gibson, Chantel Carr and Andrew Warren, "A Country that Makes Things?", *Australian Geographer* 43, no. 2 (2012): 109–13.

CHAPTER 2

Navigating Class and Populist Politics in Contemporary Oral History Practice

INTRODUCTION

This chapter contends with what it means to conduct oral histories with Australian manufacturing tradespeople, in the context of a deindustrialising economy, and more specifically in relation to populist political influence. It is by no means a definitive statement on how to conduct interviews in this context, but rather, a candid and open exploration of the ways in which class and politics wove itself into my research, and how I chose to acknowledge and work with differences of background and opinion. To work in such a context requires oral history interviewers to be flexible and open, and to keep in mind how social class, power relations and capital are experienced on everyday human levels.

I begin with a disclaimer: this chapter is something of a wild ride. First, I engage with questions around deep social divisions and populist political support, as it has emerged in the first decades of the twenty-first century. To do this, I take the reader through a thwarted interview attempt with an angry industrial craftsman—an axe-sharpener—and from there we move into an analysis of the specific class position of engineering patternmakers. Through oral history excerpts, I share contextual information about several of the interviewees in the *Reshaping Australian Manufacturing* Project. As I explain, engineering patternmakers occupy a contradictory class position, and do not fit neatly into a single class category.[1] This is partly due to their status as one of the most highly skilled industrial crafts, but also because the trade often features small businesses, and is not characterised by widespread worker collectivity. I consider the importance of

© The Author(s), under exclusive license to Springer Nature Switzerland AG 2021
J. A. Stein, *Industrial Craft in Australia*, Palgrave Studies in Oral History, https://doi.org/10.1007/978-3-030-87243-4_2

33

apprenticeship to the patternmakers' identities and class position, as well as the political attitudes of small-business and sole-operator patternmakers. Finally, various perspectives from unionised patternmakers are also highlighted. As noted by economist Michael Zweig—"classes are formed in the dynamics of power and wealth creation, and are by their nature a bit messy".[2] So too are memories. Despite the simmering resentment felt by many of those affected by deindustrialisation over the past half-century, the act of listening to, and sharing stories still has powerful generative potential for healing, mutual understanding and social recognition.

False Start (The Axe-Sharpener)

Six years ago, the only 'patternmaker' I had heard of belonged to textiles production. All this was to change in winter 2015, when I was conducting fieldwork at a steel foundry in regional Australia. I was there as part of a research team, exploring the intricacies of a family-owned steel foundry which had attracted our team's attention because the owners professed no desire to offshore to cheaper manufacturing options in Asia.[3] At the time, the research team I was part of undertook short, social-science-style interviews in an icy meeting room—not oral histories. I was nine weeks' pregnant, nauseous, freezing cold, and somewhat consumed by all of these conditions.

The workers were brought into the interview space by the foundry's administrative staff. They sat across from us—them in sand-covered high-vis work-apparel, us in black jeans and businesswear. The workers said what they thought was expected of them. Despite our 'university ethics-approved' assurances of anonymity, it came as no surprise that very few workers spoke to us frankly about their experiences or opinions. This was hardly the long-form, warm and open oral history experience that I had become accustomed to in my previous research.[4] But despite the shortcomings of this particular approach, it still provided an unpredictable springboard for the next six years of my research. The interviews marked the first time I spoke to any engineering patternmakers, and learned about what had happened to their trade. (During this process we interviewed two patternmakers, who I cannot name here due to the particular university ethics agreement used at the time. In many ways I owe a great deal to those two patternmakers, as they piqued my curiosity for the next six years of research.)

As it happened, I began not with engineering patternmaking, but with cast steel axes. We will return to the patternmakers soon, but first this chapter will delve briefly into my 'false start'—a brief journey into the world of axe-sharpening and competition woodchopping. It is rare that oral historians reflect openly on potential interviews that do not eventuate, and I certainly do not raise this as an example of best practice. The following experience is shared because it palpably points towards deeply embedded tensions in relation to social class that underpin this sort of research in the early twenty-first century.[5]

The Australian steel foundry where I began my fieldwork was a family company, which now specialises in 'consumable' parts for mining, construction and agriculture, but it also has a history of manufacturing hand tools, such as hand-sharpened axes made of cast steel. This foundry was an intriguing case because they were engaged in a delicate (and not always successful) balancing act, attempting to combine local steelmaking tradition with organisational drives towards 'design thinking' and 'innovation'.[6] Such a contradiction was exemplified by the family's decision to maintain their historical axe workshop, despite the fact that the workshop operated at a loss. While axe-making was marginal to the foundry's core business, I began with axe-making because of the value the foundry's owners placed upon this industrial craft. It was clear that there were internal dynamics at play, factors bound by locality, community, industrial craft and family. Highlighting these supposedly 'softer' concepts might seem irrational or nostalgic if interpreted solely through a frame of economic imperatives. In the current political context, and amid fears of an anticipated future of widespread unemployment or underemployment, the concepts of care, localism and maker tradition may well contain the potential—I hoped then, and I still argue now—to produce shared understandings across and between marginalised social groups.

The axes produced in the foundry's axe workshop had a long-standing reputation in the niche world of Australian competition woodchopping.[7] Competition woodchopping is an international sport, particularly popular in regions with a forestry industry, and importantly, it is a sport that has emerged out of labour practices.[8] In Australia it is a sport and a subculture characterised by whiteness, rural settler culture and hegemonic masculinity. After all, there is nothing more stereotypically masculine, agrarian and colonising than a burly 'bloke' hurling an axe into a big chunk of timber. Like most competition sports, the tools and gear are highly specialised. While most axes are forged, the woodchopping axes made at this foundry are cast in sand moulds. They are razor-sharp and specifically designed to withstand hitting knots in unforgiving Australian hardwood. After casting, the axes are hand-sharpened by a qualified industrial craftsperson.

Axe-sharpening is a skilled practice that is socially understood in the world of competition woodchopping to be a protected trade, with guarded knowledge that is often passed down generationally, along patrilineal lines. The patriarchal concept of inherited family skill was present in both the foundry's own family history and the world of competition woodchopping. These axes were hand-sharpened, often specifically by one man, who I will call Garry O'Sullivan (not his real name). O'Sullivan belongs to one of the central 'dynasties' within Australian competition woodchopping, and he is both a woodchopping competitor and an axe-sharpener. The direct involvement of O'Sullivan in the production of the cast axes indicates that this foundry has a responsibility not just to their customers and their employees, but also to the close-knit community of Australian competition woodchopping.

Following that first field trip in 2015, I formed the view that I wanted to interview O'Sullivan, to inquire about the industrial craft of axe-sharpening. O'Sullivan wasn't a foundry employee, but an independent contractor. Nonetheless, the foundry arranged for me to speak with O'Sullivan via mobile phone, and he agreed to take my call. The ethics of this research situation means I cannot reproduce the exact telephone conversation we had, but I can provide a general sense of how it went, and it did not go well. After introducing myself, and asking if I could organise an interview with him, I was told (with some aggression), "I'm not giving away any secrets!" I assured O'Sullivan that I was not interested in his trade secrets, but merely curious about his experience as a skilled craftsperson: how he found his way into this particular line of work, what his thoughts about the future might be and what his life has been like up to this point. But the conversation took an abrupt turn when he asked, "What do you think of Donald Trump?"

I was caught off-guard, and on reflection I could have answered this question more strategically. Perhaps I could have said something diplomatic, maybe referencing Trump's good intentions in his professed support of American manufacturing, "Australia could learn a thing or two from that", or something to that effect. But instead I stumbled through my response, and said something like, "Well I don't like him personally, but this isn't about me". This, I'm afraid, closed down our conversation. After that, O'Sullivan was triggered and commenced something of an angry rant. There were references to Bill Gates, and to various conspiracy theories. After some time, it became clear that there was not going to be an oral history interview with O'Sullivan, at least not at this stage. I ended the phone call as politely as I could. I remember being immensely frustrated at the time, thinking to myself, "This is so unfair! Even if I disagree with your politics, your probable attitudes to women, to race, all the rest of it … I still care! I want to know about your work. Your job. Your skills. I'm interested and I want to know what you think."

Class clanged through our disjointed conversation. To O'Sullivan—and I can only guess what he thought—but perhaps I was the very embodiment of everything he was angry with. I was the privileged urban upstart, the PhD-holding young woman, a first-generation Australian with a Jewish-sounding name. Evidently O'Sullivan couldn't have known all this, and yet my accent gave away enough: my voice may well have represented the identity politics he felt censured by. Did I also signify to him the 'elites' who supported a neoliberal economy—one that embraced global trade, high technology, and treated his industrial skills as useless cobwebs of a bygone era? Perhaps I was one of those who believed Australia's industrial decline was 'inevitable', and affected individuals need to smarten up, retrain and become entrepreneurs? (Wait, wasn't he a sole-trader, therefore more akin to the petty-bourgeoisie than the generalised notion of a 'working class bloke'?)

None of these nuances or questions were able to be communicated at the time; we never reached a mutual understanding. Evidently I did not feel disdain for O'Sullivan, but that is not the point. His world, his security and his sense of identity had—I suspect—been damaged by the localised outcomes of global capitalism, and he was angry. Moreover, it is likely that his radio station and Facebook feed were telling him who to be angry with: migrants, refugees, women, elites, aboriginal people and people on welfare. While perhaps there was no way to patch things up with O'Sullivan, I resolved to find another way to attempt to bridge the broader divide that this situation represents.

Interviewing in the Shadow of Populist Politics

This was the beginning of the path that led to the development of the *Reshaping Australian Manufacturing* oral history project. Today, in 2021 (and two babies later, for me), I still keep in touch with some of the engineering patternmakers I met on that first foundry field trip. Nowadays I speak with some of them frankly about work, life and employment challenges. But it took many years, and many different forms of communication, to get to this point. A vital part of this process was a decision I made to speak to current and former manufacturing workers—even if they all turned out to be angry, white-nationalist, Trump-supporting men, like O'Sullivan. In the end, they did not conform to this stereotype, as the rest of this book explores, in a variety of ways. Nonetheless, the act of interviewing anyone associated with Australian manufacturing necessarily means grappling with the deeply embedded tensions around class, gender and urban-regional divides that remain suspended and unresolved in Australian society and politics (as in other parts of the world).

Much has been said, in the past, on the role of oral history vis-à-vis social class, particularly in the 1970s and 1980s.[9] New currents of social history in the 1970s saw oral history as a key tool for revealing the stories of marginalised people, whose voices and experiences were not captured by official records 'from above': the working class, migrants, women, people of colour and so on.[10] Later, with the influence of poststructuralism and postmodernism, oral history analysis turned attention more towards memory, subjectivity and identity.[11] The focus fell, then, more on questions of representation and recognition, rather than on materialist aspects of the class struggle. Feminist oral historians undertook in-depth research that moved well beyond making women's voices 'heard', towards analysis of the social constructedness of gender-roles and gendered narrative positionings, showing how gendered social positions impact not only our experience but also our ways of speaking and seeing the world.[12] (See Chap. 6.)

But the present moment has another politics, a fraught one at that. The second decade of the twenty-first century features deep political fractures along the lines of class, race, sexuality and gender, which are articulated in a different key to the battles waged in the mid-twentieth century over civil rights, industrial relations, environmentalism and feminism. Old categories of the left and the right are losing their apparent cohesiveness and logic. Oral history is not separate from these political struggles. The interviewee and interviewer are bound up in a mutually constitutive act of making meaning within these existing politicised worlds, and common ground is either found or not found. Today, oral history must contend with the pervasive effects of neoliberal global capitalism, and engage with what all this might mean for our understandings of class, race and gender (among other points of difference) as these issues emerge in interviews.

Oral historians may find that some of the groups we seek to engage resent *us* as interviewers, for being who we are (i.e. academics or professional historians, and/or being otherwise affiliated with a professional class). This has implications for who we interview, how we approach particular topics and interviewees, and for how interviewers understand and present themselves.

Conservatives and right-wing political populists have since the 1970s—but even more so since the 2007–2008 Global Financial Crisis—successfully leveraged support from angry, disaffected groups that are largely working class.[13] This is the case particularly in deindustrialising regional areas such as the United States' 'rust belt' (which are predominantly white). Populist politicians such as Donald Trump, Jair Bolsonaro and Rodrigo Duterte manipulate by deliberately sowing mistrust, division and racial hatred across the public sphere. In Australia, populist politicians such as Pauline Hanson and Clive Palmer remain on the political fringe (although they sometimes have influence in passing legislation), and far-right extremist groups have been gaining confidence in social media arenas. In this local and international context, manufacturing has become a highly politicised and weaponised arena. Some (such as Trump) promised a revitalised local manufacturing sector in order to glean support for his 2016 campaign, all the while largely supporting the ruling class of whom he is a part. Meanwhile, the American Democratic Party and other heretofore centre-left parties, such as Australian Labor, have since the late 1970s embraced the neoliberal project in various ways, supporting globalised free trade, floating national currencies and boosting corporate power. While these centre-left parties tend to support progressive social justice and environmental policy platforms, they have largely abandoned their old working-class base.[14]

During the 1990s and early 2000s, the word 'class' fell from widespread use. It was seen as old fashioned, almost to the point of it being silenced entirely, or at least neutralised through terms such as 'lower socioeconomic status'.[15] However, in more recent years, 'class' has come back into circulation,[16] but sometimes in simplistic and negative way, such as a political catch-cry criticising union leaders for waging a 'class war', and references to the 'white working class' being to blame for Trump's election in 2016.[17] While this book is about Australia, discussions about Trump and his support-base remain useful because, as my 'false start' with O'Sullivan shows, similar political threads feature in Australia, as they do across the Global North and parts of the Global South. The 'white working class' *was* a key factor in Trump's 2016 victory in the United States, but it is important to ask whether this came about purely as a result of xenophobia and racism, or did the Democratic Party also fail to mobilise some of their traditional base?[18] Keen observers of North American deindustrialisation such as Steven High have pointed out that there is a clear link between Trump's growing support-base in 2016 and his (largely unfulfilled) promises of boosting manufacturing employment in the economically devastated American rust belt.[19] In short, Trump promised good jobs in deindustrialising areas, leveraging the existing powerful emotions felt in these places, as a consequence of decades of economic decline.[20]

In attempting to understand the role of social class and populist politics in manufacturing communities—particularly what that might mean for contemporary oral history practice—Zweig's contemporary class analysis provides a useful framework.[21] Rather than simply opting for income-based, fixed class categories of class, Zweig reminds us how the foundations of class are rooted in power relations: "working class people are in jobs where they have little or no control over the pace and content of their work",[22] or they have no power at all, due to a lack of work. Zweig acknowledges that power can be cultural, political and economic, but taking an essentially Marxist position on class, he notes that it is "first and foremost a product of power asserted in the production process".[23]

Recalling Raewyn Connell and Terry Irving's early work on Australian class structure from 1980, it is also important here to be reminded that class is always *relational*, and when we speak of 'power' it is to point to "structures of power", rather than simply "the business of giving and taking orders".[24] Connell and Irving's work also reminds us that class structures are "intrinsically historical concepts", bound not just by the present context but by "processes and situations" feeding from the past into the present.[25] This is especially pertinent to the practice of oral history, where an interviewee is asked to remember and retell aspects of their past, an act through which they place themselves 'in history', as they see it. It is also a relevant factor in relation to the structuring influence of trade apprenticeship, as I explore further on in this chapter.

Another key cultural factor relevant to Australia is the culture of liberalism as it exists through small-business owners and sole-traders. Small-business ownership has historically been a significant feature of the Australian manufacturing context, and this involves a culture of liberalism that values individualism, is suspicious of big government and of large organisational power (be it union-led or large corporations). Australian small-business people have tended to vote conservatively in the second half of the twentieth century, exemplified by the idea of the 'Battler' in John Howard's successful Liberal/National 1996 election campaign.[26] The 'battler', in this context, was a worker *or* small-business person, one who was 'doing it tough', at the mercy of much larger economic forces. The 'battler', then, is not strictly speaking a 'working class' character, but can also encompass aspects of the middle class.

Returning to Zweig, when power relations once are again understood as the determining factor for class position, this opens up an understanding that the 'working class' is multi-racial, mixed-gender, urban and rural, consisting of locally born and migrant workers, across different generations. Understanding power relations—particularly as they impact daily life and work—can serve as a basis for forming a potentially strong progressive front.[27] This new progressive movement could, theoretically, emerge as an allegiance of a broader working class, across stratifications of race, gender and ethnicity (among other points of difference). Zweig notes that, when understood this way, the 'working class' in the United States is much larger than is often assumed: in his terms, around 60 per cent of working Americans can be said to be working class, by virtue of their relationship to power (or lack thereof) in their working life.[28]

This identification of the mutually constitutive nature of the working class is one step. The other problem to be overcome is that of how particular demographic groups have been successfully preyed upon by populist politicians, leveraging generational racism, a fear of the 'other', and largely misplaced rage about who is 'taking the jobs'. I do not seek to apologise for white working-class racism by any means. But hatred can be manipulated, and it is not necessarily a permanent state. Unfortunately, however, at least some of the left has given up on the idea that a 'working class' is at the foundation of the progressive political movement.[29] But to treat this group with disdain—to see the rural white working class as 'deplorables' (to borrow Hillary Clinton's infamous term)—is to miss a key opportunity to challenge both global corporate neoliberal power *and* borderline fascist populist political players. This does not mean, however, that we should aim to reinstate an older (mythical) normalcy where 'men were men' in heavy industry, or pander to racist and xenophobic fears of migration, or placate misplaced concerns about 'censorship' allegedly caused by identity politics. Rather, what could unify this broader coalition is a collective understanding that only as a united front can we put forward meaningful alternatives to the worst excesses of neoliberal capitalism.[30]

42   J. A. STEIN

It was this understanding that drove my interest in interviewing current and former manufacturing workers: an understanding that oral history could have a role (albeit a small one) in articulating a generative politics across entrenched divisions. To be clear, I undertook this project imperfectly, with occasional shyness, awkwardness, with trial and error, but always with a fundamental respect for these interviewees at heart. This respect extended even when I did not agree with their politics, or their attitudes to women (etc.), or when I felt that perhaps they did not understand me (I did not feel they needed to). Underlying all this was a key desire to see any points of difference (between myself and my interviewees, or between my interviewees and wider society), as potentially generative, rather than automatically divisive.

In selecting this subject area, I also faced potential questions (from the left) about why my interview subjects were most often men, most particularly white, working-class and middle-class men. Why not focus on giving a voice to women, migrants, people with disabilities, people of colour? There are two ways to address these legitimate questions. The first is through a basic statement about demographic patterns in former manufacturing communities in Australia. Australian deindustrialisation has had particularly strong impacts upon regional areas where the dominant employed group is white, working class and male.[31] It therefore makes statistical sense that my interview group essentially reflects this demographic. The other way to address this question is to look to why it might be important to speak with potentially angry, disaffected social groups, in order to understand how particular social patterns emerge. Brazilian anthropologists Rosana Pinheiro-Machado and Lucia Mury Scalco discuss a similar challenge in relation to their research into former working-class supporters of socialist Luiz Inácio Lula da Silva, who shifted their allegiances to support the far-right populist Bolsonaro. They note:

> We were accused of humanising and giving voice to fascists. ... What is the appropriate academic posture in relation to those people who changed their votes? Should we deny this reality? Should we despise them as fascists? Our anthropological view is that we do not need to agree with people, but instead that we are to put facts in historical, contextual perspective ... understanding how rage is socially constructed and built upon a reproducing cycle of violence.[32]

Pinheiro and Scalco come from anthropology, not oral history, and Brazil and Australia are hardly political parallels, to say the least. Nonetheless, Pinheiro and Scalco's challenge is not unlike my own. They concluded that the sentiments of "hope and rage" in people's hearts come from the same place, and a close engagement with the everyday lives of low-income people provided territory where "we can reimagine new scenarios of hope".[33]

Using oral history to make similar cross-class connections makes sense. Oral history evidently has a legacy of providing a 'voice' for the working class, for the marginalised, for those whose experiences may go otherwise unrecorded and unacknowledged. Moreover, the oral history interview is literally a site of the discursive connection across and between class boundaries, and a frank confrontation of how lives are shaped. As Paul Thompson acknowledged in oral history's developing years:

> Oral sources have a much more general relevance to political history. There is a strong case for their more extensive use in the historical study of the political attitudes of the unorganised, quiescent majority of the population. Neglect of this has meant we have only the sketchiest understanding of working-class Conservatism in Britain, despite its key role in political history.[34]

Interpretations of political attitudes are no simple matter, however. It is not possible to put a microphone in front of someone in 'high-vis' and declare, "I've done it! I've given the working class a voice!" As emphasised by oral historian Alessandro Portelli in his early writings: "oral history is not the point where the working class speaks for itself ... the control of the historical discourse remains firmly in the hands of the historian".[35] This means that it is imperative that the interviewer be cognisant of the powerful role they play in relation to the class tensions emergent in the interview, and afterwards, in the stages of analysis, writing and research communication. Oral history itself, as described by Portelli, is described as necessarily a "confrontation" between two sides, the interviewer and interviewee—a disjunction on the level of class, and in terms of understandings of the world. This confrontation could emerge "as conflict", or it could be "confrontation as the search for unity".[36] This book, I hope, attempts the latter.

ENGINEERING PATTERNMAKERS IN CLASS CONTEXT

Apprenticeship and Trade Admittance

This small group of engineering patternmaker interviewees was never imagined as a 'representative sample', from which broader conclusions about Australian manufacturing could be gleaned. It nonetheless provides an example of the diversity of class-based and identity-based worlds through which industrial craftspeople pass, throughout their careers. The engineering patternmakers I interviewed were both workers and managers: they were owners of small businesses, and workers employed by large government organisations and private companies. As mentioned earlier, many patternmakers turned to other careers. They retrained as teachers, trade educators, retail employees, hospitality workers, designers, among other occupations. To that end, I am certainly not suggesting that this group uniformly represents the 'working class', and indeed many of them occupy a contradictory class location.[37] But one thing that unites them is that they undertook an apprenticeship in engineering patternmaking in their teenage years.[38] They were skilled tradespeople, first and foremost, before they shifted into anything else. While they have diverse employment pathways and relationships to power and capital, this group shares a relationship to industrial craft, to 'having a trade', which has deep historical roots, and lingering cultural influence for the rest of their lives.

What does it mean to be a skilled manufacturing tradesperson in Australia? To address this, we must look at the historical figure of the 'skilled tradesman' in Australia. In the nineteenth century (extending into much of the twentieth century), core ideals about Australian masculinity were closely tied to the concept of the fully qualified tradesman. Entry into industrial crafts was often (but not uniformly) protected by trade-specific unions.[39] Once admitted into an apprenticeship, the apprentice endured a lowly paid, five-year indenture to an employer, usually supervised by a 'master' tradesman before stepping into the trade officially. Apprentice recruitment was often a family affair: with trade skills passed along patrilineal lines, producing a hereditary aristocracy of labour. (Particular pedagogical strategies associated with apprenticeship are addressed in the following chapter.)

All this was of course a highly gendered affair: trade apprenticeship functioned to reproduce a masculinist culture of craft. Apprenticeship also operated as a form of unionised craft control, only admitting limited numbers. It also *excluded* many others, including women. The skilled tradesman was seen as a respectable figure who was practical, manually dextrous and knowledgeable, but not an intellectual.[40] In labour historian John Shields' oral histories with Australian boilermakers and engineers apprenticed in the early twentieth century, he emphasises the formative role of apprenticeship

> in sustaining ... despite major technological and workforce change, what might be termed a collective culture of craft in the Australian workplace. Its outlook was at once fraternal and sectional; labourist and masculinist.[41]

Trade apprenticeship established not only led to collective social acceptance, but also conferred upon apprentices a socially accepted form of masculinity. (I return to craft masculinity in Chap. 7.)

Other than family connections, another key factor that determined an occupational pathway towards industrial craft apprenticeship was attendance at an Australian technical high school. For much of the twentieth century, Australian public secondary education included two types of high schools: traditionally 'academic' high schools and technical high schools. Former patternmaker (and now secondary teacher) Peter Williams explained how a child's pathway was often set, from age 11 to 12:

> So the question we were asking ourselves when we were in Grade Six, the question was: "Oh, are you going to the Tech, or are you going to the High?" So, the academically-inclined kids were going to the nearest high school. (Some went on to Catholic High Schools or semi-private schools., but very few, very few of the kids in our neighbourhood did that. You either went to the high school or the Tech, and you went to the high school because you might be headed for some sort of an academic [professional] career. You went to the Tech if you felt you were headed towards being a tradesman ... somebody with some kind of a manual vocation. And I was certainly one of those. I wanted to go to the Tech. I was a hands-on person. ... I loved Lalor Tech, it was so interesting.[42]

Here, Williams suggests that there was, to some extent, a choice for boys, and a porosity between class positions that could be accessed if one had 'good enough' marks to go to an academic high school. In reality, however, a child's trajectory was generally determined by their social class and demographic background, as it was these factors that tended to determine their level of academic achievement.

46   J. A. STEIN

Williams first grew up in Wangaratta in the 1960s, which at the time was semi-rural but also dominated by textile manufacturing, but the family then moved to inner-city Melbourne (Fitzroy), where, as a child, Williams worked as a paperboy amid North Fitzroy's inner-city traffic, trams and laneways. His father Kevin was a school teacher, but also had a trade background (cabinetmaking). Kevin later became a full-time luthier (maker and repairer of string instruments), and his mother worked at a Catholic girls' college. Of his childhood, Williams said:

> We never felt that we were well-off, although we were always clothed, and we were never hungry. ... We certainly didn't live what you might call a flash lifestyle, and at times it wasn't even comfortable.[43]

From his father, Williams was exposed to fine woodworking, to the use of woodworking hand tools, to a particular work ethic, as well as to a culture of secondary education. But there were other tensions that influenced Williams' occupational pathway—he spoke of avoiding going home after selling his evening papers:

> There was no predictability about what frame of mind Dad was going to be in that particular evening, how much he might have had to drink, who was going to get a hiding for what.[44]

Avoiding going home, Williams would visit a pub in North Fitzroy, where he would sell papers and talk to the men drinking there. Alcohol consumption was a fundamental component of masculinity and collective identity within Australian working-class culture, and this was a world that Williams wished to enter:

> The hotels in those days were very different to what they are these days. I loved it. I absolutely loved the pub. ... I loved the atmosphere, I loved the camaraderie, and I really enjoyed the company of the men in there, and it was predominantly men. ... I couldn't wait to get in there as one of the men. ... This was a place where I felt safe.[45]

Apprenticeship brought not only a small wage, but also a sense of entry into this cultural milieu, when Williams did not always feel safe at home.

Within the broader Australian working class, fully qualified tradesmen saw themselves (and were seen) as attaining a form of material and moral superiority above other working-class occupations, both by virtue of their skill and by dignity as 'masters' of a craft.[46] Particular trades—such as printing and metalwork trades—understood themselves as being more highly skilled than other trades, forming part of an aristocracy of labour, a "consciously elite group".[47] The engineering patternmakers I interviewed certainly had more than just vestiges of the idea of themselves as being part of an aristocracy of labour, of being one of the more 'superior' trades. As the patternmakers often liked to remind me, engineering patternmaking emerged as an offshoot demarcation from the mediaeval all-rounder 'millwright'.[48] The specialist nature of their trade led patternmakers to favour claims about their 'exalted' status as craftsmen and artisans, inheritors of a guild-like secrecy where skills were passed on to a lucky, talented few.[49] Several patternmakers pointed me towards an oft-reproduced statement by American patternmaker Edward Leslie:

> A pattern maker is an exalted craftsman, the greatest common denominator, as well as the least common multiple of all industrial production. A pattern maker must have the creative conception of a draughtsman designer, the practical ability of a moulder, the precise skill of a machinist, the analytical judgment of a metallurgist and the specific exactness of a mathematician. He must create a plan, or design, with vision and ingenuity and build the idea from trade to trade with practical knowledge: thinking and forming inside and out with length, breadth and thickness, adjusting accurately all values and dimensions and producing with dexterous finality any conceivable form to be cast in metal. The products of the pattern maker's skill are truly surrounded by an aura of greatness which dignifies his right to assume a place of confidence, trust and honour in all industrial advance and national progress.[50]

This affirming quote was often pinned up in patternshops, serving as a reminder about patternmaking's imagined place in an industrial craft hierarchy. The form of craft prowess that is venerated here is based upon precision and intellectual clarity operating in tandem with manual dexterity, of practical and technical knowledge over bravado, of dignity over larrikinism.

While the Leslie quote is trite, this emphasis on their craft's superiority should not simply be dismissed as an exercise of posturing. As analysed by sociologist Cynthia Cockburn, the self-definition as craftspeople or artisans as superior to other members of the working class is "part and parcel of the conflict between capital and labour, not a sign of its absence".[51]

48   J. A. STEIN

The reiteration of patternmaking's superiority was in some cases a defensive gesture in a context that was devaluing manual crafts in industry. Patternmaker Tim Wighton said:

> Patternmaking was always told to me that it was a 'higher' trade If you went back to the 1800s, you know, patternmakers were on a similar footing to engine drivers. ... They were the highest you could go being blue collar without, you know, breaking through the ceiling kind of thing. ... So you were always listened to and respected that way. ... You were on a similar footing as the methods engineers, design engineers, estimators, that sort of thing.[52]

Likewise, patternmaker Peter Phipps said, "patternmaking ... was the highest trade level that you could take, so it was the most knowledgeable trade course. ... As long as I've got that behind me, I'll be able to do anything."[53] Other patternmakers told me that, in their view, the only trade that was 'higher' in the hierarchy of skill was that of the toolmaker, because that trade required the ability to transform metal into precision forms, while patternmakers excelled in timber.

While the twentieth century brought waves of industrial change that threatened the labour power of skilled tradespeople—via workplace change, technological transition and mass-production—I concur with Shields' thesis that in some trades, "craft culture and practice, including apprenticeship, remained surprisingly intact".[54] This means that when I hear stories from engineering patternmakers about their apprenticeship experience, their tales from the 1940s and 1950s are not dissimilar to stories told about the 1970s and 1980s. The similarities include: spending one's first year doing 'odd jobs' around the factory, before being allowed to handle the tools and machines, being taught by a 'master', and great pride in finally becoming a 'tradesman' at the end of one's apprenticeship. Interviewees could often recall the exact date of the beginning and end of their apprenticeship.

The late Bryan Poynton, who commenced his patternmaking apprenticeship at the International Harvester Company in Geelong in the mid-1950s, recalled that the first year of apprenticeship was spent learning "by osmosis", while "the other thing I had to do, besides sweeping, was go to the canteen with all the lunch orders, and I was eternally getting into trouble for not having the right change for everybody when I returned".[55]

Half a century after Poynton, in 2005, Wighton commenced his pattern-making apprenticeship at a Victorian foundry:

> As an apprentice you were … sweeping the floor, maintaining the machines. … You were the shop's responsibility, but it had kind of been an unspoken law that you were trained by one person, because, you know, patternmakers being a bit like artists, have their own way of doing anything, so if everyone was responsible for training the apprentice you know, you'd never get any training, because you'd be arguing all day. So he still had to do his job, while teaching me.[56]

Wighton considers himself "lucky" to be one of the last patternmakers in Australia to experience "learning the old trade, I s'pose, before it completely disappeared". He was taught manual patternmaking with hand and machine tools, before exposure to CNC machining and CAD. Whether or not that confers upon Wighton a particular sense of artisanal authority or superior status is another matter, however. In contemporary foundry work, a patternmaker's traditional skills do not command the same respect that they once did. Of his experience of management in recent foundry work, Wighton said: "You're just a labourer then, they don't wanna listen to you, or talk to you, or hear your opinion".[57] (See also Wighton's experience in Chap. 5.)

Serge Haidutschyk was apprenticed at the Victorian State Government's Victorian Railways' Newport Workshops in 1967. He described a very common apprenticeship learning experience:

> I was under the guidance of a tradesman. My bench was in a position, and right next to that was a tradesman, and every time there was a job given to me, the tradesman used to liaison with me, so I wasn't left in the lurch. … I was given the easy jobs. … So I made patterns, learning with a tradesman guiding me through, and it was excellent.[58]

Completing their apprenticeship—and receiving their indenture papers—was seen as a key life achievement. Haidutschyk said,

> I actually felt important, and I felt like I achieved something in life. … I'm a tradesman! … The most important experience was getting that paper and feeling like I'm free.[59]

'Free', perhaps, but it is worth noting that Haidutschyk then went on to work for the same employer (where he had undertaken his apprenticeship) for another 20 years, until the Workshops were closed down by the Victorian Government in a neoliberal asset sell-off in 1992. Haidutschyk's career was marked by the legacy of deindustrialisation in Melbourne: he experienced several redundancies, as recounted further on, and in Chap. 7.

Small-Business Patternmakers

As indicated earlier, patternmakers sit somewhat awkwardly within a definition of the working class, in part because of their imagined place in an aristocracy of labour, but also for reasons associated with union membership and business ownership, in short, their contradictory class position. To understand this, we must remember that patternmaking is a pre-production task in the manufacturing process. As I further explore in Chap. 4, patternmakers' hands do not touch the 'final product' and they are not, strictly speaking, part of a 'production line'. Moreover, once a pattern is made, it can be used again and again for mass-production (provided it stays intact and is not damaged in the moulding process). This means that patternmaking can be 'siphoned off' and outsourced with relative ease. You do not need a large number of patternmakers to produce a single pattern, but from there, mass-production can take place without the patternmakers' involvement. In this sense patternmakers might appear the model of alienated labour. However, from the patternmakers' perspective, as long as their *hands* make the patterns, they do not consider their labour alienated: for them, it is all about the pattern itself, not the final product.

In both the nineteenth and twentieth centuries, many larger Australian foundries had their own patternshops (particularly government-led industrial organisations). It was also common for patternmakers to set up their own, in small-business patternshops, which contracted out their services to larger foundries. These patternshops employed a small number of patternmakers (often three to ten), and often took on one or two apprentices. These small businesses were often family-run, non-unionised and managed by patternmaker tradespeople themselves. The patternmaker's spouse would often manage the accounts and administrative matters, and his sons (if there were any) were expected to follow in their father's footsteps.

Small-business patternshops were common in the twentieth-century Australian industry, and they did extremely well when Australian automotive and plastics manufacturing was booming in the mid-twentieth century. Patternshops could easily make models for plastics tooling, so they were no longer purely reliant on Australian cast metals production. These patternshops often specialised in a particular style of patternmaking, for instance, the interviewee Paul Kay's family business, W.G. Kay & Co., specialised in patterns and moulds for confectionery manufacture. Interviewee Deborah Tyrrell (and her husband Greg) runs Kimbeny Pty Ltd., which used to specialise in vacuum-formed plastic trays for cosmetics retail displays, among other things.

My interviewees included both current and retired employees *and* business owners, so I was conscious that I was, at times, talking to 'bosses'. But here is where it is useful to go back to the concept of power relations: to be a patternmaking business owner in the twenty-first century is not to command a great deal of power at all. The business owners I spoke with (formally and informally) had an almost uniform experience of precarity, loss of livelihood and grave concerns for their future. Some still employed a small number of patternmakers, while others, like Kay, had been reduced to sole-operators—closing their factory and moving the workshop to their domestic dwelling. The aforementioned, Peter Phipps, a third-generation patternmaker and business owner, said, "Where we used to, at one stage, have 10 people [employees], now there's 3 of us and a robot".[60] He explained:

> I'd love to put on more staff. I want to advance. I want to do more, but I need a growing industry around me. But ultimately, it's a shrinking industry. ... If you went to the local village here in Thirroul, there's probably eight or nine, there'll be a tenth coffee shop open tomorrow, and they still sell coffee ... vibrant and making money, because the culture is booming and people are doing that. But we're not in that position. I'm in a different part of society that isn't advancing. We're going backwards.[61]

Here, Phipps shows a keen awareness of the intersections between class, culture and the economy, and where his business fits in this picture. Phipps' desire for a 'way out' of the neoliberal capitalist cycle is clearly expressed:

> I'd like someone to think outside the square, that's a politician, to work out a way that struggling industries such as manufacturing can help the staff. Like at the moment, I can't pay my staff much, their wages are not good. ...

Both parties have thrown us away a long time ago. Our two, the Liberal and Labor parties, they've both given up on us. That's how we all feel. We're just not necessary any more.[62]

It is clearly apparent how views such as these are ripe fodder for populist politicians offering a 'solution', in order to gain support. There is a deep sense of disillusionment with contemporary economics and existing party politics.

When I asked Kay what he'd like the government to do, to help support his industry, he looked at me, a little exasperated, and said: "It's way too late for that".[63] There were times in Kay's interview where he seemed to be describing the problems of neoliberal capitalism, without necessarily being aware of this:

Everything's profit driven. ... I think that this constant drive for efficiency and this constant search for profits, I think also share-listed companies and investors looking for a return. ... I think it's pushed a lot of small businesses out of the way. I think the current situation is in favour of large companies.[64]

Kay's position recalls Erik Olin Wright's class analysis of the contradictory class location of small-business owners. In relation to class consciousness, Wright states, "there may be many petty bourgeois who take a quite anti-capitalist stance".[65] These patternmaking small businesses are completely at the mercy of larger manufacturing corporations. When large local manufacturers went bust, or shifted offshore, patternmakers lost much of their business in one hit.

Patternmakers and Unionisation

Historically, patternmaking has not been a highly unionised trade in Australia, which evidently impacts the patternmakers' sense of solidarity, as well as their bargaining power as an occupational group. It is also an extremely small trade, in terms of numbers, as outlined in the Introduction. The survival of the trade into the twenty-first century is more by virtue of its craft-based material qualities, and relative imperviousness to technological change (until CNC), not by virtue of its collective power. The small-business nature of many patternmaking enterprises added to this lack of unionisation. However there were (and are) patternmakers in Australian unions. In the twentieth century, the unionised patternmakers tended to be in the Amalgamated Engineering Union (AEU), among other metalworkers such as fitters and turners, blacksmiths, toolmakers, welders and so on.

As noted by labour historian Thomas Sheridan in his history of the AEU, patternmakers were a small group of highly skilled AEU members, but the vast majority of members were in other metal trades and occupations. For instance, in 1966, patternmakers made up only 0.4 per cent of the AEU metal workforce members.[66] Today, the remaining unionised patternmakers tend to be in the Australian Manufacturing Workers' Union (AMWU), an amalgamated union which represents the full gamut of (what is left of) unionised Australian manufacturing workers. These patternmakers tend to be foundry employees, employees of medium- to large-size foundry businesses. It is interesting to note that through the ongoing process of union amalgamation, the remaining unionised patternmakers have shifted from a more conservative union (the AEU), into a more left-wing union (the AMWU).

In the United Kingdom, engineering patternmakers were represented by the United Patternmakers' Association (UPMA), which differed from the Australian model inasmuch as the patternmakers in the UK organised separately from other metalworkers. The UPMA was envisaged as a union for patternmakers alone. This tells us something of their view of themselves, vis-à-vis the rest of the working class. This approach was not without its critics. Recalling the 1904 article in *The Socialist* mentioned in Chap. 1, here an anonymous patternmaker describes the general problem of capitalism, as it specifically relates to patternmakers:

> The patternmaker boasted that he was an aristocrat of labour. … If he had thought very much at all he would have seen that he had absolutely no property, with the exception of his hand tools and his *skill as a pattern-maker*, that is, his *labour power*. … At the end of the week, however, he was not in possession of the pattern he had made—that belonged to his master—but instead he got paid … wages instead. … The wages he received in exchange for *his skill as a patternmaker* represented less in value than one half of the wealth he had produced.[67]

The article goes on to specifically criticise the UPMA, stating that the union "is no longer of any use to the working class in their work of emancipation", in part because it had been founded on the idea that it was a union *only* for patternmakers, and not allied to the broader working class.

54   J. A. STEIN

Among my interview participants, discussions of union membership prompted a variety of responses, and not always a great deal of detail. It seemed a peripheral experience for most of them, or, rather, something external that happened to them, rather than something of which they were constitutive. Peter Phipps' father Bruce (a second-generation patternmaking business owner) said that union membership "wasn't compulsory, and I never did". He added:

> I couldn't see the benefit in our trade, so I just kept out of it. And I don't like—I've always tried to keep peace. I don't like getting involved in arguments. ... Very rarely were the unions involved in small shops.[68]

Bruce Phipps conceded that when he commenced his apprenticeship at Sydney's shipbuilding Cockatoo Island in the late 1940s: "the whole island was sort of run by unions, so you more or less had to be in it".[69] (Apprentices, however, were not required to be union members, so Bruce's statement here is not actually a contradiction of his earlier declaration.)

As a government employee, Haidutschyk remained a union member for as long as he worked at the Newport Railways (in his case, in the Australian Society of Engineers). He expressed union loyalty, but for him, union membership did not necessarily lead to a keen sense of class consciousness. This was most apparent in his discussion of 'closed shops'. Haidutschyk had referred to his patternshop as being a closed shop, so I asked him about it. I assumed he was going to explain that only union members were allowed to work there. Instead he said:

> Well, what my interpretation of a close shop is, where's one building, a factory, it's seventy-five metres by twenty-five metres long. All the equipment's in there, front door, back door, and nobody was allowed ... in there, to be honest. Nobody was allowed in there. If you worked in another section of that factory, you weren't allowed to just open the door and walk in there. ... This was a closed shop, and the only people working in this area were the tradesmen. ... I stayed under one roof for twenty-five years, and that was it.[70]

Haidutschyk endured three redundancies in his career, working as a tradesman patternmaker, then when patternmaking roles proved too difficult to find, he worked as a maintenance worker at an aged care facility. (See also Chap. 7.) Thus Haidutschyk's experience, throughout his lifetime, has

2 NAVIGATING CLASS AND POPULIST POLITICS IN CONTEMPORARY ORAL... 55

been as a working-class tradesman and as the son of Ukrainian refugee migrants to Australia. Haidutschyk's decades of union membership did not lead to him becoming classically 'left wing'. Instead, he expressed a relatively conservative personal politics: he is a staunch Australian nationalist and expressed concerns that more recent refugee migrants to Australia were not assimilating or contributing as he felt his parents' generation had. His proud Australian nationalism was enfolded with a passion for Australian native flora and timbers, intertwined with pride in his refugee migrant parents' capacity to survive and thrive in their new country.

Wighton was another patternmaker with union experiences to recount. He has recent experience working as a patternmaker at two separate Victorian foundries: one that was unionised (AMWU), and a family-run foundry without a union presence. Wighton observed that at his first employer:

> The patternshop tended to have the most highly trained, highly intelligent members of the foundry ... they always wound up being a union rep ... which was good, but it was also bad, because the management would seem to take their frustration out on us.[71]

Of his first employer, Wighton said, "the union kept them honest, so they didn't get away with too much".[72] He also noted that his first employer "had a very strong union presence and an inclusive, proactive OH&S [Occupational Health & Safety] framework, thanks to which I know my legal rights and how to enforce them".[73] Of the next foundry Wighton worked at, he felt that the fact that it wasn't a unionised workplace was detrimental to workplace conditions and wages. His earlier experience in the union enabled him a level of consciousness of his situation that he felt other workers might be lacking. Like Kay, Wighton spoke to a larger exhaustion with the current economic system:

> Neoliberalism and globalisation are ... reducing the breath of skills the individual has, and trying to reduce labour down to 'plug and play' style workplace arrangements.[74]

> I think the past 20 years of all this business push, you know, this neocapitalism 'outsource it, service economy and get a degree', I think all of that has been a failed experiment. We're left now with no manufacturing. ... It sounds melodramatic but I don't know how people are putting up with it at the moment.[75]

56   J. A. STEIN

His own personal situation encapsulated this problem well. When I interviewed Wighton in 2017, he said:

> I've been working 10 years. I have no house deposit, you know, and that's through no fault of my own. I don't live lavishly, I don't smoke. I don't really drink. I don't have subscriptions to 2 dozen streaming services, you know, there's no, there's none of that. We live quite frugally. We op-shop, we make things ourselves. I can't tell you where the money is going. There was no money to begin with.[76]

I return to Wighton's story at several other stages in this book, particularly Chaps. 3 and 5. As the youngest patternmaker interviewed here—and the father to three young children—his particular experience seemed the most contingent, the most at risk, in the current economic context. Wighton's reflections were less in the realm of 'history' and more concerned with contemporary issues and an uncertain future.

CONCLUSION

Evidently, the patternmakers I interviewed did not turn out to be as angry as O'Sullivan had been, but if they had been, they would have had good reason. Or, put it this way: the patternmakers I interviewed all experienced frustration, grief, loss and anger in relation to the disintegration of their trade. Perhaps they were not as outwardly aggressive as O'Sullivan, but they all understood themselves in relation to a wider social and political context; they recognised their relative powerlessness, and their fleeting moments of agency. There is a role for oral history in articulating this, as it is inherently a 'slow' medium, allowing interviewees the time to reflect, time to articulate their position. It does not subject participants to the fast-paced, scattergun immediacy of so many other aspects of contemporary interactions and social media. Using the life history form in oral history also enables a deeply contextual approach: allowing us to see how class, gender, ethnicity, education and other relevant factors are all relevant components shaping how people understand their lives and their place in history. This enables understandings to emerge on both materialist and symbolic levels (i.e. the capital and power people have access to, and how they understand their identity in relation to the rest of society).

The act of interviewing and then interpreting the material is never straightforward. I am just as enmeshed in the present politics as everyone else is. As an interviewer I had to forge a path that used our respective differences positively and generatively. The interviewees were 'narrators' of their experience, and they constructed their place in the world as they spoke.[77] In this way, the interviewees were active protagonists in the making of history. These histories of industrial craft in Australia were not something to be completely defined *by me*, but something that would emerge through discourse and interaction.

As oral historians know from experience, 'discourse and interaction' is not just something that happens when the audio recorder is running. Interactions that occur when the recorder is switched off can be just as important (and sometimes frustratingly so!). In the middle of the interview, after the first or second recording session, we would often stop for lunch. The lunchtime conversations were often very different. The tables turned: often the interviewees wanted to ask about my situation. Was I in precarious employment in the university sector? How did I manage childcare and work? Was childcare expensive in the city? Did the baby sleep at night? (Would they have asked some of these questions if I was a man? I did wonder.) But they also asked: Was it hard to find an affordable home in the city? Where was I from—was I the child of migrants? Did I have a craft or making practice? These sorts of conversations were a way to find shared-ground, and for the most part this was not difficult to do.

Throughout this project I have engaged with my interviewees not only from the point of view of their manufacturing labour but also in relation to other aspects of their lives: their occupational pathways, their other responsibilities beyond their paid labour, their creative practice and their culture. The following quote from the interviewee Peter Watts (former patternmaker, now an artist) is shared here not so much as an endorsement, but to indicate that some of the interviewees understood that their stories were significant, as their experience was an 'unmapped' transition:

> Your willingness Jesse to go where others have dared not is most appreciated. You have chosen a most obscure field of enquiry and have examined this with great care and clarity. Beyond defining what patternmaking is or was, you honour us all with this insightful account of individual transitions beyond 'the patternmaking bench'. To have listened and given witness to us who traversed that unmapped path … is both astonishing and very gratifying.[78]

58   J. A. STEIN

Industrial craft in Australia spills out into the domestic sphere, into education and career pathways, into the arts and into communities.[79] Listening out for how it operates means understanding that there will be contradictions and overlaps, and places where industrial craft hides in other, apparently 'non-industrial' practices. In deindustrialising contexts, the culture of industrial craft cannot be wrestled into singular categories of 'craft', nor 'skilled', nor simply 'working class' experience. It is all of these things, but it is also much more, as the following chapters explore.

NOTES

1. Robert Weil, "Contradictory Class Definitions: Petty Bourgeoisie and the 'Classes' of Erik Olin Wright", *Critical Sociology* 21, no. 3 (1995): 3–37; Erik Olin Wright, *Class Counts* (Cambridge: Cambridge University Press, 2000 edition).
2. Michael Zweig, *The Working Class Majority: America's Best Kept Secret* (Ithaca and London: Cornell University Press, 2012), 2nd edition, 39.
3. Fieldwork conducted in July 2015 with A.V. Simpson, M. Berti & A. Hermens, UTS Business School, UTS Human Ethics Approval #ETH16-1004.
4. For example, my interviews with print-workers from the NSW Government Printing Office, as part of the *Precarious Printers* research project (2011–2014).
5. I focus less on race and ethnicity in this particular research, due in part to the relative ethnic homogeneity of the cluster of interviewees I encountered. Some of the best recent work that engages with deindustrialisation, race and ethnicity in oral history (in a post-Brexit context) is Ben Rogaly, *Stories from a Migrant City: Living and Working Together in the Shadow of Brexit* (Manchester: Manchester University Press, 2020); Jason Hackworth, *Manufacturing Decline: How Racism and the Conservative Movement Crush the American Rust Belt* (New York: Columbia University Press, 2019).
6. Ace Volkmann Simpson, Marco Berti, Jesse Adams Stein, and Antoine Hermens, 'Sensemaking in managing a family firm's "tradition of innovation"', conference paper, *32nd EGOS Colloquium—Organizing in the Shadow of Power* (Naples: 7–9 July 2016).
7. Mark Adams, "On the Road Again", *The Cutting Edge* 94 (April 2013).
8. Richard Cashman, "Book Review: Reet A. and Maxwell L. Howell's *The Genesis of Sport in Queensland: From the Dreamtime to Federation*", *Sporting Traditions* 10, no. 1 (1993): 116–18; Kate Kruckemeyer, "'You Get Sawdust in Your Blood': 'Local' Values and the Performance of

2 NAVIGATING CLASS AND POPULIST POLITICS IN CONTEMPORARY ORAL... 59

Community in an Occupational Sport", *American Folklore Society* 115, no. 457 (2002): 301–31; Rupert Tipples and Jude Wilson, "Work-Sport Competition: The Role of Agricultural Contests in New Zealand", *Rural Society* 17, no. 1 (2007): 34–49.

9. Joan Sangster, "Politics and Praxis in Canadian Working Class Oral History", in Robert Perks and Alistair Thomson (eds), *The Oral History Reader*, 3rd edn (London and New York: Routledge, 2016), 59–72. See also earlier oral history writing such as Luisa Passerini, *Fascism and Popular Memory: The Cultural Experience of the Turin Working Class* (Cambridge: Cambridge University Press, 1987); Elizabeth Roberts, *A Woman's Place: An Oral History of Working Class Women 1890–1940* (London: Basil Blackwell, 1984); Michael Frisch, *A Shared Authority: Essays on the Craft and Meaning of Oral and Public History* (New York: SUNY, 1990); Paul Thompson, *The Voice of the Past: Oral History* (Oxford and New York: Oxford University Press, 1978, second edition 1988); Alessandro Portelli, "The Peculiarities of Oral History", *History Workshop Journal* 12, no. 1 (1981): 96–107.

10. Sangster, "Politics and Praxis".

11. Sangster, "Politics and Praxis", 60; Alastair Thomson, "Fifty Years On: An International Perspective on Oral History", *Journal of American History* 85, no. 2 (1998): 581–95.

12. Sangster, "Politics and Praxis"; Catherine Daley, "'He Would Know, but I Just Have a Feeling': Gender and Oral History", *Women's History Review* 7, no. 3 (1998): 343–58.

13. Steven High, "Right Wing Populism and the Realignment of Working Class Politics in Canada", *Canadian Dimension* (19 November 2020). See also Michael Zweig, "White Working-Class Voters and the Future of Progressive Politics", *New Labour Forum* 26, no. 2 (2017): 28–36; and from an urban policy perspective, see Hackworth, *Manufacturing Decline*; Tracy Neumann, *Remaking the Rust Belt: The Postindustrial Transformation of North America* (Philadelphia: University of Pennsylvania Press, 2019).

14. Zweig, "White Working-Class Voters"; Bjarke Skærlund Risager, "Neoliberalism is a Political Project: An Interview with David Harvey", *Jacobin* (23 July 2016), https://www.jacobinmag.com/2016/07/david-harvey-neoliberalism-capitalism-labor-crisis-resistance/, accessed 2 June 2021. See also William Mitchell & Thomas Fazi, *Reclaiming the State: A Progressive Vision for Sovereignty for a Post-Neoliberal World* (London: Pluto Press, 2017).

15. Zweig, "White Working-Class Voters".

16. The author would like to acknowledge the significant multilingual work currently being undertaken in Canada, Europe and the United Kingdom, shared through the collaborative partnership *Deindustrialization and the*

Politics of Our Time (DéPOT), which includes the re-analysis of working-class issues and a critical rethinking of deindustrialisation. See https://deindustrialization.org/.

17. Zweig, *The Working Class Majority*.
18. High, "Right Wing Populism".
19. High, "Right Wing Populism".
20. Steven High, "Deindustrialization and its Consequences", in Michele Fazio, Christie Launius, and Tim Strangleman (eds) *Routledge International Handbook of Working-Class Studies* (London and New York: Routledge, 2020), 169–79.
21. Zweig, *The Working Class Majority*.
22. Zweig, "White Working-Class Voters", p. 28.
23. Zweig, *The Working Class Majority*, p. 10.
24. R.W. Connell and T.H. Irving, *Class Structure in Australian History: Documents, Narrative and Argument* (Melbourne: Longman Cheshire, 1980), p. 1.
25. Connell and Irving, *Class Structure*.
26. See Judith Brett, *Australian Liberals and the Moral Middle Class: From Alfred Deakin to John Howard* (Cambridge University Press, 2008).
27. Michael Zweig, "Six Points on Class", *Monthly Review Press* 58, no. 3 (July–August 2006).
28. Zweig, *The Working Class Majority*, p. 3.
29. Even worse, as suggested by David Harvey, some of the left are in fact "reinforcing the endgame of neoliberalism" by only focusing on symbolic and recognition-based forms of identity discourse, at the expense of materialist and redistributive goals. In other words, paying lip service to identity politics without acknowledging that symbolic inequality stems from materialist inequality. See Harvey in Risager, "Neoliberalism is a Political Project". See also William Mitchell and Thomas Fazi on the divided left, in Mitchell and Fazi, *Reclaiming the State*, 10–11.
30. Zweig, "White Working-Class Voters".
31. Jennifer Rayner, *Blue Collar Frayed: Working Men in Tomorrow's Economy* (Melbourne: Redback, 2018).
32. Rosana Pinheiro-Machado and Lucia Mury Scalco, "Anthropology in Times of Hatred Politics", *Fieldsights* (Society for Cultural Anthropology, 28 January 2020), https://culanth.org/fieldsights/anthropology-in-times-of-hatred-politics, accessed 10 March 2021.
33. Pinheiro-Machado and Scalco, "Anthropology in Times of Hatred Politics". See also, High, "Deindustrialization and its Consequences".
34. Thompson, *The Voice of the Past*, p. 82.
35. Portelli, "The Peculiarities of Oral History", p. 104.
36. Portelli, "The Peculiarities of Oral History", p. 106.

37. Weil, "Contradictory Class Definitions"; Wright, *Class Counts*.
38. The interviewee Deborah Tyrrell is the exception here, but her business partner and husband *is* an engineering patternmaker by trade.
39. The United Kingdom and Australian trade apprenticeships in the nineteenth and twentieth centuries tended to be more tightly protected by unions than was the case in places such as Canada. See John Charles Wren, *Skilled Trades' Work and Apprentice Training in the Manufacturing Industry with a Primary Focus on the Millwright Trade*, PhD Thesis (Toronto: University of Toronto, 2008); Marilyn Zapf, *The Making of Industrial Artisans: Training Engineers in Britain, 1964–1979*, Masters Thesis (London: RCA, 2012).
40. Andrea Waling, *White Masculinity in Contemporary Australia: The Good Ol' Aussie Bloke* (London and New York: Routledge, 2020), p. 29.
41. John Shields, "Craftsmen in the Making: The Memory and Meaning of Apprenticeship in Sydney between the Great War and the Great Depression", in Shields (ed), *All Our Labours: Oral Histories of Working Life in Twentieth Century Sydney* (Sydney: New South Wales University Press, 1992), p. 88.
42. Peter Williams, interview with author, *Reshaping Australian Manufacturing*, 26 November 2017 (Canberra: NLA), https://nla.gov.au/nla.cat-vn7540153.
43. Williams, interview with author.
44. Williams, interview with author.
45. Williams, interview with author.
46. Shields, "Craftsmen in the Making", p. 89.
47. Thomas Sheridan, *Mindful Militants: The Amalgamated Engineering Union in Australia 1920–1972* (London, New York and Melbourne: Cambridge University Press, 1975), pp. 13–14.
48. Joseph G. Horner, *Pattern Making: A Practical Treatise Embracing the Main Types of Engineering Construction* (London: Crosby Lockwood and Son, 1902), p. b; Sheridan, *Mindful Militants*, p. 2; Wren, *Skilled Trades' Work*.
49. John Looker, *I Want to be a Patternmaker* (Melbourne: Memoirs Publishing, 2011).
50. Edward Leslie, quote reproduced in *Kindt Collins Master Products*, catalogue (Ohio: Kindt Collins Ohio, n.d.).
51. Cynthia Cockburn, *Brothers: Male Dominance and Technological Change* (London: Pluto Press, 1983), p. 32.
52. Tim Wighton, interview with author, *Reshaping Australian Manufacturing*, 27 November 2017 (Canberra: NLA), https://nla.gov.au/nla.cat-vn7540155.

53. Peter Phipps, interview with author, *Reshaping Australian Manufacturing*, 11 May 2018 (Canberra: NLA), https://nla.gov.au/nla.cat-vn7765727.
54. Shields, "Craftsmen in the Making", p. 90.
55. Bryan Poynton, interview with author, *Reshaping Australian Manufacturing*, 22 February 2018 (Canberra: NLA), https://nla.gov.au/nla.cat-vn7580610.
56. Wighton, interview with author.
57. Wighton, interview with author.
58. Serge Haidutschyk, interview with author, *Reshaping Australian Manufacturing*, 4 December 2018 (Canberra: NLA), https://nla.gov.au/nla.cat-vn7889878.
59. Haidutschyk, interview with author.
60. Peter Phipps interviewed by audio producer Olivia Rosenman for 'Invisible Hands', *HistoryLab* podcast, Season 2, Episode 2, December 2018, https://historylab.net/s2ep2-invisible-hands.
61. Phipps, interview with author.
62. Phipps, interview with author.
63. Paul Kay, interview with author, *Reshaping Australian Manufacturing*, 30 April 2018 (Canberra: NLA), https://nla.gov.au/nla.cat-vn7765725.
64. Kay, interview with author.
65. Wright, *Class Counts*, p. 221.
66. Sheridan, *Mindful Militants*, p. 9.
67. Anon., "Patternmaking and Capitalism", *The Socialist* (November 1904): 7.
68. Bruce Phipps, interview with author, *Reshaping Australian Manufacturing*, 31 May 2018 (Canberra: NLA), https://nla.gov.au/nla.cat-vn7765732.
69. Bruce Phipps, interview with author.
70. Haidutschyk, interview with author.
71. Wighton, interview with author.
72. Wighton, interview with author.
73. Wighton, personal communication with author, 19 May 2017.
74. Wighton, pers comm., as above.
75. Wighton, interview with author.
76. Wighton, interview with author.
77. Portelli, "The Peculiarities of Oral History".
78. Peter Watts, personal communication with author, 4 March 2021.
79. Chantel Carr, "Maintenance and Repair Beyond the Perimeter of the Plant: Linking Industrial Labour and the Home", *Transactions of the Institute of British Geographers* 42, no. 4 (2017): 642–54.

CHAPTER 3

The Patternmaker's Toolbox: Making Things on the Side in Industrial Craft Apprenticeship

INTRODUCTION

Within half an hour the fire was in Airey's Inlet. So we really had no time. Inadequate water facilities, no sprinklers, only a small 1500 gallon tank of water. The town water supply was just a tiny dribble, so there's no way of fighting or impeding that fire. ... I had a chance to chuck my toolbox on somebody's car, get that out, and then the family spent the rest of the night in the water, down at the beach closest, up to our necks, luckily it was low tide and a calm sea, and we had our T-shirts pulled up over our heads because the embers were all dropping around us, and the noise was fearful. Lots of explosions. You know it was just a huge roar. ... So there was my wife and our two children, and I think they had a cat with them, the cat survived as well.[1]

These are the recollections of Bryan Poynton (Fig. 3.1), a woodwork artisan who originally trained as an engineering patternmaker. Poynton and his family survived the Ash Wednesday bushfires, a 1983 disaster in the Australian states of Victoria and South Australia, which had claimed 75 lives. During the bushfires, Poynton lost his house, his wood workshop

© The Author(s), under exclusive license to Springer Nature Switzerland AG 2021
J. A. Stein, *Industrial Craft in Australia*, Palgrave Studies in Oral History, https://doi.org/10.1007/978-3-030-87243-4_3

63

Fig. 3.1 Bryan Poynton, photograph by the author, 2018

and many works in progress. The most important things survived, however: his family, and his original patternmakers' toolbox (Fig. 3.2). What was it about this toolbox that made it so precious? Poynton made this toolbox during his patternmaking apprenticeship at the International Harvester Company in the mid-1950s, in the Victorian town of Geelong. The custom of requiring (or at least encouraging) woodwork-related apprentices to make their own toolboxes was widespread in Australia, among other places, throughout the twentieth century.

This chapter examines the social and educational significance of industrial workplace practices that resulted in objects being crafted 'on the side', both by apprentices and fully qualified tradespeople. My focus here is how engineering patternmakers designed and crafted timber toolboxes, and bespoke tools, during work time, using workplace materials and scrap. In particular, I highlight how apprentices made timber toolboxes during their four- or five-year apprenticeship. Of all the patternmakers I interviewed and spoke to informally, only two had *not* made their own toolbox,

Fig. 3.2 Bryan Poynton's first toolbox, c. mid-1950s. Photograph by the author, 2018. Toolbox and hand tools now held with Museums Victoria, Melbourne

and *all* had spent at least some of their time at work making things on the side. While making objects such as a toolbox was never a formal requirement of the Australian apprenticeship system, their production—particularly in the patternmaking trade—was widespread, forming part of the cultural reproduction of industrial craft identity. The chapter traces both ends of a tradesperson's career: the early days in a patternmaker's apprenticeship, and the final days before retirement, when tradespeople begin to contemplate life at home, making things, this time without the machinery, space and tools available at their workplace.

The chapter demonstrates how, for apprentices, quietly crafting supposedly 'unproductive' objects at work formed a vital pedagogical process of 'learning by doing'; it represented a staged marker of apprentice achievement. By the completion of their apprenticeship, twentieth-century patternmaking apprentices were expected to have a complete set of their own hand tools, and a handmade toolbox in which to keep them. Other than a very small tool allowance as part of their pay, apprentices received no other formal or financial support to meet these implicit workplace expectations. Hand tools were expensive, and machine tools even more so. But in an apprentice's first year it was customary for an apprentice's 'master' (or the shop Foreman) to give their apprentices the task of building a toolbox, and at least some work time (and sometimes materials) for this purpose.[2] Some patternshops gave apprentices a set of standard technical drawings to use as a guide. Others encouraged their apprentices to design their own.

Initially I took these toolboxes somewhat for granted. Histories of craft have already explored handmade boxes made by amateur and professional woodworkers.[3] Existing studies have also investigated the specific and evolving meanings of craft tools for their makers.[4] So at first I did not quite know how to fully appreciate these patternmakers' toolboxes. After my first few interviews, however, some nagging questions arose. I soon ascertained that the patternmaker's toolbox was typically made in the first year of their apprenticeship, when the apprentice was usually only 16 years old. (There were of course exceptions, and some patternmakers continued making toolboxes throughout their careers.) But, typically, the timber toolbox was an apprenticeship task. The handmaking of other hand tools often came later, when a specific need arose. What, I wondered, was the formal status of this toolbox, in relation to the production output of the patternshop or foundry? Was the toolbox and its contents owned by the apprentice or by their employer? Were they produced during work time?

The patternmakers soon set me straight: toolboxes and bespoke tools were generally produced during work time (after their required daily tasks were complete), and were often made using workplace materials and recovered scrap timber. One key point emerged throughout my interviews: this act of making things on the side was a pedagogical exercise; it was viewed as an opportunity for apprentice skills development. The toolboxes were ultimately seen as the apprentice's property, and they were treasured—many still are. As objects, these toolboxes were seen to convey and contain key aspects of the patternmaker's life history and industrial craft achievement. Nowadays, these boxes exist as objects of pride, but also a profound sense of sadness: representative as they are of a trade that is no longer accorded the recognition it once was. For individual patternmakers, their handmade toolboxes—and the tools therein—later became potent symbolic vectors for patternmakers' personal, collective and professional identities.[5] The valences attached to these boxes shifted in the late twentieth and early twenty-first centuries, when Australian patternmakers faced two aforementioned threats: a declining manufacturing sector and the increasing uptake of digital fabrication technologies which usurped patternmakers' craft control (as explored in Chap. 5).

The following section provides an overview of the specific Australian apprenticeship context. From there, the chapter shifts to the oral history material, featuring patternmakers discussing their toolbox and bespoke toolmaking experiences. The chapter then engages briefly with the experiences of several patternmaker educators in the final years of their careers: they made custom-built lathes, at work on the side, in preparation for life beyond the workplace. Finally, I consider what has happened to these covert making practices in the contemporary context (particularly toolbox making). Current manufacturing business management methods can have unforeseen and significant impacts for apprentice training, as well as transforming the material culture of the shopfloor.

Industrial Craft Training Through Making Foreigners

As briefly discussed in Chap. 2, in the Australian apprenticeship system, patternmaking apprentices were traditionally indentured to an employer for four years (formerly five).[6] The same applied in other industrial trades, in a system largely inherited from the United Kingdom. The apprentice was trained in-house by their employer, and as their skills increased they were given harder tasks to complete. The apprentice's experience varied a

68   J. A. STEIN

great deal, depending on the nature and size of their employing organisation. For example: an apprentice assigned to a small commercial patternshop might have learned a highly specialised type of patternmaking, but not been exposed to a broader sense of patternmaking as it operates in a broad swathe of manufacturing sub-sectors. That apprentice might learn how to work fast and accurately, in order to get orders made for an unforgiving private sector. An apprentice assigned to a large government-led industrial organisation, however, may spend their first year learning about all of the various industrial trades at their organisation, before being introduced to speciality skills in patternmaking. In this way the government apprentice may gain a wider understanding of a complete industrial process, but may not work as fast as some commercial patternmakers expected.

This variation in apprenticeship experience meant that one aspect of every apprentice's experience was absolutely vital: public education. During their apprenticeship, Australian trade apprentices also attended technical education classes at an approved training facility (previously known as 'technical colleges', colloquially known as 'trade school', now commonly referred to as 'TAFE'—essentially public educational institutions for formalising trade skills). Apprentices attended either 'night school' or a particular regular pattern of attendance, such as 'block release'.[7]

Histories of nineteenth- and twentieth-century apprenticeship can be problematic because, while apprenticeships effectively served to pass on craft skill, they also involved child abuse, patriarchal masculine rituals (known as 'initiations' or 'hazing') and vastly uneven power dynamics.[8] Furthermore, apprenticeships are difficult to generalise about, as they featured fluid and ever-changing customary practices that differed from one geographical location to another and from one trade to the next.[9] As noted by labour historian John Shields, even in the mid-twentieth century Australian apprenticeship agreements "echoed the paternalistic language and class inequities of nineteenth century 'master and servant' law".[10] Some apprentice processes served to bring an apprentice into a powerful unionised collective, while other processes produced a free-roaming individual. This largely depended upon the size of their first employer, and whether that patternshop was unionised. It can be said, however, that in general industrial craft apprenticeships became powerful sources of a person's identity and achievement. As noted in Chap. 2, an apprenticeship situated a person's class position, and in some cases limited their future career prospects. But it also endowed their hands—and their minds—with

3 THE PATTERNMAKER'S TOOLBOX: MAKING THINGS ON THE SIDE... 69

their own particular material 'super-power'. This was certainly the case for engineering patternmakers, who continue to deeply value their (now rare) capacity to materialise precise three-dimensional forms manually.

For the patternmakers I interviewed, trade school provided a vital exposure to a broader world beyond the troubles and technologies pertaining to their particular employer. Patternmaking apprentices were able to speak to other students and staff with expertise in different aspects of the patternmaking trade—from plastics, to automotive modelmaking, to foundry work for mining and the agricultural machinery. For example, at the George Thompson School of Foundry Technology (part of the Royal Melbourne Institute of Technology [RMIT], Melbourne), apprentices were able to use the school's own foundry, and engage with the process of metal casting from technical drawing, through to patternmaking, moulding, casting, the after-cast process, to the final product. Peter Williams commenced his patternmaking apprenticeship in 1978 and attended the George Thompson School at the same time. Like many others I interviewed, Williams was extremely positive about his educational experience:

> It was a *fascinating* place, I *loved* it. ... It was the only purpose-built foundry and pattern-making training facility in the Southern Hemisphere. There was nothing else like it in the Southern Hemisphere. To find a better place for patternmakers and foundrymen to do their technical schooling, you'd have to go to London, or maybe Philadelphia or somewhere like that. ... Because the school was well staffed you didn't have to wait for help. ... They would roam the room. ... They would stop and demonstrate, it was all very practical and hands-on.[11]

Later, in the mid-1990s, Williams became a patternmaking teacher at this very school. We will revisit his story in Chap. 5. While trade schools did not tend to teach toolbox making—as this was often done by the apprentice's employer—this practice changed in the late twentieth century. Patternmaking educator Anthony Freemantle indicated that his patternmaking school (TAFE Queensland) did in fact teach toolbox making for a period of time—to pick up the practice that some commercial employers had dropped—but toolbox-making has now ceased at TAFE too.

I want to dwell a little longer on apprenticeships because, in recent years, these forms of technical education have been grossly devalued and misunderstood, almost to the point of being 'written off' entirely, particularly in Australia. The incremental defunding of publicly owned training institutions (such as TAFEs) is one example of this current lack of value accorded to trades and their skill-development requirements. The economic and political shifts that prompted deindustrialisation did not simply mean a loss of jobs in the manufacturing sector. With it, there emerged an attitude that devalued manual trades as an educational and vocational pathway. TAFE institutions were underfunded, resulting in poorer and poorer educational outcomes, making them easy targets for restructuring. Likewise, disappearing local manufacturing facilities also meant a loss of educational spaces: places where working-class and middle-class young people had previously gained life-long skills and qualifications. This devaluation of trades education also entails a misunderstanding of what such education entails in practical terms. Trades education is so often a hands-on process, and employers alone cannot be expected to provide the full remit of an apprentice's training. Trade skills are material, practical and embodied. They are gained through the cumulation of hundreds of hours of exposure to wide-ranging practical tasks as well as theoretical knowledge about materials, technologies and processes. Core to these embodied and material pedagogical practices was the making of things 'on the side', as the next section will explain.

MAKING THINGS ON THE SIDE: EXISTING ANALYSIS

The workplace practice of making objects on the side—in work time, using shop materials and factory space—is a global practice, known by a variety of colloquial names. In the United States it is sometimes called making *homers*.[12] French theorist Michel de Certeau drew attention to the equivalent term *la perruque*.[13] In places colonised by Britain, the terms *government job* and *private job* have been used.[14] Sociologist Michel Anteby—who has examined the practice in factory French settings—noted that the labels *bousilles*, *pinailles* and *bricoles* were used in factories, and he has also used the terms *side productions*.[15] In Australia the most common twentieth-century labels for making things on the side are *foreign orders* and *foreigners*.[16] The precise derivation of the term is unclear; however, it could be suggested that the terms point to an undercurrent of racism in twentieth-century Australian society—suggesting something from 'outside' that is not-quite proper, on the fringe. On the other hand, 'foreigners' were also celebrated, albeit discreetly, by the workers who made them, so the term is not necessarily pejorative. Disclaimers aside, 'foreigner' is the term most commonly used by the patternmakers I spoke with, so I will use it here.

Over the past two decades, a scattering of sociological and historical studies have examined the practice of making things on the side at work.[17] It has been established that foreigner production is a prevalent but seldom publicly acknowledged practice, part of workplace culture across industrialised economies.[18] In making foreigners, workers use workplace machinery, scraps or new materials and factory time, to produce objects. Former boilermaker and academic Stephen Smith (not to be confused with the patternmaker Stephen Smith in Fig. 3.3) has identified four categories of foreigner: "a semi-legitimate foreigner as indicator of knowledge and skill"; personal objects for home or friends; a "network foreigner" to establish relations with particular workers or groups or a "commercial foreigner" intended for money or barter (the latter category was not common).[19] The objects made include gifts, toys, furniture, household knick-knacks, tools and contraptions for the workplace—and boxes. Existing research into foreigner production has established its significance in the moral economy of industrial workplaces, and its value as a subtle form of political resistance prompted by the threat of deindustrialisation.[20] As Anteby has established, foreigner production does not easily fit into established narratives relating to labour history, nor business history.[21] To this I would add, we are still in the early days of understanding the

Fig. 3.3 Stephen Smith's toolbox, 1990s. Photograph courtesy of Stephen Smith

72 J. A. STEIN

importance of these practices to histories of design and craft. More specifically, little has been written on the educational role of foreigner-making, particularly within craft apprenticeship, nor on how deindustrialisation and standardisation principles may have transformed or eradicated these expressions of creativity.

Patternmakers are an intriguing example for examining foreigners. The level of skill they possess has led to their reputation, in some quarters, as the worst (or best) offenders in terms of foreigner production.[22] As originally shared by labour historian Bobbie Oliver, Western Australian patternmaker Patrick Gayton reflected: "if they ever closed the patternshop then we would re-open it ... and call it 'Foreigners Incorporated'".[23]

MAKING TOOLBOXES: AN APPRENTICESHIP EXERCISE

One of the most common foreigners produced in patternshops was the patternmaker's toolbox. Using Smith's categories, the timber toolbox would often have been "semi-legitimate" as a foreigner, generally produced with the approval and assistance of the tradespeople in charge of an apprentice. Building toolboxes contributed to the development of skilled industrial craftspeople, enhanced workplace cultures and provided obvious practical benefits. Smith explains that foreigners "acted as an indicator of individual skill and craft, by which the tradesman, sub-foreman and foreman could measure your progress and development of knowledge".[24]

Heritage advocate Ric McCracken shared an example of twentieth-century industrial workplaces regulations, specifically pertaining to foreigner production:

> An employee shall not convert to his own use any material or article the property of the Department, however small its value; and, under no circumstances, may an employee make any tool, pattern, model or article of any description ... for private purposes.[25]

Notwithstanding official organisational policies such as the example above, the production of private articles in work time was widespread in Australian industry. Drawing on the example of the Western Australian Government's Midland Railway Workshops, Oliver made a distinction between foreigner production by apprentices, and by qualified tradespeople:

3 THE PATTERNMAKER'S TOOLBOX: MAKING THINGS ON THE SIDE… 73

Apprentices were required to make their own tools as part of their training, and they then kept these as their tools of trade, so opportunities doubtless existed for making "extra" items. Rules 53 and 55 were the most specifically aimed at combating foreigner production, however. The former prohibited employees from ordering 'work of any description' without the authority of the foreman, and the latter stated that employees must not convert to their own use "any material or article".[26]

In this way, we can see how apprentices were not subject to the same restrictive rules as fully employed tradespeople. However, my anecdotal experience talking to patternmakers suggests that foreigner-making did not markedly change on completion of an apprenticeship. Some patternmakers were frequent foreigner-makers: like Poynton ("they used to call me Homer"), while patternmaker Bruce Phipps described himself as a "good boy", implying he did not make many.[27]

While there was no particular agreed style for patternmakers' toolboxes, the Australian and New Zealand toolboxes I encountered have key similarities. The boxes most commonly featured dovetail joints and a series of shallow sliding drawers, sometimes concealed behind a removable vertical face panel. (See e.g. Fig. 3.3) Woodworking author Jim Tolpin stated that "there doesn't seem to be any hard evidence that there existed … any formal rite of passage concerning the building of tool chests".[28] The main terms of interest here are 'hard evidence' and 'formal'. While such practices were customary and widespread, at least in Commonwealth nations, little was formally recorded in apprenticeship guidelines.[29]

There is one intriguing parallel in recent literature: craft scholar Marilyn Zapf's study of twentieth-century British engineering craftspeople gives attention to the toolmaker's toolbox.[30] Some of Zapf's interviewees described having timber toolboxes presented to them as gifts at the completion of their apprenticeship, in a customary acknowledgement of mastery. As Zapf explains, such toolboxes were loaded with symbolic significance:

> On the shopfloor, these wooden toolboxes serve as an acknowledged reminder of the toolmaker's skill. Therefore, they are a symbol of professionalization, a marker of socially accepted boundaries set around the idea of skill, and arguably the toolmaker's perceived status within the company. Because of their visual distinction and conceptual implications, the toolboxes, and the skills they represent, are a source of pride.[31]

Why did toolmaker apprentices not make their own toolboxes, why were they gifted them? While Zapf does not answer this, the answer may prove materially specific: toolmakers worked with metal, while patternmakers were traditionally timber-workers. A timber toolbox was highly preferable to a metal one, in order to protect the metal tools therein, avoiding instruments becoming blunt and damaged.

Patternmaking toolboxes were evidently cherished by their makers, in Australia and elsewhere, and they were transported globally, if the patternmaker moved.[32] Freemantle started his apprenticeship in 1990 at the South African Railways, before moving to Australia. He explained:

> As a patternmaking apprenticeship it was part of our job to make a toolbox. Which was ... quite an exciting thing and I still have my toolbox sitting in my garage which I still use today.[33]

Likewise, Peter Phipps recalled: "That's one of the first things that you did. ... My father did that, my grandfather did that. Everyone did that."[34] Peter's father, Bruce Phipps, recollected:

> I made my toolbox, to start with ... it had ... mortise and tenon joints in it, all hand-done ... and it had all drawers in it with a door that came down ... that was all made out of Cedar, which was pretty expensive timber in those days, and that was one of the things that we made. I got two of them ... because I had more tools, and I needed them.[35]

Visits to patternmakers' home workshops quickly indicated one toolbox was only the 'tip of the iceberg' in terms of their requirements for tool storage, and patternmakers often made more than one. The time taken to make a first toolbox seemed to vary, and it was also dependent on the lenience of the patternshop. For former patternmaker Jon-Michael Rubinich (apprenticed in the early 2000s at a Melbourne patternshop): the "boss let me work on it for an hour or so every afternoon".[36] The fact that Rubinich made a toolbox at all is important evidence demonstrating of the persistence of the practice into the twenty-first century, an issue I will return to further on.

Once packed with tools, the toolbox was extremely heavy, and not intended as a mobile unit. The toolbox most often remained at the patternmaker's workplace, on the floor, often underneath a patternmaker's bench or on top of it (Fig. 3.4). Australian patternmaker John Looker spent some time working in England in the mid-1950s, and transported

3 THE PATTERNMAKER'S TOOLBOX: MAKING THINGS ON THE SIDE…   75

Fig. 3.4 Paul Kay and his toolbox, under his workbench. Photograph by the author, 2018

his toolbox by ship, from Melbourne to London. In his memoir, Looker described arriving at his new London workplace, Singer Motors:

> I needed to take my bench-top toolbox with me. Loaded with tools it was heavy, and it was an effort to carry it to the bus stop. … The problem started at the Coventry bus station. … It was a long way … to the Singer Works, and it involved many rest stops. I finally got there … [but then] I surprised myself by saying that I could not lug my toolbox any further and would need assistance.[37]

Patternmaker Debra Schuckar, who undertook her apprenticeship in the 1980s at the Victorian State Electricity Commission, also made her toolbox during her apprenticeship (Fig. 3.5). While she was keen not to make her gender the focus of her interview, Schuckar's unusual status as a female patternmaker has given her a sense of critical distance. (See also Chap. 6.) Where male patternmakers tend to assume a kind of "natural" craft identity, she identifies the constructedness of craft masculinity. She said, "I've still got [my toolbox] today. … It's almost like a male version of a glory

Fig. 3.5 Debra Schuckar's toolbox. Photograph by the author, 2018

3 THE PATTERNMAKER'S TOOLBOX: MAKING THINGS ON THE SIDE... 77

box (laughs)."[38] Here, Schuckar shows an implied understanding that, as Shields notes, "learning to be a tradesman meant growing into a particular socio-cultural identity; into a gendered language of craft".[39] With their toolbox complete, apprentice patternmakers could proudly see tangible evidence of their progression towards becoming the 'craftsman' they imagined their future selves to be.

Schuckar emphasised that making one's own toolbox was fundamentally an educational process. While the value of 'learning by doing' is a firmly established pedagogical concept, unfortunately recent trades education in Australia has devoted less time to technical exposure in classrooms and workshops.[40] Making a patternmakers' toolbox is difficult: the box must be strong enough to hold a patternmaker's extensive tool collection, and the box was supposed to last a lifetime. Viewed in this way, the requirement to produce a timber toolbox was a substantial expectation to be placed on inexperienced, teenage apprentices.

I asked patternmakers about this challenge. New Zealand patternmaker Stephen Smith reflected: "I think being the freedom to make it, made it feel like it wasn't so difficult"[41] (Fig. 3.3). Schuckar also underplayed the difficulty of the task, explaining how she was supported by other tradespeople:

> We used Sugar Pine, and the boss taught me how to machine it … then we clamped up some pieces together in the big sash clamps—which I'd never seen before in my life—and glued those up and then you re-machine them. Then he taught me how to do dovetailing … and you make one big solid box. Then once you've made the box you cut the box on the circular saw and cut the lid off … it makes the lid exactly the same as the box. Then you make the surrounds on it, and then make all the drawers inside. That was the first thing you spend time making before you get all your tools.[42]

The process for making the toolbox proved to be a revelation for some of the patternmaker apprentices: it demonstrated how to join timber without the need for nails or screws, and trained them to plan and execute a complex task with precision.

Patternmaker Serge Haidutschyk also understood toolbox making as an educational exercise:

> I made my own toolbox … which I've still got at home now, and I've got all my patternmaking, carving tools in there now, and that toolbox was made

78   J. A. STEIN

by me in my first year of apprenticeship. It took me, like, it took me about two months to make, and I was doing it in between making patterns. ... I made this beautiful toolbox which was about a meter long, half a meter wide, with a beautiful lid on it, and it had shelves and drawers in it. Every apprentice had to make their own toolbox.[43]

As an interviewee, Haidutschyk was energetic, arms waving wide, full of enthusiasm about his former employment as a patternmaker at the Newport Railway Workshops. Haidutschyk was thrilled that someone was finally taking the time to ask him about it. As Haidutschyk explained, patternmaking apprentices at the Newport Railways were provided toolbox instructions:

The toolbox what had to be made to a specific specification and dimension ... all the framing and all the drawers was made out of Queensland Maple ... and also White Beech and a few other timbers ... local timbers. Australian timbers.[44]

Not all patternshops had toolbox specifications, however, and some apprentices extended the toolbox project much further, exercising their own unique design and materials judgments. Bruce Phipps stated, "you could go to a lot of trouble, or not a lot of trouble".[45]

Poynton certainly went to a lot of trouble. His toolbox was the most elaborate I encountered. This box was the one that was "magically preserved" after the Ash Wednesday bushfires, as referenced at the beginning of this chapter (Fig. 3.2). Poynton's toolbox process extended well beyond an apprentice-training exercise, and he is quoted at length below, to do justice to his craft labour:

I made it during the course of my apprenticeship, probably took a period of about three years ... it's made from Queensland Maple, which we sometimes used in patterns. And unlike patternmaking—where you're looking for really nice straight grained timber, you don't want any character in the timber as such. I've specially chosen what we call figured timber. ... So it's all carefully joined with sliding dovetail panels so they all lock together. There's no nails or screws holding the box together, only in the hinges. The lid, which hinges up from the back, there's a piano hinge on the back, once the lid is released there are two pins that go through the front panel on top of the box, on the front, and they're spring-loaded. And by shutting the lid, they're forced down into the top of the panel. And they locate in little brass

3 THE PATTERNMAKER'S TOOLBOX: MAKING THINGS ON THE SIDE... 79

inlays in the edge of the panel ... once you open the lid, it exposes all the drawers ... all with really nicely figured timber, and all dovetail joins in the corners. So it's quite a thing ... to still be able to have after the traumas of bushfire, it was magically preserved.[46]

Making a delicate toolbox with figured timber provided a much-needed creative outlet for Poynton as an apprentice, whose creative instincts were never entirely answered by the strict dimensional accuracy of patternmaking. One of the most poignant and bittersweet moments in this project was when I was able to help facilitate the transfer of Poynton's toolbox (among other items) to the collection of Museums Victoria, after he passed away in 2020.

Making and Acquiring Hand Tools

Having made their toolbox, the next task for patternmaking apprentices was to fill it. The patternmakers I interviewed who trained in the mid-twentieth century spoke of the challenge and expense of acquiring good quality woodworking hand tools. In the immediate post-war period, materials were scarce, and imported goods were expensive. A patternmakers' toolkit included chisels, planes, various contraction rules, a sharpening stone, paring gouges, swan neck gouges, spoon gouges, clamps, radiuses, dividers, callipers and a sliding bevel.[47] It also included mallets, spoke shaves, clamps, knives, hand-routers, hammers, saws, files and hand-sanders, etc. In some periods, Australian apprentices received a small tool allowance from the government, as part of their salary. As Peter Phipps recalled of his boss, "he'd always check on me that I was spending that tool allowance".[48] Other apprentices borrowed tools from their patternshop's Foreman, and some were the lucky inheritors of a retiring patternmaker's hand tools.[49]

Alternatively, patternmakers found ways to make tools at their workplace. It helped if the patternshop also had a foundry attached, so you could cast your own. Poynton said:

Patternmakers require some unusual tools and not ones commercially available. So I was ever making tools even when I was sorta in the later stages of my apprenticeship. They used to call me Homer, because I was making so-called homers, or foreigners, and I'd spend at least an hour of my day somehow contriving to make part of a tool that I was working on or finishing.[50]

80   J. A. STEIN

He later explained, "I made sometimes little wooden patterns for tools". These patterns could be taken to the adjacent foundry. Poynton added, conspiratorially, "we could talk the foundry into making these castings for little spoke shaves, and little planes and things".[51]

This final comment by Poynton corroborates existing studies of foreigner production, acknowledging how the making of foreigners was often a reciprocal, cooperative activity involving multiple trades.[52] Bruce Phipps described certain conditions for making foreigners: "when you were a bit slack, you were allowed to do it then. You had to get permission. 'Can I make this?'"[53] By contrast, Poynton preferred a wilier approach:

> There was a wood store at the back and ... I used to go down, looking all official with my contraction rule and a rolled up drawing, out to the timber yard—and a handsaw—and I'd haul all the maple boards out of the rack and I'd cut off all the fiddle-back places and I'd take those ... just enough to fit in my bag, which is highly illegal really.[54]

Reflecting more generally on the production of foreigners in the workplace, patternmaker Tim Wighton also emphasised the training potential of 'learning by doing':

> I got a lot of free rein to make foreigners, you know, things that I want to make. ... And it wasn't frowned upon, as you weren't spending all day on it, as long as you were using scraps, and you were doing a bit here and there, it was okay ... as an apprentice as that was okay because you were learning so through doing, you're learning how to use the wood machinery and you're learning how to carve, learning all those techniques.[55]

Wighton's interview is particularly significant because it refers to a relatively recent apprenticeship experience—between 2005 and 2008. Even in the twenty-first century, where business efficiency and 'lean manufacturing' increasingly dominate, foreigner production was, to some extent, tolerated in the patternshop. I return to Wighton's experience in the next section.

Handmade patternmaking tools were a product of the patternmakers' need to create patterns to precise dimensions; bespoke measurement tools were often produced as a solution to a specific problem in pattern planning. Handmade gauges and radiuses were regularly mentioned, in addition to other bespoke tools that had no official name. Peter Phipps explained:

> Some things you used to measure, like depth ... we'd make like these long fingers out of plywood. ... I guess we'd call them 'long fingers' ... you would make those tools specifically for those jobs.[56]

Likewise, when I visited Haidutschyk, he directed me to inspect a bench in his workshop, which he had prepared before our interview. It was covered with carefully laid out handmade tools (Fig. 3.6). Haidutschyk said:

> As my apprenticeship was heading towards the fourth year, I also made a lot of tools that were specifically made for those jobs, like there was special radius gauges. There was a flat long router ... there was a special carved hand plane for different diameters. There was a ... little centre-finding tool. ... I made about ten tools ... which you couldn't buy.[57]

Fig. 3.6 Serge Haidutschyk's handmade tools. Photograph by the author, 2018

82   J. A. STEIN

Haidutschyk had carefully labelled each item, and he explained the specific use of each tool in meticulous detail. His pride in creating these objects was obvious, and it again reminds us that patternmakers craft much more than patterns.

It is important to reiterate that these individual and collective foreigner-making activities were, to a large extent, outside of the control of business owners and management. Supervisors sometimes turned a 'blind eye', or tacitly endorsed particular foreigners if they stood to benefit ("Can I have one too?") But there was nothing official about these practices: they operated outside of the system of productivity and profit. Rather, such practices existed in something of a workers' commons: a moral economy of craft labour.[58] Furthermore, the production of hand tools was part of a system wherein industrial craftspeople such as patternmakers were expected to *own their own tools*. For employee-patternmakers, this gave them a degree of independence from their employer. However, as emphatically argued by that 1904 socialist patternmaker encountered in previous chapters, for patternmakers, tool ownership is not the same thing as owning the means of production:

> [The patternmaker] would point with pride to his miserable collection of puny hand tools huddled together in his tool chest, and tell you that they were his own—they belonged to him—and that if he was dissatisfied with any particular employer he could lift his tools and seek another master. Quite true, oh wage slave! … Unfortunately for him, capitalism could not stand still, but had to go on developing.[59]

While this patternmaker certainly makes some accurate predictions about the future precarity of the patternmaker (and it is true patternmaking was always at the mercy of other manufacturing industries), they neglect to mention one key factor. Tool ownership gave patternmakers the freedom to themselves become capitalists. It enabled patternmakers to set up their own businesses with relative ease, resulting in a proliferation of small patternmaking businesses (in Australia) by the twentieth century.

Hand tools, however, were rarely enough. Most self-respecting patternmakers desired a full suite of woodworking machine tools as well, including, importantly, a lathe. The following section briefly delves into another tale of workplace making on the side, this time at the end of the patternmakers' careers, rather than at the beginning. It is included so as to demonstrate how embedded making practices punctuate the working lives of industrial craftspeople long after their apprenticeships are complete. It also demonstrates how some foreigners emerged collectively.

THE TRADE EDUCATOR'S SYNDICATE: MAKING LATHES FOR RETIREMENT

In 1985 in Melbourne, a group of trade educators gathered at a meeting at the George Thompson School. These teachers trained apprentices in patternmaking, foundry moulding, metallurgy, woodwork, machining and welding. It is certainly not a good time to be employed as a public educator of manufacturing apprentices. These teachers gather for a lunch-time talk on the lowering of the retirement age for state government employees. They learn that if they take early retirement at age 55, they could retire on half-pay through their superannuation. It is not a lot, but it is a little better than the aged pension. Looker, by this stage a pattern-making teacher, was 50 at the time. While passionate about teaching the craft of patternmaking, he felt the George Thompson School had changed in recent years. There were pressures to rationalise the content: to teach more in less time.[60] Faced with rising administrative work, and time con-straints, his colleagues grumbled that they had become more like "clerks" and less like tradespeople.[61] At this stage, in the mid-1980s, Looker knew that the likelihood of finding a patternmaking job in a rapidly deindustri-alising Melbourne would become increasingly difficult. Retirement seemed a more attractive option. Looker turned his mind to what his retirement might involve:

> One of my first thoughts was the realisation that I would no longer have use of a fully equipped workshop. … My immediate concern was to have a lathe. … The thought of retiring and not having a lathe was not acceptable.[62]

This emphasis on a lathe shows the importance of wood-turning to a retir-ing patternmaker. A lathe was an expensive piece of equipment, and given his future would be more financially restricted, Looker was reluctant to buy one:

> After some thought I came to the realisation that I was working in the very place where I could produce one. I could make the patterns. The foundry downstairs could produce the castings in iron, and the small machine shop

attached to our department was just the place to machine and fit all the components together.[63]

Looker's lathe project required the assistance of others: he needed the foundry staff on board, and the machine shop staff. Word spread swiftly among the department. The Head of Patternmaking, Jim Walker, was also considering retirement in the near future, and felt he needed a lathe at home. Added to this, Walker was tired of the rising bureaucracy and felt beset by stress: "We had too many teachers for the student numbers, and they were at me to sack some of them. ... But, you know, I didn't want to sack them."[64] Walker needed a 'Staff Development' project to keep his staff busy (and therefore avoid making them redundant), and Looker's lathe idea suited this purpose. In this way, Looker's project began 'on the sly'—as an unauthorised project—but it emerged with tacit institutional approval from one of the bosses.[65] Looker was asked to "collect money from each syndicate member on a fortnightly basis".[66]

Ultimately, nine trade educators joined the Syndicate. They decided to make ten lathes, so as to defray the materials costs by selling the tenth machine. As Walker explained, the project involved the full production of bespoke lathes, from start to finish: "We made the drawings, the patterns, the castings, machined them, and we made the lathes over a period of about eighteen months."[67] Looker worked throughout lunchtimes and trade school teaching breaks to get the lathes finished in time for Christmas.

Like most organisations or collectives, the Syndicate was not without its tensions or difficulties. Looker explained that:

> When it became obvious that all members would get a lathe as long as people kept up their payments, the majority of the work was done by John Noke, our machine-room supervisor, and myself. ... The tenth lathe was taken by a member of the Syndicate who said he might have a buyer for it. We could have reasonably expected $1500 for it, but we never saw it again, or any money.[68]

In the end, Walker was disappointed with his lathe, believing he got the "lemon", with a fault in the transmission: "You had to hold your hands just right to get it to work properly." Meanwhile, Looker's lathe was akin to a "Rolls Royce" and worked beautifully.[69] This story is shared not so much as a story of ingenuity or skill, but as an example of the ways in which manufacturing tradespeople have strategised and collectivised, in unpredictable ways, when faced with impending change.

WORKPLACE STANDARDISATION BRINGS THE DECLINE OF THE HANDMADE TOOLBOX

As a result of decades of funding cuts to the TAFE training system,[70] the formal education of patternmakers (among other trades) has suffered in a number of ways. Freemantle—who now teaches patternmaking to some of the few remaining apprentices at TAFE Queensland—explained: "We insist still on teaching our students those traditional skills … [but] they keep on reducing the [teaching] hours. We don't actually get them to make a toolbox anymore."[71] This has meant that the toolbox project remains up to the whim of the apprentice's employer. Patternmaking business owner Paul Kay previously employed and trained apprentices:

> I used to give my first-year apprentices a week, a solid week, to make their toolboxes, and you know, just get fully into it, because I knew how long it was going to take them.[72]

These days, however, Kay does not hire apprentices. He concedes that there is little interest from younger people, and inconsistent work available, which makes hiring any employees difficult.

Without foreigners (and toolbox making in particular), an apprentice's experience could feel dull and hollow. In their first year, patternmaking apprentices were (and still are) generally given menial tasks, such as sweeping and cleaning, and fetching lunch for the other tradespeople.[73] Another factor in recent years is the increasing availability of affordable, mass-produced metal toolboxes—such as JV or Rhino boxes—and heavy-duty tool bags. While Tolpin correctly notes that metal toolboxes tend to blunt tools, they have nonetheless become popular.[74] As the following example will illustrate, the increasing proliferation of the metal toolbox is not only a consequence of personal preference, or offshored mass-manufacturing, it also has a specific relationship to corporate rationalisation trends.

What has happened to this culture of making things on the side in the neoliberal culture of 'lean manufacturing'[75] and corporate standardisation? As argued by vocational training researcher Karen Reilly-Briggs, "The ghost of Taylor is still alive in the twenty-first century", where scientific

86   J. A. STEIN

management "continues to underpin much of contemporary management thinking" in manufacturing.[76] A useful illustration is Tim Wighton's experience. Wighton was trained in traditional (manual) methods of patternmaking, but he began his apprenticeship in 2005, at a time when CNC machines were increasingly being introduced into patternshops. While this training in manual patternmaking methods (both timber carving and pattern process planning) is something Wighton values, it also made him keenly aware of how management intersects with automated processes. As we have seen, Wighton's apprenticeship featured some of the same kind of industrial craft adventures as, for example, Poynton's in the mid-1950s (and Wighton himself appreciated listening to Poynton's interview for this reason). But for Wighton, other key apprenticeship experiences were missing. Here is why: during Wighton's apprenticeship, his employer (a large Australian foundry) instituted the popular '5S' business strategy on the shopfloor.

5S is a Japanese organisational method and philosophy that earned international recognition after its application in the Toyota production system.[77] 5S stands for *seiri* (organisation), *seiton* (neatness), *seiso* (cleaning), *seiketsu* (standardisation) and *shitsuke* (discipline).[78] 5S appeals to managers partly because it provides quick, visible results of active 'management' with little effort. The concept puts a high value on tidiness, requiring—among other things—workers to 'clean up' their factory areas, removing all unnecessary items, standardising furniture and machinery, and changing the way tools are stored and displayed.

At the foundry where Wighton undertook his apprenticeship, 5S involved installing shadow-boards for tool storage, alongside other standardisation and safety strategies. One result of this institutionalised tidying was that the patternmakers' handmade toolboxes had to be removed from the shopfloor. Wighton reflected:

> Everything had to be standardised. Everybody had to have the same metal toolbox, which was way too small, to be honest. It was just a single toolchest that had about three drawers … and the other three drawers or top. And you were expected to try and fit everything of yours in there, which was impossible.[79]

The patternmakers' workbenches were also standardised, introducing small mobile steel workbenches, which the patternmakers also felt were inadequate (Fig. 3.7). Ironically, this new storage system often produced

3 THE PATTERNMAKER'S TOOLBOX: MAKING THINGS ON THE SIDE... 87

Fig. 3.7 Tim Wighton's workbench and red metal toolbox after 5S standardisation, foundry patternshop, Victoria. Photograph by Wighton, c. 2007

88   J. A. STEIN

messier spaces: without adequate storage space, tools and objects overflowed onto other surfaces. There was understandable resistance to this imposition of standardisation. It was not only impractical, but also separated patternmakers from a meaningful object that was core to their identity. But this was also a period of precarious work: whatever was left of Australian manufacturing during the 2007 Global Financial Crisis was on unsteady ground. Good manufacturing jobs were scarce. In this context, most patternmakers begrudgingly complied with the standardisation policies, with the exception of a few stalwart older-generation tradespeople. Wighton continued:

> I think there was only two people in the 'shop that got away with actually keeping their original toolboxes, because they kicked up such a fuss that it wasn't worth trying to pry it out of their hands basically. ... It's why I never got to make my patternmaker's toolbox.[80]

This is how I first learned of the significance of the patternmaker's toolbox: from a patternmaker who was never given the chance to make one, as an apprentice. Wighton's story is shared here to indicate the palpable effects of apparently innocuous managerial strategies such as 5S. Not only do such strategies transform spaces, they also alter the ways in which managers and business owners regard industrial craftspeople.

The arrival of workplace rationalisation and technological change had consigned the patternmaking toolbox largely to the domestic sphere. Once there, these boxes became lingering physical reminders of trade identity. Human geographer Chantel Carr has explored how, in the context of deindustrialising communities, skilled labour practices "spill out" of the workplace, reappearing in the domestic material culture, and emergent through maintenance and repair practices.[81] This example demonstrates how some of this 'overspill' can occur as a result of a managerial drive for sleek factory uniformity. Haidutschyk and Schuckar's apprenticeship toolboxes now reside in their respective home workshops. The same applies for Kay and patternmaker Scott Murrells. Likewise, Peter Phipps said laughingly, "there's a couple of coffee tables in our house here that are old toolboxes".[82]

CONCLUSION

With the increasing use of technologies such as CAD and CNC machines, hand tools and their toolboxes have evidently receded in importance. Peter Phipps summed this up: "Yeah, the toolkit's short-changed these days because I'm so used to CAD work, and CNC now ... [I've] got a computer screen! (laughs)"[83] Most contemporary patternmakers no longer carve timber to make patterns. Instead, their tasks revolve around CAD programming and machine set-up: digitally fabricating patterns out of timber or polyurethane, and hand-finishing them, as analysed in Chap. 5.

This chapter has drawn upon oral histories in order to highlight how toolboxes, hand tools and bespoke machines—foreigners—were quietly produced in the industrial workplace, in a tacitly accepted form of industrial craft enculturation. My choice in emphasising toolbox production is a conscious attempt to demonstrate the cultural and pedagogical value of supposedly 'unproductive' practices in workplaces. To this end, I hope to encourage positive attention towards a broader spectrum of 'non-economic' or 'unproductive' examples of craft and creative activity. Foreigner-making is a form of craft stewardship and care.[84] It is about developing skills, materials knowledge, problem-solving ability and community connections. As mentioned in Chap. 1, all these capacities may be sorely needed in the future, in an increasingly resource-constrained and degraded environment in need of infrastructural maintenance and repair.[85] The making of foreigners—whether they be semi-official or entirely under the radar—represents a set of practices that value making and repair over consumption, and value knowledge-sharing over corporate control, sustainably maintaining resources, culture, community and place.

NOTES

1. Bryan Poynton, interview with author, *Reshaping Australian Manufacturing Oral History Project*, 22 February 2018 (Canberra: National Library of Australia [NLA]), https://nla.gov.au/nla.cat-vn7580610. This chapter is a substantially revised and amended development upon the article: Jesse Adams Stein, "The Production of Toolboxes and Hand Tools in Industrial Craft Apprenticeship," *Journal of Modern Craft* 12, no. 3 (2020): 233–54. This chapter also contains revised and amended extracts from the journal article: J. A. Stein, "The Trade Educators' Syndicate: Making 10 Retirement Lathes in the Twilight of

Australian Manufacturing", *Digital Culture & Society* 6, no. 1 (2020) (Special issue: *Alternative Histories in DIY Cultures and Maker Utopias*, edited by Cindy Kohtala, Yana Boeva, Peter Troxler, 2020): 203–6. Reprinted by permission of De Gruyter.

2. Serge Haidutschyk, interview with author, *Reshaping Australian Manufacturing*, 4 December 2018 (Canberra: NLA), https://nla.gov.au/nla.cat-vn7889878.

3. Stephen Knott, *Amateur Craft: History and Theory* (London: Bloomsbury, 2015), 61–2; Jim Tolpin, *The Toolbox Book* (Newtown CT: The Taunton Press, 1995).

4. See Jon Wood, "Tools of Trades," *The Journal of Modern Craft* 3, no. 3 (2010), 277–8; Celine Johnson Soliz, "Clay, Tools and Tooling," *The Journal of Modern Craft* 3, no. 3 (2010): 349–54; Ethan W. Lasser, "Factory Craft: Art and Industry in Conversation," *Journal of Modern Craft* 6, no. 3 (2013): 315–20. See also industrial craft tools discussed in Thomas L. Steiger, "Construction Skill and Skill Construction," *Work, Employment & Society* 7, no. 4 (1993): 535–60.

5. See also Marilyn Zapf, *The Making of Industrial Artisans: Training Engineers in Britain, 1964–1979* (Masters Dissertation, RCA, V&A History of Design, London, 2012), 82–8.

6. Brian Knight, *Evolution of Apprenticeships and Traineeships in Australia: An Unfinished History* (Adelaide: National Centre for Vocational Education Research [NCVER], 2012).

7. While I have used past-tense here, this is generally still the case in contemporary apprenticeships. Although, for patternmaking apprentices, in-person TAFE experiences are not as frequent, due to geographical distance and more recently, Covid-19 restrictions.

8. Merle Patchett, "Historical Geographies of Apprenticeship: Rethinking and Retracing Craft Conveyance over Time and Place," *Journal of Historical Geography* 55 (2017): 31.

9. Patchett, "Historical Geographies".

10. John Shields, "Craftsmen in the Making: The Memory and Meaning of Apprenticeship in Sydney between the Great War and the Great Depression," in Shields, ed., *All our Labours: Oral Histories of Working Life in Twentieth Century Sydney* (Sydney: University of New South Wales Press, 1992), 95.

11. Peter Williams, interview with author, *Reshaping Australian Manufacturing*, 26 November 2017 (Canberra: NLA), https://nla.gov.au/nla.cat-vn7540153.

12. Michel Anteby, "Factory 'Homers': Understanding a Highly Elusive, Marginal, and Illegal Practice", *Sociologie du Travail* 48 (2006): 233–8.

13. Meaning "the wig". Michel De Certeau, *The Practice of Everyday Life*, trans. Steven Rendall (Berkeley & London: University of California Press, 1984), 24–8.

14. Michel Anteby, "The 'Moralities' of Poaching: Manufacturing Personal Artifacts on the Factory Floor," *Ethnography* 4 (2003): 219; Graham Seal, "Foreigners in Workplace Culture," in Jennifer Harris, ed., *Foreigners: Secret Artefacts of Industrialism* (Perth: Black Swan Press, 2009), 38.
15. Anteby, "The 'Moralities' of Poaching"; Anteby, "Factory 'Homers'", Anteby, *Moral Gray Zones: Side Productions, Identity, and Regulation in an Aeronautic Plant* (Princeton: Princeton University Press, 2008).
16. Key studies of the practice in the Australian context include: Patrick Bertola and Bobbie Oliver, eds., *The Workshops: A History of the Midland Government Railway Workshops* (Perth: University of Western Australia Press, 2006); Harris, *Foreigners*; Jesse Adams Stein, *Hot Metal: Material Culture & Tangible Labour* (Manchester University Press, 2016).
17. In addition to the previously cited examples, see also: Miklos Haraszti, *A Worker in a Worker's State* (New York, Universe Books, 1978); Robert Kosmann, "La Perruque ou le Travail Masqué," *Histoire* 11 (1999): 20–7.
18. Bobbie Oliver, "Making Foreigners at the Midland Government Railway Workshops, 1904–1994", in Harris, *Foreigners*, 26.
19. Stephen Smith, "Foreigners: 'The Forbidden Artefact'", in Harris, *Foreigners*, 21–3.
20. See Ibid., also Bertola and Oliver, *The Workshops*.
21. Anteby, "Factory 'Homers'", e23.
22. Oliver, "Making Foreigners", 36.
23. Oliver, "Making Foreigners", 36.
24. Smith, "Foreigners", 22.
25. The rules of the Midland Government Railway Workshops, Western Australia, cited by Ric McCracken, "The Workforce Cultures", 209–10.
26. Oliver, "Making Foreigners", 33.
27. Poynton, interview with author; Bruce Phipps, interview with author, *Reshaping Australian Manufacturing*, 31 May 2018 (Canberra: NLA), https://nla.gov.au/nla.cat-vn7765732.
28. Tolpin, *The Toolbox Book*, 10.
29. Zapf, *The Making of Industrial Artisans*, 85.
30. Zapf, *The Making of Industrial Artisans*, 82–8.
31. Zapf, *The Making of Industrial Artisans*, 87.
32. Anecdotal evidence from interviews and social media analysis suggests patternmakers in the United Kingdom and New Zealand also made toolboxes during their apprenticeship.
33. Anthony Freemantle, personal communication with author, 4 September 2018.
34. Peter Phipps, interview with author, *Reshaping Australian Manufacturing*, 11 May 2018 (Canberra: NLA), https://nla.gov.au/nla.cat-vn7765727.
35. Bruce Phipps, interview with author.

36. Jon Michael Rubinich, Patternmakers' Facebook Group, 29 January 2018, www.facebook.com/groups/502920693172756.
37. John Looker, *I Want to be a Patternmaker: A Memoir* (Melbourne: Memoirs Foundation Publishers, 2011), 84–5.
38. Debra Schuckar, interview with author, *Reshaping Australian Manufacturing*, 23 February 2018 (Canberra: NLA), https://nla.gov.au/nla.cat-vn7580622.
39. Shields, "Craftsmen in the Making", 106.
40. Karen O'Reilly-Briggs, *National Training Reform and the Impact on Vocational Education for Metal Engineering Trades in Victoria* (PhD diss. La Trobe University, 2016), 39.
41. Stephen Smith, personal communication with author, 27 February 2019.
42. Schuckar, interview with author.
43. Haidutschyk, interview with author.
44. Haidutschyk, interview with author.
45. Bruce Phipps, interview with author.
46. Poynton, interview with author.
47. Brian Williams, "Patternmaking and Tools of the Trade", *The Tool Chest* 133 (August 2019): 1–8.
48. Peter Phipps, interview with author.
49. Williams, interview with author.
50. Poynton, interview with author.
51. Poynton, interview with author.
52. Smith, "Foreigners".
53. Bruce Phipps, interview with author.
54. Poynton, interview with author.
55. Tim Wighton, interview with author, *Reshaping Australian Manufacturing*, 27 November 2017 (Canberra: NLA), https://nla.gov.au/nla.cat-vn7540155.
56. Peter Phipps, interview with author.
57. Haitudschyk, interview with author.
58. Seal, "Foreigners in Workplace Culture," 46.
59. Anon., "Pattern Making and Capitalism", *The Socialist* (November 1904), 7.
60. Looker, *I Want to be a Patternmaker.*
61. Jim Walker, interview with author, *Reshaping Australian Manufacturing*, 7 December 2018 (Canberra, NLA), https://nla.gov.au/nla.cat-vn7889849.
62. Looker, *I Want to be a Patternmaker*, 245.
63. Looker, *I Want to be a Patternmaker*, 245.
64. Walker, interview with author.
65. Smith, "Foreigners".

66. Looker, *I Want to be a Patternmaker*, 246.
67. Walker interview with author.
68. Looker *I Want to be a Patternmaker*, 246.
69. Walker interview with author.
70. Reilly-Briggs, *National Training Reform*.
71. Anthony Freemantle, interview with author (telephone interview), 4 September 2018.
72. Paul Kay, interview with author, *Reshaping Australian Manufacturing*, 30 April 2018 (Canberra: NLA), https://nla.gov.au/nla.cat-vn7765725.
73. Shields, "Craftsmen in the Making", 100.
74. Tolpin, *The Toolbox Book*, 3.
75. Steven Imp, "Leak Test Process: Using Lean and 5S to Drive Manufacturing Process Improvements," *Quality* (September 2011): 30–4.
76. Reilly-Briggs, *National Training Reform*.
77. Kaoru Kobayashi, Ron Fisher & Rod Gapp, "Business Improvement Strategy or Useful Tool? Analysis of the Application of the 5S Concept in Japan, the UK and the US," *Total Quality Management and Business Excellence* 19, no. 3 (2008): 245–62.
78. Kobayashi, Fisher & Gapp, "Business Improvement Strategy", 245. English translations vary slightly.
79. Wighton, interview with author.
80. Wighton, personal communication with author.
81. Chantel Carr, "Maintenance and Repair Beyond the Perimeter of the Plant: Linking Industrial Labour and the Home," *Transactions of the Institute of British Geographers* 42, no. 4 (2017): 642–54.
82. Peter Phipps, interview with author.
83. Peter Phipps, interview with author.
84. Frances Flanagan, "Climate Change and the New Work Order," *Inside Story* (February 28, 2019), https://insidestory.org.au/climate-change-and-the-new-work-order.
85. See Chantel Carr, "Repair and Care: Locating the Work of Climate Crisis", keynote address, Institute of Australian Geographers & New Zealand Geographical Society Combined Conference (9 July 2021).

CHAPTER 4

Industrial Craft as Design Knowledge: Hidden Intermediaries of Design and Production

INTRODUCTION

There's a lot of work and art in understanding how things are actually moulded … it's not just making a simple pattern. You've got to actually make it on an angle to withdraw out of sand so the whole system works.[1]
Serge Haidutschyk

This chapter makes a claim about a particular kind of *design knowledge* that is possessed by industrial craftspeople who work in fields that are related to, but are not, strictly speaking, industrial design.[2] More than other chapters in this book, this chapter engages with the disciplines of design history and design studies. In this chapter I encourage us to remember that deep understandings of the human-made world are not merely the purview of those with the privilege to call themselves professional designers; a great deal can be learned from others, for example industrial tradespeople. While we have come some way, in recent years, towards appreciating the involvement of amateurs, collectors and enthusiasts in design and design history,[3] less has been said about the contributions of industrial craftspeople, whose work is fundamentally linked to the production of designed things.

As noted in Chap. 1, patternmaking is an industrial craft that remains almost invisible—within the discipline of design history and also in

© The Author(s), under exclusive license to Springer Nature Switzerland AG 2021
J. A. Stein, *Industrial Craft in Australia*, Palgrave Studies in Oral History, https://doi.org/10.1007/978-3-030-87243-4_4

95

96   J. A. STEIN

popular understandings of manufacturing—despite patternmaking's former centrality to many manufacturing processes. Mainstream understandings of mass-manufacturing tend to rely on the tropes of sweatshop labour and/or highly automated production settings—and both scenarios are cause for concern, for different reasons. Despite criticisms, the image of the 'star' industrial designer remains influential. But it is the highly skilled, craft-based intermediate stages of production that receive far less attention. Accordingly, this chapter focuses on what engineering patternmakers *know* through practice. Patternmakers harness comprehensive understandings of design form, materials, geometry and manufacturing processes. Far more than being 'process workers' following orders in factory settings, patternmakers play a distinct and influential role in bringing things into being.

My use of the term 'design knowledge' is playfully drawn from Nigel Cross' *Designerly Ways of Knowing*, which, although the subject of ongoing debate, is consistently returned to as a standard definitional anchor for describing design knowledge.[4] In summary, Cross demarcates design as a "third area" of knowledge (humanities and sciences being the other two arenas):

> Designerly ways of knowing rest on the manipulation of non-verbal codes in the material culture; these codes translate 'messages' either way between concrete objects and abstract requirements; they facilitate the constructive, solution-focused thinking … they are probably the most effective means of tackling the characteristically ill-defined problems of planning, designing and inventing new things.[5]

As I will outline in this chapter, many of these aspects of design knowledge can also be identified when examining the skills of engineering patternmakers (with the exception of the final category, tackling 'ill-defined problems'). In comparing Cross' conceptualisation of design knowledge with my research into patternmakers' knowledge through practice, I demonstrate a degree of interconnectedness between the conceptual and practical arenas of patternmaking and design in practice. Presented this way, design and patternmaking operate across a *spectrum of practice*, rather than within bounded, polarised limits that might otherwise be strictly labelled by some as 'craft' and 'design'. (For further discussions on 'craft' and its limits, see Chaps. 3 and 7)

4 INDUSTRIAL CRAFT AS DESIGN KNOWLEDGE: HIDDEN INTERMEDIARIES... 97

In this chapter I intend to be careful about my claims: I am not arguing that patternmakers *are* designers, in an authorial, 'original-creator' sense. Rather, patternmakers are design-affiliated professionals who thoroughly understand many aspects of design, and historically (and even to some extent today), their expertise has been important to designers. Patternmakers are not generally involved in the original authorship of a new design, but their role in pre-production for many manufacturing processes often results in collaborative design changes, to ensure production is achievable. Such changes may not be obvious, but they are often essential for ensuring a successful production run. With this in mind, I argue that patternmakers' accumulated understandings of form, materials, problem solving, production planning and three-dimensional visualisation constitute a form of design knowledge, which extends far beyond the oversimplified notion of a technician who is 'good with their hands'.

This chapter surveys how patternmakers' design knowledge manifests in the specificity of their labour practices. It provides a subtle but important challenge to design history's (and design studies') sometimes designer-centric framing of industrial design and manufacturing. This chapter can be seen as a response to design theorist Lucy Kimbell's calls for an understanding of design that "de-centres the designer as the main agent in designing", and acknowledges design as "involving diverse and multiple actors".[6] This has broader implications for how design history and design studies frames and values the knowledge, skills and influence of those engaged in industrial production.

Before examining Cross' conception of design knowledge—chosen for its clarity and for its widespread influence—I have another caveat to make. It is important to point out that idea of design knowledge itself is contested. As design theorist Ken Friedman has described, defining design knowledge is complicated by design's roots. Design as a codified, professionalised field emerged from craft and vocational training sectors, becoming gradually professionalised (and shifted into university education) throughout the late twentieth century. Friedman states,

> On the one hand, design is anchored in a range of trades or vocations or crafts. ... On the other hand, the design profession is a contemporary field growing within the university. Having few historical roots in the philosophical tradition deeper than the last few decades, we have yet to shape a clear understanding of the nature of design. We do not agree, therefore on

98   J. A. STEIN

whether design knowledge constitutes a discipline, a field, or a science, one of these, two, or even three.[7]

As I hinted earlier, my approach in this book deliberately eschews strict disciplinary distinctions. I am not concerned, for instance, with any need to draw a line between what is 'craft' and what is 'design'. My observations of industrial design and patternmaking suggest that the situation is far blurrier in practice.

As noted by design theorist Tony Fry, design history risks being "historically dislocated" and restricted by its own disciplinary boundaries.[8] It is imperative, Fry argues, that new forms of design history engage with

> [the] huge complexity of the 'world-within-the-world' of human fabrication, wherein everything within this world has been created by design: as such, it is often invisible, mostly anonymous.[9]

This means that it is possible to say, for instance, that patternmakers practise an industrial craft, *as well as* possessing specialised understandings of design, through their knowledge of three-dimensional form, materials and manufacturability. From this position, design knowledge and craft practice need not be seen as mutually exclusive. Certainly, one realm should not be considered superior to (or worthy of higher remuneration than) the other.

This chapter situates us within the context of the growing discourse about industrial craft, both within and beyond design history. I then draw upon oral history material in order to outline the process of making a pattern. A close engagement with these processes allows us to compare Cross' conceptualisation of 'designerly ways of knowing' with patternmaking in practice. The final section of this chapter provides a brief discussion about patternmakers' relative freedom to make changes to a design. It concludes by reflecting on the continuing value of trades knowledge, in the context of digital fabrication technologies.

INDUSTRIAL CRAFT IN DESIGN HISTORY

Where once 'craft' was understood as the antithesis to industrial factory production, in recent years, historians of western design and craft have stepped beyond this false dichotomy.[10] We are no longer subject to the long-standing assumption that craft practices and industrial production are at opposing ends of a polarised binary, a notion that can be traced from

4 INDUSTRIAL CRAFT AS DESIGN KNOWLEDGE: HIDDEN INTERMEDIARIES... 99

John Ruskin and the Arts and Craft Movement's reaction against the industrial revolution.[11] There is a small but growing appreciation of the interconnectedness of design, production and craft, both past and present. As explained by Glenn Adamson, it is possible to understand craft not as an "eternal" tradition rooted in the distant past but as a "modern invention" that emerged in close connection with industrial design and factory production.[12]

As observed in Chap. 1, craft is now experiencing a revival in terms of popular consumption and academic analysis, across humanities disciplines.[13] Recent years have seen a burgeoning study of craft not only in modern craft studies and design history[14] but also in sociology, human geography and anthropology.[15] This has broadened the questions being asked and challenged narrower notions of craft as regional, colonised, nostalgia-laden, gendered and/or amateur.[16] Fashionable craft practices such as beer brewing, surfboard-making and hair-dressing have recently received attention as skilled activities worthy of academic analysis.[17] It is fair to say that we are moving in the direction of a more comprehensive understanding of the complexity of craft, both in historical and in contemporary terms.

But there remain some 'blind-spots'. Craft still tends to be more readily identified with the artisanal handcrafter, while the unglamorous, grubbier, more apparently working-class industrial practices remain less recognised.[18] It is worth asking whether design history and modern craft studies replicate social class structures, through this unequal emphasis. Craft's role in heavy industrial production remains relatively unexamined territory for design historians and social scientists alike.

As Ezra Shales has argued, we must move past the perception that industrial manufacturing is a realm almost exclusively dominated by machines and unskilled labourers.[19] The *idea* of heavy industrial manufacturing still generally invites mental images that seem to be craft's antithesis: conveyor-belt production lines in some far-away low-wage nation or fully mechanised robotic factories. Shales has questioned this, directing our attention to the skilled craft production that is *ongoing* in factories, noting that "most of us still live within an hour's drive of factories, even if we might conceptually define our society as 'post-industrial'".[20] What could we discover if we look to the "extraordinariness of an 'ordinary' hand", he asks.[21] This is where my own research has taken me: into industrial patternshops, metal foundries and wood workshops in suburban and regional Australia.

100   J. A. STEIN

At this point it is important to acknowledge that 'production' has a long and contested past within the discipline of design history.[22] In design history's earlier years, 'production' was often used as a term to describe the *design* stages, with less attention given to the industrial processes enacted to bring manufactured objects into being.[23] With this in mind, Marilyn Zapf called for an expansion of design history's understanding of 'production', to encompass labour and training well beyond the "well researched area of the star-designer, manufacturer, or object".[24] Zapf's approach corresponds with my own inclusion of industrial craft labour as an area suitable for design history study.

Why is engineering patternmaking a particularly interesting trade from which to explore design knowledge in industrial craft? As Sarah Fayen Scarlett and Adamson have separately argued, patternmaking well exemplifies the significance of craft knowledge within industrial production.[25] Patternmaking reveals how deeply interconnected manual craft, design planning and automated production can be in practice. From Scarlett we learn that patternmaking was perceived as a working-class trade, one that American furniture designer Charles Rohlfs (1853–1936) wanted to conceal from his personal history, so as to avoid his popular Arts and Craft designs being tarnished by his trade background.[26] Adamson notes that patternmaking is "a good example of the way a mass production system can increase the importance of craft skill rather than diminishing it".[27] Further, Adamson states that the pattern itself is an unfamiliar object for a design or craft historian to analyse, as

> patterns and prototypes are not copies, strictly speaking, but they are mimetic objects, in which craft skill is tested not on the basis of originality, but by its ability to approximate an external ideal.[28]

We can therefore see how a pattern—as an object—can exceed the value of a single mass-produced thing, as it will, in part, dictate the quality of the manufactured object.[29] While Robin Holt and Andrew Popp's revisionist study of Wedgwood has helped overturn some of design history's earlier false dichotomies between 'craft' and 'industry', the craft-industry relationship has only begun to be explored in academic analysis of craft, design and manufacturing.[30]

My focus on patternmakers' expertise, then, carries wider implications for how we frame and value the knowledge, skills and influence of those involved in industrial production. Phillip Pacey's early suggestion for

4 INDUSTRIAL CRAFT AS DESIGN KNOWLEDGE: HIDDEN INTERMEDIARIES... 101

design history to emerge "in relation to a broader picture which encompasses the non-professional designing which preceded and has co-existed with professional design" is helpful here.[31] Patternmakers fall within this 'broader picture', as their practices are based in a form of design actualisation—transforming a two-dimensional image into three-dimensional form. To ignore a patternmakers' skill, knowledge and experience would be to overlook a significant and under-appreciated form of craft practice that is deeply engaged with questions of form, materiality and process—all elements that are at the crux of how designed objects come into being.

DESIGN KNOWLEDGE AND PATTERNMAKING IN PRACTICE

The following sub-sections focus on the patternmaking process in detail, as a way of engaging with the design-oriented expertise that patternmakers possess and enact (and narrate as they speak, through oral histories). For the sake of simplicity, the rest of this section will refer to the patternmaking process for foundries, in a 'traditional' patternshop. In other words, this section will refer to patternmaking process prior to the widespread introduction of CNC machines into patternshops in the 1990s and early twenty-first century.

Patternmakers Read and Write in 'Object Languages'

A patternmaker began a new 'job' with a set of engineering or design drawings on paper (or on a stable material such as mylar film) (Fig. 4.1). After studying the drawings and specifications, the patternmaker then produced a 'layout', marking out their drawing to scale, on Plywood or on wooden board. (A more detailed description of the patternmaking workflow is provided in Chap. 5) Former patternmaker Peter Williams, reflecting on his apprenticeship experience in the 1970s and 1980s, explained how a 'job' commenced:

> One of the most exciting parts of my job, and I can remember it as an apprentice ... was going up ... the manager's office, tapping on the door, and saying,
> "Dave, I need a job, whaddya you got for me next?" and Dave would go to the plan file, and take out the next job, and we'd roll that drawing out onto the bench, and I'd look at it and go,

102 J. A. STEIN

Fig. 4.1 Patternmaking process for a dead lever brake bracket, including layout, pattern, corebox and casting, 2009. Pattern and photographs by Tim Wighton

4 INDUSTRIAL CRAFT AS DESIGN KNOWLEDGE: HIDDEN INTERMEDIARIES... 103

"Yep, yep, righto," ... Sometimes we'd sit there and look at a drawing for two hours on a bench, and nut that out, and see it in our minds, and agree on things. And then I'd go away and get started. And that—I found that just *enthralling*. And then to go away and make it happen was ... making it happen was almost secondary to that initial excitement of reading a drawing, and seeing the thing in three dimensions in my own mind ... to make a full-size layout—which is virtually another drawing—we would make that on a sheet of plywood ... we would use a scribe and dividers, and engineer's marking out equipment, to inscribe that object.[32]

Bryan Poynton described a similar scenario (approximately two decades earlier, in the 1950s):

The foreman would come along ... with a new drawing, and put it in front of you, and say, "There's your next job." ... He would explain what it was, and any little ... difficulties that there might be with interpreting the drawing, and then he'd walk away and leave you. The first thing, when all the patternmakers got a job ... they would make what we'd call a layout, so you joined up a number of boards. It was before the days of plywood ... you'd make a nice flat board, plane it down ... then you'd proceed to mark out all the dimensions of this particular object that the pattern would be, including the contraction, so you'd be using the contraction rule for the various metal that it was to be cast in ... very accurate layout, and included all the draft angles, and all the holes that had to be bored, any surfaces that had to be machined subsequently, ... And so that was the prime drawing that you worked from. From then on, you discarded the paper ... the wooden parts that were supposed to fit on this layout very accurately ... and then you could start assembling them into the final job.

The process of reading a drawing, then *re*-drawing the pattern and therefore *visualising* what was to be constructed was extremely important.

Patternmakers often emphasise that being able to read a design or engineering drawing is a key skill that they possess (and they often express surprise at design and manufacturing professionals who nowadays have less ability to understand technical drawings). Debra Schuckar said,

The only thing that makes me feel confident in doing this job is that when I see a drawing, I can visualise it three-dimensionally in my head. It just comes to me. Even if I look at something to draw, I can see the finest detail. I can see the grain in the timber. I can see everything to record it at the same time.[33]

In this quote, Schuckar is describing how she spoke about drawing when she was interviewed for her patternmaking apprenticeship, as a 15-year-old. Reflecting on drawing in this way was part of what got her the job. (See Chap. 6)

Let's now return to Cross' 'designerly ways of knowing'. Cross states that designers "use 'codes' that translate abstract requirements into concrete objects", and they "use these codes to both 'read' and 'write' in 'object languages'".[34] Certainly, in this respect, patternmakers speak—and make—in that same language. Patternmakers understand form, geometry, light and visuality in a comparable way to a designer. Schuckar even used the same terminology, 'language', as Cross:

> Patternmakers speak another language, and it's very hard to describe. I don't know if I described it well to you today, what a patternmaker does. It's a language within itself. often at parties you don't tell anyone what you do, because it's too long-winded to tell anyone the whole process, because they look at you blankly after you've spoken for half an hour anyway![35]

In sum, patternmakers possess an understanding of the material world that is embodied, visual and object-oriented, enabling them to both 'speak' (draw) and 'read' the coded language of design form. Like designers, patternmakers make sense of their tasks through the process of drawing.

A Solution-Focused Approach

Returning to the 'nutting out' that Williams referred to, this is about how patternmakers must plan for *how* the object was to be moulded and cast—what they referred to as the 'methods'. While this planning process was partly undertaken by other specialists (e.g. engineer, toolmaker, moulder, industrial designer and 'methoder'), patternmakers were traditionally very involved in the planning process. Patternmaker Tim Wighton explained,

> [My former employer] was very collaborative in [their] design processes. I was on equal footing with the product designers and methods engineers. They understood and took advantage of patternmaking being a multidisciplinary trade, not just on the crafting side but on the intellectual side too. I can not only read drawings but understand and reinterpret them to make the object castable. Adding allowances for machining, contraction and taper. Designing cores, coreboxes, joint lines and loose pieces.

4 INDUSTRIAL CRAFT AS DESIGN KNOWLEDGE: HIDDEN INTERMEDIARIES... 105

Then there [are] all the methoding considerations: How many castings can fit in a moulding box? Where/how will we feed the casting? Ingates, runners, risers, chills, vents, tie-bars. All this before you even get to actually making the tooling.

The methoder handed me a drawing, told me how many castings he wanted in a mould box, and suggested how the job was to be methoded. From that point the job was wholly mine; design, crafting, trailing and altering (it's a rare pattern that works first time without any modification) ... the pattern-maker still had control over the design and construction of the tooling.[36]

I retained a long quote here because of Wighton's intriguing use of the word *design*: for him, design is closely tied to the autonomy he was once afforded as a patternmaker at this particular foundry. It is about judgement, decision making and iterative testing. As Wighton explains, patternmakers not only make patterns but also plan and design the pattern's cores, joint lines, taper and so forth. They help plan how the pattern will sit in the moulding box. These terms and concepts may not be familiar terms outside of the foundry industry; essentially they are production considerations that are necessary for an effective mould and resultant casting to be produced. We will return to Wighton's experience further on.

When considered from this perspective, we are not far from Cross' position that designers' "mode of problem-solving is 'solution focused'",[37] compared to, for example, scientists, who focus on *understanding* the problem at hand. In this respect, patternmakers are more akin to designers, because their motivation is to produce the solution, rather than to articulate what the impeding issues are (unless this articulation is necessary in order to convince an engineer to alter a design, more on that further on). For a patternmaker, the solution to the 'problem' is the realisation of the design in a physical form, one that enables a mould to be successfully created. Former patternmaker Scott Murrells reflected,

I guess, in a way, patternmakers solve problems. There's a design, that comes along, and it gets turned into a drawing, or a sketch, or whatever it is. And you solve that problem, you turn it into the three-dimensional object that they want.

Murrells added—discussing both patternmaking and clay modelling:

106   J. A. STEIN

> You're told what shape you have to do from a drawing and you're problem solving, and I think that at the end of the day you're probably 50 per cent a shape-maker, and 50 per cent a problem-solver. That's how I saw myself. … So how do I make this? How do I do this? [38]

Bruce Phipps similarly reflected on the problem-solving thought process that he experienced when planning a pattern. Sometimes it could consume him completely, keeping him up at night:

> Well, it is a creative job … And it's a worrying job, you know? … To me, it was. I've always—I'll get a drawing, and working it out, I've got a nervous stomach, I've got to go to the toilet! … Because you've got to actually study it. So all your life, you're studying. You've got to make this job work. I wake up in the middle of the night, three o'clock in the morning, and I'll actually work it out in bed, because there's nothing else going on around me.[39]

Patternmaking, then, is cohesion of manual craft, tacit knowledge, technical interpretation and even aesthetic consideration. This process results in a myriad of decisions that the patternmaker must make, all of which could impact upon the form of the final product. Nonetheless, patternmakers are rarely recognised as possessing design expertise. Patternmaking may not constitute 'design' in the authorial sense of original creativity. But this type of process planning—enabled through experience, iteration and experimentation—embeds and actualises design at every stage. The 'craft' of patternmaking is not only present in the workshop, it is also constantly whirring through industrial craftspeople's minds.

Constructive Modes of Thinking

Cross claims that a designers' "mode of thinking is 'constructive'".[40] In making this argument, he contrasts the 'analytic' approach from the sciences, with the 'constructive' nature of designing. Cross identifies what has now become a clichéd characteristic of design thinking: designers are well known for redefining questions, rather than simply analysing stated problems. Cross explains, "design is a process of pattern synthesis, rather than pattern recognition … it has to be actively constructed by the designer's own efforts".[41] Intriguingly, were we to insert the term 'patternmaker' in place of the word 'designer' in the above quote, and it would still make sense, although a subtly different kind of sense.

In my interviews and discussions with patternmakers, many noted that in the pattern planning process, the problems identified by engineers, moulders and managers were often quite different from the problems and solutions identified by patternmakers. One of the most frequent ways that the problem was reframed was to do with the limitations of materials and their affordances. For example, the most significant consideration for patternmakers is usually metal shrinkage: accounting for the amount that metal contracts as it cools. One of a patternmaker's most prized tools, therefore, was their set of 'contraction rules', known in different regions as a 'shrink rule', 'shrink gauge' or 'patternmakers' scale' (Fig. 4.2). There were rules (gauges) for steel, copper, bronze, aluminium, and so forth. Shrinkage meant, for example, that a pattern needed to have different dimensions to the desired end-product, a factor that sometimes troubled clients and designers, who did not always recognise their intended 'final

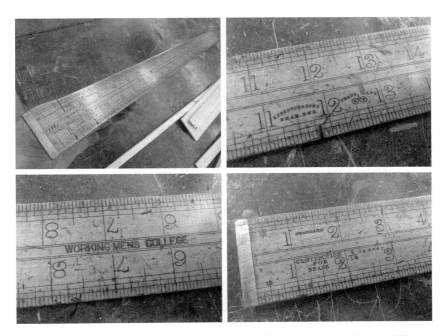

Fig. 4.2 E. Preston & Sons brass contraction rule. Photograph by Peter Williams, reproduced with permission

108   J. A. STEIN

product' in the pattern they saw patternmakers producing. Patternmaking educator Anthony Freemantle explained,

> The other people from other trades and other skill areas ... didn't understand the concept of shrinkage, they didn't understand the concept of taper, they didn't understand the concepts of contraction and so forth, and they didn't understand the concept of actually how you could split your pattern up, and where you should place the joint line, which half is going in which half of the box, when are we going to add a third moulding box in the middle, and we found it was too hard to train these people.[42]

In sum, a patternmaker's understanding of material properties meant thinking about product form very deeply: a temporal, design-conscious and process-based understanding of object formation.

This brings us to the act of pattern construction itself. Having planned the pattern and casting methods, a patternmaker then used hand and machine tools to construct the pattern, alongside building the corebox, plate, cores and so on. Murrells described patternmaking (prior to CNC):

> It was all just all hand and machinery, and all your work was done off a bandsaw, or a sander, and then chisels and planes and that sort of thing. All hand work, the majority of it.[43]

As explored in the previous chapter, patternmakers tended to have larger tool collections than carpenters or cabinetmakers, often taking up several handmade toolboxes, and including tools they made themselves.[44] In a mid- to late twentieth-century patternshop, the machinery often included a circular saw, lathe, bandsaw, buzzer, sanding machine, router and a thicknesser: all machinery that requires an active and careful handling by a trained user. The actual making of the pattern itself was an exercise in precision (to the degree that timber will allow). When describing his colleague 'Colin', Poynton observed:

> There seem to be two types of patternmakers: one who likes to get a block of wood and start taking things out, like he might have a sculpture, pieces out to find the model ... then people like Colin, who had actually fabricate it out of small blocks. ... So his patterns were very accurate but they were no visual works of art, you know they're sort of patchy looking but, you know, beautifully made. I sort of fitted somewhere in between those two methods

4 INDUSTRIAL CRAFT AS DESIGN KNOWLEDGE: HIDDEN INTERMEDIARIES... 109

of making. … It's not sensible to make some things out of a solid block. It's much more accurate and quicker to build them up from pieces.[45]

Here patternmaking is shown to be a constructive process requiring the individual judgement of the patternmaker. There is generally more than one way to build a pattern, although one method might be more efficient or accurate than another.[46]

Patternmakers, Designers and Ill-Defined Problems

I was initially surprised to learn that patternmakers are often not particularly interested in the final product—which of course designers and design historians *are*. In fact, often patternmakers never saw the final, mass-produced object that their pattern was used to produce. Poynton reflects the views of many I spoke to in this quote:

> To be honest I was never all that interested in the final product. I was totally interested in the wooden aspect of it. If I was making component I didn't care what it was for basically … of course, having a mind to the way it was successfully going to mould, and then my job was done.[47]

Williams similarly reiterated that the actual function of the manufactured object—out in the world—was not usually a concern of his, unless it specifically affected the form of the pattern (e.g. if a surface needed to be machined). Williams said,

> Quite often you wouldn't even care what it was. You know, you'd be making a pattern for an object, and you'd look at the object and you might not even recognise it, not even know where it's going, what purpose it's serving in industry or manufacturing, you know, you really didn't think about it, you'd just make it.[48]

The patternmakers' focus was on achieving the best quality pattern and mould for the manufacturing process in use. In that respect, the *form* had to be just right, but the ongoing life of the thing was less relevant (and not part of their 'solution').

Other patternmakers had subtly different views about this. Paul Kay, for instance, said that he enjoyed it when he worked on patterns such as rail-welding equipment, because it was not just more mass-produced plastic junk and confectionery products. Of rail-welding patterns, Kay said, "[Y]ou could actually say, well this is something decent, it's required, it's useful. The general population, or industry, is getting something really worthwhile here."[49] Exceptions aside, this still remains a rather different disposition to a designer: patternmakers *make forms*, not ideas.

This brings us to Cross' final category of 'designerly forms of knowing', where he states that designers "tackle ill-defined problems".[50] This point is a key divergence between the knowledge structures of designers and patternmakers, at least in terms of their paid labour. The required task of a patternmaker is highly specific and structured, rather than open-ended. Kay was quite clear about this:

> We weren't designing the product. We were working from a drawing that was designed by someone else and it was using our knowledge of a product's mouldability. That was really the only part where we were being creative.[51]

From here we can understand that patternmaking was not creative in a loose, free, 'ill-defined' sense. As noted earlier, a key distinction is the fact that patternmakers were not the 'authors' of the designed objects, but intermediaries who played an important role in the production process. Accordingly, all my statements about the 'design knowledge' of patternmakers must be understood not as a claim towards their creative, individual acts of designing new things, but their collaborative function in the actualisation of design. This highlights my earlier clarification in the Introduction—I do not intend to conflate two professional categories. Rather, I am arguing that these industrial craftspeople and designers have shared forms of design knowledge in many, but not all, respects. It was within the restrictions of their professional tasks—to accurately produce a pattern, mould or tooling—that patternmakers exercised a considerable amount of decisional autonomy and judgement. There are moments, however, where patternmakers stepped beyond this, where their expertise resulted in subtle but often important changes to the final product, as the next section will explain.

Making Changes

We have established that patternmakers did not mindlessly create mere copies of the 'real thing', but carefully planned and produced a pattern, which was a functional interpretation of a drawing in subtly different dimensions to the original. In this section, we explore how patternmakers' expertise often resulted in modifications to the form and moulding methods, so as to make production viable.[52] Such alterations had to be negotiated with the engineer or designer (or client), in a process of collaborative design (although it would almost never be called this). Wighton explained that, at one of the foundries where he worked:

> If through staring at the drawing longer than [the engineers] did, you found something, it wasn't a big issue to say, 'Look, I reckon maybe you could squeeze an extra one in the [moulding] box if you did it this way', or 'maybe can we adjust that?' ... So that was the planning stage, and then the actual pattern was made was more or less the patternmaker's decision.[53]

Similarly, patternmaker Peter Phipps explained that his patternshop often "redesigned" (his term) a customer's part (one could also use the term 'co-design', but for overuse I will avoid it). Peter emphasised that dialogue was an important part of this process:

> If you can sit down with a customer and they say,
> "I want this. Do that," and I say,
> "Well, that's good, but let's get a good quality one. Let's talk to the foundry if they think they're going to be able to get you a good casting." ...
> I'll say,
> "Well, can we redesign that and make it this shape? It won't affect what you're trying to do with it, and you'll get a good casting from there."
> A three-way conversation always gets a good result.[54]

Bruce Phipps described a similar scenario, and again uses the term 'designing':

> Quite often, a customer will come in and leave the drawing, "This is what I want made." ... so you sit there and study the drawing of what he wants, and then you advise him what you agree that the pattern will need to be ... and you design the pattern. ... You've got to have loose pieces that pull in and out as the sand comes away. ...There's lots of different designs that get pretty complicated, and sometimes they just can't do what they ask for. ... So, there's a lot of designing, which we do help them to get up what they want.[55]

112   J. A. STEIN

Patternmakers such as Bruce and Peter Phipps understood how the object needed to be shaped in order for a metal casting to be successful and could speak the language of the foundry.

They also rapidly learned the 'language' of other manufacturing sectors, when approached by customers who wanted a pattern made. Note here, again, Peter Phipps uses the term "redesign":

> Often you'll redesign the customer's part, and ... they often come to you and they expect you to know everything about their industry, as if you're an expert in their industry. One minute you know all about petrol tankers; the next minute you know all about mining; you're an expert [for] the guy who wants a mould made for a shampoo bottle; you're the expert with the guy who wants the headlight of a car made.[56]

This shared communication between those involved in the pre-production and manufacturing stages is not just a contemporary phenomenon and has also been described by technology historian John K. Brown, in relation to the nineteenth-century drafting work by the engineer Robert Hawthorn. Brown noted, "when skilled patternmakers interpreted Robert Hawthorn's sketches, they necessarily exerted a substantial influence over the full-sized design".[57] Likewise, patternmaker John Looker described the close relationship between patternmakers and draughtsmen in 1950s Australia and the United Kingdom: "The daily visit between the drawing office staff was interesting to me. ... There was a mutual understanding between both groups."[58] This close—daily!—connection between design and pre-production workers resulted in mutual understandings that have arguably eroded in more recent years.

Through the process of bringing a drawing to life, patternmakers were sometimes frustrated by the engineers and industrial designers with whom they worked. Murrells explained how his tacit understanding of how light bounces off a curved surface was something that he learned over time, as a patternmaker and an automotive clay modeller:

> Designers are great at illustrating and ideas, but when it comes to three dimensions not all of them really have a clear understanding. But coming from a patternmaking background, having a good understanding of shape and form and how to actually create that ... a lot of [designers] have an understanding of what they want it to look like, but not necessarily how to get to that finished product. ... Working in three dimensions is different to working on a sketch or on a computer's instructions. ... The designer may

4 INDUSTRIAL CRAFT AS DESIGN KNOWLEDGE: HIDDEN INTERMEDIARIES... 113

want a surface to do a certain thing and, I use the term, 'light up' in a certain way ... it creates a differentiation between surfaces hence gives you that proportional value. As a modeler [and patternmaker], you understand that sometimes it's not achievable. So you have to try and convince [the designers], and nine times out of ten you would put in what they want, and then you could explain to them in visual terms why it doesn't work, and then we attack that problem with a different solution.[59]

Some designers, Murrells felt, did not possess this form of three-dimensional comprehension. Murrells was not alone in his gentle critique of designers. Others had similar views, variously describing designers as "a bit precious",[60] and sometimes decrying their ineptitude:

Every day I'm asked to make or modify tooling in ways that I *know to be wrong*, that what I do today will come back some time in the future to be redone, either due to poor design or engineering.[61]

The above quote, which I have shared anonymously, reflects a frustration that patternmakers often express—where their technical and design knowledge surpasses that of the designers or engineers they are working with.

In another example, patternmaking business owner Deborah Tyrrell outlined similar processes of negotiation with designers and clients, before a pattern was produced. Tyrrell observed that with the introduction of CAD, industrial designers have become less au fait with the actual material and technological capacities of manufacturing processes:

This is where they [designers] don't understand. ... One of our manufacturing companies has just employed a new industrial designer and it has taken him probably six to 12 months to get up to speed to understand the restrictions. ... Some of the people coming out [of university], they think, "we're industrial designers, *we know*." And you think, "No, you don't."[62]

As Tyrrell recounted, designers and engineers sometimes sent them CAD files that included unworkable forms and shapes which simply could not be produced, or did not have appropriate tolerances, curves or undercuts. The forms would then have to be reworked, through a collaborative process that was not always a positive experience, hampered by economic stresses, power relations, technological challenges and time constraints.

I return now to Wighton's story, as it offers a striking illustration of how, more recently, some of the decisional autonomy afforded to patternmakers has been transferred out of their hands. When Wighton changed jobs, moving to another steel foundry, he found that the agency and autonomy he was accorded, as a patternmaker, also changed:

> [This foundry] just presents me with the finished pattern and accompanying methods. ... All I have to do is post-process it (sanding, painting, branding) and stick it in a moulding box. No designing, no methoding consultation.[63]

This organisational dynamic is closely connected with the increasing use of CNC machines, 3D printing and CAD/CAM software in the patternmaking process. With the introduction of these technologies, a common result is that more decisional autonomy tends to be afforded to engineers and managers, with less agency given to tradespeople on the shopfloor.[64] Like Tyrrell, Wighton felt that his shopfloor experience meant that he understood far more about how to plan a pattern's methods, than, for example, a recently graduated engineer who sat in front of a computer all day and rarely visited the shopfloor. The engineer, however, commanded a bigger salary, a higher organisational status and more decisional rights in the industrial processes compared to the patternmakers. (See also Chap. 5)

These tensions are underwritten by social class in the Australian context. As established earlier, patternmakers are qualified tradespeople with apprenticeship backgrounds. Industrial designers and engineers are, certainly for the past four decades in Australia,[65] tertiary educated, white-collar professionals. Designers, engineers and managers may well ignore the advice of skilled tradespeople on this basis, dismissing tradespeople as old fashioned, under-qualified and uneducated.

Undoubtedly, tensions between occupational groups are not unusual in workplaces,[66] but the relationship between designers and tradespeople is yet to be thoroughly explored in design history and elsewhere.[67] The patternmakers' critique of designers (and engineers) is an important element to acknowledge. The twenty-first-century enthusiasm for 'design thinking' and 'innovation' has placed designers' knowledge and skills on a pedestal, with the inferred meaning that other professional groups are perhaps not as capable, creative or clever. More often than not, manufacturing tradespeople, when they are considered at all, are thought to be 'lower' process workers, inflexible traditional thinkers, somehow not in keeping

4 INDUSTRIAL CRAFT AS DESIGN KNOWLEDGE: HIDDEN INTERMEDIARIES... 115

with the times. As this chapter has shown, the material particularity of object production (past and present) is far more collaborative and entangled, where a variety of specialised groups work together to bring an object into being.[68] It is important to be reminded of the complexities of authorship and production in industrial manufacture—intricacies that are easily overlooked, for instance, when we name an industrial designer as *the* creator of a design.

CONCLUSION

Returning to Scarlett's account of late nineteenth-century patternmaking, she notes that patternmaking was "a greatly respected skill that required a significant degree of individual creativity, precision, and intimacy with materials".[69] In spite of this, Scarlett highlighted how designers such as Rohlfs hid this background, because of the social perception of class, and the negative reputation of industrial production within the world of artisanal craft, at the time. While the denigration of factory production may have had its roots in the industrial revolution, it has reverberated throughout the twentieth century, and still lingers today, within and beyond design. The generalised lack of appreciation of the skills and knowledge of industrial craft practitioners has also contributed to a largely uncritical embrace of technologies such as CNC machines and 3D printing.[70]

The deskilling of specialist crafts and industrial trades is usually seen as an inevitable consequence of technological change. However if we amassed a deeper understanding of industrial craftsworkers' capacities—including their design knowledge—then perhaps we would not be so swift to undermine them through the introduction of new technologies. This is why I have chosen to draw attention to invisible actors in production processes—those who are key players in making objects materialise, but who are rarely acknowledged, let alone highly valued, in academic writing about manufacturing and design, and in society at large. While businesses, governments and teaching institutions race to embrace digital fabrication technologies and robotic production, I urge us to pause and look to the recent past, asking not only what have we lost but also what might be revalued and reimagined in the present context.

Notes

1. Serge Haidutschyk, interview with author, *Reshaping Australian Manufacturing*, 4 December 2018 (Canberra: NLA), https://nla.gov.au/nla.cat-vn7889878.
2. This chapter is a substantially revised and amended development upon the article: Jesse Adams Stein, "Hidden Between Craft and Industry: Engineering Patternmakers' Design Knowledge", *Journal of Design History* 32, no. 3 (2019): 280–303.
3. Paul Hazell & Kjetil Fallan, "The Enthusiast's Eye: The Value of Unsanctioned Knowledge in Design Historical Scholarship", *Design and Culture* 7, no. 1 (2015), 107–23.
4. Nigel Cross, *Designerly Ways of Knowing* (London: Springer, 2006). See also Bryan Lawson & Kees Dorst, *Design Expertise* (Oxford: Architectural Press, 2009); Bryan Lawson, *How Designers Think: The Process Demystified* (Boston: Elsevier/Architectural Press, 2005).
5. Cross, *Designerly Ways*, 10.
6. Lucy Kimbell, "Rethinking Design Thinking: Part II", *Design and Culture* 4, no. 2 (2012): 129.
7. Ken Friedman, "Creating Design Knowledge: From Research into Practice", Keynote paper from IDATER99 and IDATER2000 (Department of Design and Technology, Loughborough University, 2001).
8. Tony Fry, "Whither Design/Whether History", in Fry, Clive Dilnot & Susan Stewart (eds), *Design and the Question of History* (London & New York: Bloomsbury, 2015), 1–97.
9. Fry, "Whither Design", 4.
10. Robin Holt & Andrew Popp, "Josiah Wedgwood, Manufacturing and Craft", *Journal of Design History* 29, no. 2 (2016), 99–119; Sarah Fayen Scarlett, "The Craft of Industrial Patternmaking", *Journal of Modern Craft* 4, no. 1 (2011): 27–48; Ezra Shales, "A 'Little Journey' to Empathize with (and Complicate) the Factory", *Journal of Modern Craft* 4, no 2 (2012): 215–20.
11. Glenn Adamson, *The Invention of Craft* (London & New York: Bloomsbury, 2013), xv.
12. Adamson, *The Invention of Craft*, xiii.
13. Susan Luckman, *Craft and the Creative Economy* (New York: Palgrave Macmillan, 2015); Richard E. Ocejo, *Masters of Craft: Old Jobs in the New Economy* (Princeton: Princeton University Press, 2017); Clare M. Wilkinson-Weber & Alicia Ory DeNicola (eds), *Critical Craft: Technology, Globalization and Capitalism* (London & New York: Bloomsbury, 2016); Mark Banks, "Craft Labour and Creative Industries", *International Journal of Cultural Policy* 16, no. 3 (2010): 305–21; Richard

4 INDUSTRIAL CRAFT AS DESIGN KNOWLEDGE: HIDDEN INTERMEDIARIES... 117

Sennett, *The Craftsman* (London & New York: Penguin, 2008); Matthew Crawford, *Shop Class as Soulcraft: An Inquiry into the Value of Work* (New York: Penguin Books, 2009).

14. Holt & Popp, "Josiah Wedgwood"; Scarlett, "The Craft of Industrial Patternmaking"; "Modern Craft Studies: The Decade in Review" (editorial), *Journal of Modern Craft* 10, no. 1 (2017): 5–18; Ezra Shales, *The Shape of Craft* (London: Reaktion Books, 2017); Louise Valentine (ed), *Prototype: Design and Craft in the 21st Century* (London & New York: Bloomsbury, 2013); Glenn Adamson (ed), *The Craft Reader* (Oxford & New York: Berg, 2010); Glenn Adamson, *Thinking Through Craft* (Oxford & New York: Berg, 2007).

15. See, for example, Laura Price & Harriet Hawkins (eds), *Geographies of Making, Craft and Creativity* (London: Routledge, 2018); Merle Patchett, "The Taxidermist's Apprentice: Stitching Together the Past and Present of a Craft Practice", *Cultural Geographies* 23, no. 3 (2016): 401–19; Chris Gibson, "Material Inheritances: How Place, Materiality, and Labor Process Underpin the Path-Dependent Evolution of Contemporary Craft Production", *Economic Geography* 92, no. 1 (2016): 61–86; Chantel Carr & Chris Gibson, "Animating Geographies of Making: Embodied Slow Scholarship for Participant-Researchers of Maker Cultures and Material Work", *Geography Compass* 11, no. 6 (2017): 1–10.

16. For earlier discussions on craft's definitional limits, see Tanya Harrod, "Introduction", *Journal of Design History* 10, no. 4 (1998): 341–2; Tanya Harrod, "Introduction", *Journal of Design History* 11, no. 1 (1998): 1–4; Peter Dormer (ed), *The Culture of Craft* (Manchester: Manchester University Press). See also: Stephen Knott, *Amateur Craft: History and Theory* (London, New Delhi, New York & Sydney: Bloomsbury, 2015).

17. Ocejo, *Masters of Craft*; Andrew Warren & Chris Gibson, *Surfing Places, Surfboard Makers: Craft, Creativity and Cultural Heritage in Hawai'i, California, and Australia* (Honolulu: University of Hawai'i Press, 2014); Helen Holmes, "Transient Craft: Reclaiming the Contemporary Craft Worker", *Work, Employment and Society* 29, no. 3 (2014): 479–95.

18. Shales, "'A Little Journey'", 217; Crawford, *Shop Class,* 3; Banks, "Craft Labour and Creative Industries", 37.

19. Shales, "A 'Little Journey'", 216.

20. Shales, "A 'Little Journey'", 219.

21. Shales, "A 'Little Journey'".

22. Grace Lees-Maffei, "The Production-Consumption-Mediation Paradigm", *Journal of Design History* 22, no. 4 (2009): 354.

23. Lees-Maffei, "The Production-Consumption-Mediation Paradigm". See also Marilyn Zapf, *The Making of Industrial Artisans: Training Engineers in Britain, 1964–1979,* MA Dissertation, V&A History of Design (London:

RCA, 2012), 10. Tony Fry is one early exception: Tony Fry, *Design History Australia: A Source Text in Methods and Resources* (Sydney: Hale & Iremonger, Power Institute of Fine Arts, 1988), 70.

24. Zapf, *The Making of Industrial Artisans*, 11.
25. Scarlett, "The Craft of Industrial Patternmaking", 30; Adamson, *The Invention of Craft*, 145–6.
26. Scarlett, "The Craft of Industrial Patternmaking".
27. Adamson, *The Invention of Craft*, 145.
28. Adamson, *The Invention of Craft*, 146.
29. Adamson, *The Invention of Craft*.
30. Holt & Popp, "Josiah Wedgwood".
31. Philip Pacey, "'Anyone Designing Anything?': Non-professional Designers and the History of Design", *Journal of Design History* 5, no. 3 (1992): 217–25.
32. Williams, interview with author.
33. Debra Schuckar, interview with author, *Reshaping Australian Manufacturing*, 23 February 2019 (Canberra: NLA), https://nla.gov.au/nla.cat-vn7580622.
34. Cross, *Designerly Ways of Knowing*, 12.
35. Schuckar, interview with author.
36. Tim Wighton, personal communication with author, 19 May 2017.
37. Cross, *Designerly Ways of Knowing*, 12.
38. Scott Murrells, interview with author, *Reshaping Australian Manufacturing*, 25 November 2017, (Canberra: National Library of Australia [NLA]), https://nla.gov.au/nla.cat-vn7540149.
39. Bruce Phipps, interview with author, *Reshaping Australian Manufacturing*, 31 May 2018 (Canberra: NLA), https://nla.gov.au/nla.cat-vn7765732.
40. Cross, *Designerly Ways of Knowing*, 12.
41. Cross, *Designerly Ways of Knowing*, 8.
42. Anthony Freemantle, interview with author (telephone interview), 4 September 2018.
43. Murrells, interview with author. Minor note: CNC machinery of various kinds has existed since the late 1940s, but in terms of its uptake in Australian patternmaking, the shift did not occur until the 1990s and early 2000s.
44. Brian Williams, "Patternmaking and Tools of the Trade", *The Tool Chest* 133 (2019): 1–8. See also Raphael Samuel, "Workshop of the World: Steam Power and Hand Technology in mid-Victorian Britain", *History Workshop* 3 (Spring 1977): 38–9, for a discussion of whether or not a patternmaker's much prized (and almost always privately owned) toolkit meant that patternmakers owned their own means of production. I tend to think it did not, as patternmakers were always reliant upon other industries (e.g. foundries) in order to effectively sell their labour.

45. Bryan Poynton, interview with author, *Reshaping Australian Manufacturing Oral History Project*, 22 February 2018 (Canberra: NLA), https://nla.gov.au/nla.cat-vn7580610.
46. Throughout the twentieth century, patternmakers have adapted to use more timber repair fillers—'bog filler'—making the process less about carving and more about building up a form gradually.
47. Poynton, interview with author.
48. Williams, interview with author.
49. Paul Kay, interview with author, *Reshaping Australian Manufacturing*, 30 April 2018 (Canberra: NLA), https://nla.gov.au/nla.cat-vn7765725.
50. Cross, *Designerly Ways of Knowing*, 12.
51. Kay, interview with author.
52. J. K. Brown, "Design Plans, Working Drawings, National Styles: Engineering Practice in Great Britain and the United States, 1775–1945", *Technology and Culture* 41, no. 2 (2000): 202.
53. Tim Wighton, interview with author, *Reshaping Australian Manufacturing*, 27 November 2017 (Canberra: NLA), https://nla.gov.au/nla.cat-vn7540155.
54. Peter Phipps, interview with author, Reshaping Australian Manufacturing, 11 May 2018 (Canberra: NLA), https://nla.gov.au/nla.cat-vn7765727.
55. Bruce Phipps, interview with author, *Reshaping Australian Manufacturing*, 31 May 2018 (Canberra: NLA), https://nla.gov.au/nla.cat-vn7765732.
56. Peter Phipps, interview with author.
57. Brown, "Design Plans, Working Drawings", 202.
58. John Looker, *I Want to be a Patternmaker: A Memoir* (Melbourne: Memoirs Foundation Inc., 2011), 51.
59. Murrells, interview with author.
60. Poynton, interview with author.
61. Anon, personal communication with author, 2016.
62. Deborah Tyrrell, interview with author, *Reshaping Australian Manufacturing*, 19 October 2018 (Canberra: NLA), https://nla.gov.au/nla.cat-vn7861536.
63. Wighton, personal communication with author.
64. See David F. Noble, "Social Choice in Machine Design: The Case of Automatically Controlled Machine Tools, and a Challenge for Labor", *Politics & Society* 8, no. 3–4 (1978), 313–47.
65. Simon Jackson, "Institutionalising Design Education and Design Promotion in Australia: From early British influences to wider international engagement", *Design & Technology Education* 21, no. 3 (2016): 8–14.

66. Peter Cook, *The Industrial Craftsworker: Skill, Managerial Strategies and Workplace Relationships* (London and New York: Mansell, 1996).
67. There is a relevant parallel in architecture, see Christine Wall, *An Architecture of Parts: Architects, Building Workers, and Industrialisation in Britain 1940–1970* (London & New York: Routledge, 2013).
68. Kimbell, "Rethinking Design Thinking".
69. Scarlett, "The Craft of Industrial Patternmaking", 30.
70. Paul Atkinson, "Boundaries? What Boundaries? The Crisis of Design in a Post-Professional Era", *The Design Journal* 13, no. 2 (2010): 137–55.

CHAPTER 5

'Just Finishing': From Manual Patternmaking to CNC Machine Milling

Introduction

I'm not sure what it's like in other parts of the world. I haven't travelled overseas much at all, but I know in Australia, as Australian men, we identify personally very, very strongly with what we do. For example, if I go to a barbeque and I meet somebody, meet a bloke, the conversation will probably go along the lines of,

"Oh, g'day Jim, I'm Peter."

"Oh, g'day Peter, how are you?"

"Yeah, I'm pretty good, yeah, mate."

"What do you do, Jim?"

"Oh, I'm a bricklayer."

"Oh, right! Bricklayer!"

So … that's usually among the first questions we'll ask when we meet somebody new, and it's usually where we will go with our conversation. And to me that's a real indicator of how we identify … that's our place in the world. "I'm a patternmaker, and this is my spot in the world."

And then the follow-on from that,

"If I'm a patternmaker and I'm not making patterns, then what am I?"

© The Author(s), under exclusive license to Springer Nature Switzerland AG 2021

J. A. Stein, *Industrial Craft in Australia*, Palgrave Studies in Oral History, https://doi.org/10.1007/978-3-030-87243-4_5

And that hit me like a train. It hit me like a freight train. ... And it was a really sobering thought, and that was when I thought,
"Well, you're going to have to be something else, because patternmaking is not going to be around for much longer. Get used to it. So, what *are* you going to do?"
... I did not have an immediate answer for that.[1]

—Peter Williams

Here, patternmaker turned-school teacher Peter Williams describes the moment—in the 1990s—when he realised that his trade was no longer going to provide him security for his working life, and with it, his identity must also change. In this quote Williams indicates a shrewd understanding of the particular importance of paid employment to normative masculinity in Australia. But he also implicitly refers to the devastating impact of technological change on the industrial craft of engineering patternmaking. It is a moment of realisation that digital fabrication was going to replace his hands in the making of patterns. The threat went beyond employment security, to something more existential.

The story of workers' struggle against the introduction of labour-replacing technology is one of the oldest and most enduring narratives in the realm of work, and it has been explored time and again in existing histories of labour, technology and industrial relations.[2] The replacement of labour by machinery was such a dominant feature of twentieth-century industry that it surprises some people when I explain that similar issues are *still occurring* in Australian manufacturing in the present day. "Isn't manufacturing production all run by robots now anyway?" seemed to be the prevailing attitude (at least from outside of manufacturing). Nowadays, automation—widely understood as technological 'progress'—is so accepted as the norm that it is seen as positively 'old hat' to question the roll-out of further automation.[3] Yet I would argue that today, more than ever, it is crucial to remind ourselves how and why technology is deployed by business owners and by large organisations, and continue to ask: in whose interest this does this technology operate? This is particularly the case when we consider the increasing global power of corporations such as Google and Amazon, and the celebrated use of so-called disruptive innovation to challenge existing spheres of work and life.[4] Despite attempts in the 1970s and 1980s to reject technologically determinist understandings,[5] the idea of technological change as an inevitable, linear progression—hurtling along outside of human influence—nonetheless prevails in the media, managerial agendas and in mainstream political discourse.

As I established in Chap. 1, there is also a widespread political and journalistic assumption that deindustrialisation is a finished process, that manufacturing is simply over in Australia. This is by no means the case. Manufacturing is a broad term for a wide variety of diverse industries, and while some are certainly in decline, not all are, and manufacturing workers and business owners continue on, despite the economic challenges caused by globalisation, economic restructuring and swiftly changing technological spheres. This is, in part, why I have also chosen to tell the stories of some businesses and patternmakers who are *still working*, as I write this in 2021. This is an historical story, but it is not exclusively history, and the legacy of technological decisions made in the late twentieth century continues to reverberate in the present.

Many of the patternmakers I spoke with felt that the arrival of computer numerically controlled (CNC) milling machines—and the CAD/CAM software (Computer Aided Design and Computer Aided Manufacturing) that accompanied them—was the defining story of their trade's decline. This was framed in much the same way that printing compositors saw computerisation as the central narrative of the demise of letterpress and hot metal typesetting.[6] This chapter examines how this relatively recent technological change was experienced, from the perspective of some of the engineering patternmakers who saw it unfold.

CNC essentially disrupted patternmakers' control of their craft on the shopfloor. In practice, the use of CNC meant that patternmakers no longer made the patterns themselves, using hand tools and manually controlled machine tools. Instead, their role was reduced to machine set-up, and then manual finishing (sanding) and painting the digitally milled pattern. In short, patternmakers no longer made patterns, their tasks became 'just finishing': sanding and painting. Furthermore, the new technologies and software programs also meant that the pattern planning ('methoding') was sometimes taken off the hands of the skilled patternmakers, and shifted to white-collar engineers and methods planners. This latter change is not always the case, but it was certainly a feature of the altered division of labour in larger foundry enterprises, for example. Small-business patternmakers, on the other hand, have tended to retrain their patternmakers to use CAD/CAM programs and plan pattern methods digitally. Ultimately I argue that CNC continues to dehumanise and alienate industrial craft workers. Yet other pathways could be taken, approaches which incorporate a mix of newer and older technologies, and operate with respect for human labour and industrial craft knowledge.

In this chapter I first outline how CNC technologies transform the patternmaking labour process. I also acknowledge previous research on CNC and NC machinery (relating to its introduction to other manufacturing sectors). The chapter then moves to examine the experiences of two patternmakers who left the trade after they saw the impact of CNC technology. In this section I focus on the stories of Peter Williams and Scott Murrells, who retrained into other occupations following their shift away from patternmaking. From there we consider the experience of a younger patternmaker, Tim Wighton, who continues to work in patternmaking in a CNC environment. The stories of small-business patternmakers Deborah and Greg Tyrrell, and Peter and Bruce Phipps are also recounted, as these businesses invested in CNC in an effort to keep their enterprises running: the technology enabled their business to survive a little longer than it might have otherwise. Finally, it explores how a small number of patternshops proudly continue to operate *without* CAD/CAM and CNC, boasting that their patterns are still made manually, with precision, care and speed, demonstrating that alternative technological paths are possible. Paul Kay's workshop-in-the-basement also features here as a curious recursion of an early industrial 'putting out' craft system.

TECHNOLOGICAL PREDICTIONS

Despite the lack of unionisation and collectivity among Australian patternmakers (as we saw in Chap. 2), manual patternmaking endured long after many other industrial crafts had disappeared from Australian shopfloors. As we have seen in the previous two chapters, engineering patternmaking was a trade that was marked by particular in-built defences against incursions of automation. Factors that made patternmaking relatively resistant to automation included the fickleness of timber as a medium: the direction of woodgrain, timber knots and timber's variation in terms of density and expansion were all factors that the manual patternmaker knew how to work with, while CNC machines mill all material in the same way. Other factors that initially protected patternmakers from technological change included the precision required for, and the complexity of, three-dimensional patterns with undercuts and cores, which initially CNC machines were not complex enough to produce (although this is generally

5 'JUST FINISHING': FROM MANUAL PATTERNMAKING TO CNC MACHINE... 125

no longer the case). The individualised, bespoke nature of each pattern, the immense size of some patterns and the localised nature of pattern-shops' relationships to their clients were other key factors that slowed automation in this sector.

A century before Peter Williams realised his patternmaking days were drawing to close, patternmakers felt a great deal more certainty about the resistance of their craft to technological incursions. An 1885 technical patternmaking manual contained this fateful aside:

> I love this trade because the continual change of work requires a constant exercise of the mental faculties, at once pleasing and healthful, and invests subjects apparently dry with an ever-new interest. Pattern-making is also of very high antiquity, since some Neolithic fellow-craftsman must have modelled the pattern of the metal mould, with its gate and runner and dowels, from which the first bronze user made his first hatchet or chisel of metal. And it can never be superseded, since *no machine can ever take the place of intelligence in the construction of patterns whose types and dimensions are seldom exactly alike.*[7] (My emphasis)

This quote is from a patternmaking manual by foreman patternmaker Joseph Horner. It is not unusual; many extracts such as this were often pinned up in patternshops. This particular quote also appears in Geoffrey Needham and Daryl Thomson's 1998 chronicle of South Australian metal casting, *Men of Metal.*[8] Needham and Thomson note that "100 years later, the silicon chip changed that for all time", although they reason that the uptake of digital technology is because of the "increasing demand for dimensional accuracy",[9] rather than considering the broader economic structures pushing employers' uptake of digital technologies. Needham and Thomson's text is nonetheless useful, because it provides an indicator of a mid-1990s mindset in the foundry sector. At this stage, digital fabrication technologies were seen as being in their 'early days' for foundries and patternshops, and there was widespread expectation that significant disruption was on the horizon.

Referring to a conference paper by John Stapleton in 1986, Needham and Thomson state,

> This is just the beginning of what will eventually become a way of life for patternmakers ... 12 years on, a patternmaker can sit at his PC and create an electronic model of a part he wishes to manufacture.[10]

At the time of writing it is 23 years later, not 12, and it is possible to say that this 1986 prediction has essentially come to pass. However, things are not necessarily the way Stapleton (or Needham and Thompson) might have predicted. Stapleton emphasised 3D printing technologies, such as selective laser sintering (SLS), laminated object manufacture and stereolithography as being the most considerable harbingers of change in the foundry sector. Additive manufacturing has certainly had some influence, but over the past two decades, it is CNC milling machines (alongside CAD/CAM software) that has made the biggest change to patternmakers' labour.

From the 1990s onwards, but particularly in the first decade of the twenty-first century, Australian patternmakers increasingly faced the introduction of CAD/CAM and CNC into patternshops (Fig. 5.1). CNC milling machines come in many sizes and differing capacities, but to describe them simply: they are programmable robotic arms that mill material

Fig. 5.1 Thermwood CNC machine nicknamed 'Woody', with patternmakers, Victorian patternshop, 2017. (Photograph by the author)

subtractively, in order to produce a form. Today, such machines can operate at many axes, moving around material to produce complex undercuts and highly detailed shapes. CNC machines can mill a broad variety of materials, including (but not limited to) timber, dense polyurethane modelling board and metal. CNC has been used in the toolmaking sector for much longer than in patternmaking, to cut metal tools for high production-run plastics manufacturing.

It is not possible to discuss the introduction of CNC machines into patternmaking without considering the broader political and economic shifts in Australian manufacturing, as these were of key influence in business decisions regarding technological adoption. Put very simply, when I asked patternmakers what were the factors that caused the decline of their trade, the employee patternmakers tended to tell me it was technological change, while the small-business patternmakers often pointed towards political-economic transitions (Australian tariff reductions, the offshoring of local manufacturing to Asia, and the 2007–2008 Global Financial Crisis). These challenges, in the small-business owners' view, necessitated their investment in the technology. But ultimately they found that the technologies did not solve their problems.

How CNC Changes the Patternmaking Workflow

Most patternmakers I spoke to tended to view the introduction of CNC into patternshops as 'inevitable' (in a technologically deterministic sense). Many, however, criticised *how* CNC was introduced, as well as questioning the capacity of the technology itself, compared to their own skilled hands. There was a shared understanding among the patternmakers that it did not matter how 'high tech' a machine was—if it was not in skilled, knowledgeable hands, the end-result would be poor. To understand how CNC machines have transformed patternmaking, it is necessary to first be familiar with the workflow for traditional patternmaking.

The manual patternmaking process starts with an engineering blueprint or a design drawing, usually provided by the client. As briefly outlined in Chap. 4, a skilled patternmaker was then assigned the 'job', and they studied the drawing. In this planning process, the patternmaker had to account for metal shrinkage. They also had to make allowances for the pattern's taper, vents, runners, cores and so on—these are all technical patternmaking terms, but the essence of the plan is this: a pattern must effectively

128   J. A. STEIN

produce a mould and must be able to be removed without damaging that mould. The patternmaker's decisions were usually checked with the patternshop's foreman or other patternmakers, and often there was an open communication process with the foundry (if relevant), to check particular details about the methods for casting the object.

The patternmaker then developed their own 'layout', drawing the pattern up on a board using precision measuring instruments (not blunt pencils!). Once the pattern's form was planned, the patternmaker also had decisional autonomy over how they were to produce this shape (usually out of timber), including planning where the glued joins would be, and how many pieces of timber would be needed. The patternmaker made the pattern, using hand tools and manually operated machine tools. This could take a few days, or up to several weeks, depending on the complexity of the pattern. In traditional patternmaking, the main medium used for pattern construction was timber, using a dimensionally stable timber such as Malaysian Jelutong, Kauri, Sugar Pine or King William Pine. Once complete and dry, the pattern was checked with precision measuring tools, then sanded and painted by patternmakers or assistants (painted markers tell the moulders how to handle the pattern), and checked again. Once the pattern was transferred over to the foundry, patternmakers did not want to see it again. If they did, it usually meant there was something wrong with it, and the arguments between moulders and patternmakers could be unpleasant, with each group blaming the other. As mentioned, patternmakers tend not to be concerned about seeing the finished, cast or moulded product. While this could be interpreted as a form of worker alienation from the full production process, for patternmakers, their focus was on having decisional autonomy over the form of the *pattern*, not the final product.

The CNC process, on the other hand, *is* an alienated, and arguably deskilled, labour process. With CNC, the patternmaking process starts with a CAD drawing (usually provided by the client). From there, retrained patternmakers, or engineers, convert the original design into another CAD file, one that is usable for CNC to produce the pattern itself. The CAM side of the software involves the toolpathing—that is *how* the robotic arm will travel to produce the form. This new file must take into consideration how the pattern is to be used in a foundry (or in plastics production), allowing for those same pattern planning principles mentioned above: metal shrinkage, cores, taper and so on. The patternmaker (or engineers) must also decide which material to use for the pattern (e.g.

timber, metal and polyurethane modelling board), depending upon the final production method. Once decided, the CNC machine is set up by patternmakers or sometimes non-trade-qualified staff. The CNC machine then mills the shape, which can take a few hours, or a day, depending on the form. This generally happens with supervision, but CNC machines are also run overnight, in un-manned factories. Once milled, the pattern is checked, hand-finished and sometimes painted by patternmakers or assistants. Overall, the process takes from a few hours to two days, rather than several weeks (in the manual process). This means that patternshops have a much faster pattern turnover (and theoretically require fewer workers).

The adoption of CNC in the patternmaking sector was largely a decision made by owners of foundries and patternshops, who chose this technological path in response to overseas competition, where CNC machines were already commonplace. Employers also sought out CNC because they were bound up in a wider manufacturing landscape that increasingly shared expectations about how tools and product designs were to be communicated across business platforms (i.e. the increasing use of CAD for product designs). Remember here that patternmaking is a pre-production industry: it is reliant on other manufacturing clients and their preferences for how work was to be developed. This meant that patternmaking business owners lacked a certain degree of agency, even when they knew how the new technology may impact on their patternmaking employees. It is also possible to say that, in the case of Australian patternmaking, CNC machines were not generally deployed with the pure intention of replacing labour, but more often because business owners felt they had little choice if they wanted to continue to participate in the fast-paced, global market.

While the introduction of CNC did not necessarily lead to widespread unemployment for Australian patternmakers, it was in most cases experienced as a form of worker alienation and dehumanisation of labour. As noted, in some cases this transition reduced industrial craftspeople's control over the shopfloor, handing that control up to management and tertiary-trained engineers. As a result, some patternmakers felt disrespected and not listened to. The introduction of CNC also led to a generalised 'speeding up' of production, and small-business patternmakers felt pressured to embrace the technology so as to stay afloat in an increasingly competitive, globalised manufacturing market. This meant making significant financial investments in machines that soon required expensive maintenance and software updates, as well as a massive retraining effort for patternmaker business owners. The reaction of employee patternmakers also diverged, but tended to reflect their age: in the 1990s and early 2000s, older patternmakers tended to resist the technological transition, and sought a way out, often retraining in other occupations or retiring from paid work altogether. Younger patternmakers tended to actively seek retraining in CAD/CAM and CNC, but many also left the trade. Significantly, in almost all cases, retraining was not generally provided by employers or government, in a meaningful or useful sense. Retraining was something that individual workers had to seek out in their spare time and pay for themselves. Before engaging with the specific stories shared here, it is important to acknowledge the wider, multi-industry context in which CNC technology has operated for several decades.

CNC in Context

CNC as a technology has a much longer history. Numerically controlled (NC) machinery can theoretically be traced to the 1804 Jacquard loom. More relevant though are the NC tools that were developed after World War II in the United States at Bell Aircraft and MIT.[11] It is difficult to generalise here, as there are a variety of NC tools with a range of applications. CNC milling machines, specifically, are designed as a precision tool that produces a shape using subtraction. CNC milling machines were certainly in use in patternmaking and toolmaking in Japan and the United States in the later decades of the twentieth century. As noted earlier, Australia experienced something of a technological time-lag when it came to CNC adoption in patternmaking.

Before we venture further into the Australian patternmakers' story, it is notable that David F. Noble's influential 1978 critique of technological determinism, 'Social Choice in Machine Design', focused on the case of CNC technology into the American metalwork sector (then called NC machines).[12] The CNC milling machines being used in Australian patternshops today are distinct from the NC technology discussed in Noble's work. Nonetheless, the essential transformation to workers' craft control—from the hands of industrial craftspeople into the hands of management and engineers—is a continued pattern. Beyond this, as Noble points out, with the installation of CNC technology comes a particular "engineering ideology of profit making and management" which displaces an industrial craft ethic based on skilled, manual control and tacit knowledge.[13]

CNC technologies have been a present force in many woodwork and metalwork industries for several decades now, across the Global North. The cabinetmaking trade, for example, has been completely transformed by CNC for a significant period of time. A study from 2008, by former millwright-turned-academic John Charles Wren, focuses on the impact of CNC and CAD technologies on the skilled work of Canadian millwrights, welders, machinists and toolmakers.[14] Wren notes,

> Computerization and CNC machines are doing to the metal-cutting trades what computerization did to the printer's trade in virtually eliminating the necessity of human labour in the printing industry.[15]

Echoing Noble, Wren agrees that the introduction of CNC means that the skilled craftsperson is no longer in control and "management succeeds in regaining control of the production process", with millwrights, machinists and toolmakers becoming "little more than CNC machine minders".[16] To give some extent of the scale of this impact, Wren notes that 30 per cent of toolmaker shops in the United States closed down between 2000 and 2003.[17]

For a more contemporary parallel, human geographers Andrew Warren and Chris Gibson's have charted the impact of CNC machines and globalised economic shifts on surfboard-making in Australia, California and Hawaii.[18] CNC entered surfboard-shaping workshops at around the same time as it was adopted in patternshops. Board-shapers and patternmakers are also similar inasmuch as they tend not to be unionised. As noted by Warren and Gibson, the adoption of digital fabrication methods has changed the workforce, resulting in new workers with specialisations in CAD/CAM programs, computer engineering and information technology.[19] They note, "[C]omputer shaping surfboards remains dependent on the knowledge and experience of hand shapers for the inputting of design features".[20] But, as with patternmaking, there is little or no secession plan for passing manual shaping craft knowledge onto younger surfboard shapers. As time passes, the ageing workforce and attendant knowledge loss will become an increasing problem for industrial crafts such as surfboard-making and engineering patternmaking.

Leaving the Trade

This section focuses on the lives of former patternmakers Scott Murrells and Peter Williams. While other patternmakers also discussed leaving the trade, it makes sense to focus in detail on particular life stories so as to have the space to explore the various stages of realisation, life-shifts and retraining strategies in sufficient detail.

Scott Murrells

Scott Murrells (Fig. 5.2) undertook a patternmaking apprenticeship in the late 1970s at John Williams Patterns, a private 'jobbing' patternshop in Melbourne, which provided Murrells exposure to a variety of different types of patternmaking. Murrells loved the work, and he was good at it. He discovered that he could make patterns fast and accurately, making his skills ideal for commercial patternshops. During his apprenticeship, Murrells also attended technical training at the George Thompson School of Foundry Technology, as did all Victorian patternmaking apprentices. Reflecting on his time at the George Thompson School, Murrells remarked about the patternmaking teaching staff: "I think they were there because

Fig. 5.2 Scott Murrells. (Photograph by the author, 2017)

5 'JUST FINISHING': FROM MANUAL PATTERNMAKING TO CNC MACHINE...   133

I think they could see the end of patternmaking and they ... needed to get into something else."[21] However this reflection was made in retrospect, it was not something he was aware of as an apprentice. Murrells recalled,

> When I first started as a patternmaker, I remember a tradesman saying, "Why'd you pick this trade? It's not gonna be around in the next few years." They knew it was coming. ... The teachers knew it was coming to an end. I think it's just normal human nature to just hang on until you're pushed over the edge.[22]

Murrells described how he observed a decline in metal casting components for machinery in the 1980s, and a concurrent rise in plastics production, particularly for the automotive manufacturing sector. This had follow-on impacts for what patternshops were required to produce. Murrells stated what happened bluntly, almost as if it occurred without human involvement: "Then CNCs came in."[23] Indeed, this is how technology can be experienced for workers: one minute they are there, working on a bench. The next minute a space in the patternshop is being cleared, and a large machine is installed.

As I have argued elsewhere,[24] technological change in a broader societal sense is rarely a sudden 'rupture', and more often it comes in gradual and inconsistent waves, moving in one direction, and then doubling back in another. Murrells described how the early CNC machines he saw installed did not always produce great results, and patternmakers were all "very sceptical":

> [T]his pattern hadn't been machined properly, obviously something had moved and it had made a mistake. So we had to fix it up by hand. "This'lll never take off" [they said]. Well, it has. It took a while, but it has taken off.[25]

Once CNC really 'took off', Murrells had to decide what he wanted to do. At first, the problem for him was not job security (although that came later on). The initial problem was boredom:

> I wasn't really frightened of it, but ... the work became less and less fun. Because ... all you were doing was, you know, making sharp corners round and the round corners sharp, sort of thing. So it was boring. I guess that's the reason I didn't stay in patternmaking, because it became boring.[26]

At this point it is important to note that Murrells is discussing the specific quality of work for patternmakers, and how this changed, to the extent that he did not want to be a patternmaker any more. There is a clear need for a deeper research focus on 'decent work' in the manufacturing sector. The decline of automotive manufacturing in Australia—particularly between the 1980s and the early 2000s—has presented challenges not only in terms of providing base-level employment for retrenched automotive workers. The 'spillover' impacts experienced within affiliated automotive manufacturing sectors (such as patternmaking) also include the decreasing availability of "decent work".[27] Decent work is work that is appropriately remunerated, *satisfying to undertake*, and with suitable and humane worker conditions.

For Murrells, being an engineering patternmaker had been, prior to the introduction of CNC, a more than 'decent' fusion of creative, intellectual and manual challenges. With the introduction of CNC machines, that dynamic dissolved into fine, uniform, automatically machined sawdust. Murrells said,

> You know there was no real ... problem solving ... That was all taken off you. You were just doing what the machine didn't have the ability to do at that time. ... You no longer became the problem solver or the creator of the pattern. ... You become the finishing of the pattern. ... All that creativity comes away from it. ... There's no fun in it anymore.[28]

Murrells' first response to this problem was to 'chase' the manual work in non-CNC patternshops, before they too brought in the new technology:

> Like you're on top of a domino, and you've gotta jump the next one before that domino falls over. ... That's what my career's been like, jumping from one domino to the next, as the one behind it falls over.[29]

Murrells initially retrained as a clay modeller for automotive design, where he worked for around seven years (for General Motors Holden and Ford). Clay modelling was a manual and mental challenge, which Murrells appreciated, but automotive design was not without its own politics and class tensions between the tradespeople (clay modellers) and the professional class (designers and engineers). (Murrells' clay-modelling experience is described in further detail in Chap. 4.)

5 'JUST FINISHING': FROM MANUAL PATTERNMAKING TO CNC MACHINE... 135

Unfortunately, automotive design also soon featured a push to have their design modelling undertaken digitally, a shift encouraged by the engineers, designers and managers. Added to this, Murrells' employment situation was becoming more precarious: short-term contracts were all that was on offer with the car manufacturers, not long-term security. Murrells sought another retraining avenue. He enrolled in an Advanced Diploma of Engineering Design. This was self-funded, and undertaken at in his own time, at night:

> I was working eight hours a day, and going to Swinburne [University] and doing four hours. You know there was a lot of work, but you did it. I didn't have kids back then.[30]

It almost goes without saying that working for over four hours at night, in addition to your day job, is near impossible when you have parental responsibilities and young children (although many do attempt this).

Ultimately, Murrells found that working as a tool designer did not suit him because he did not enjoy sitting at a computer desk all day: "So I turned around and said, this is not for me. I realised I was never going to have a sit-down-in-front-of-a-computer job."[31] Murrells now works in regional Victoria in hardware retail. He reports that life is far more relaxing than it was during his years chasing the "falling dominoes" of manual work in patternmaking and automotive clay modelling. But there is an element of societal knowledge loss going on here—where skilled patternmakers end up working in retail, their in-depth knowledge of manufacturing processes, of materials, of woodturning, of tools and so on are not able to be shared or utilised to their fullest extent.

Peter Williams

Williams also undertook a patternmaking apprenticeship at roughly the same time as Murrells. Williams first learned about CNC machines as an apprentice at a private patternshop in Melbourne, but he did not take CNC very seriously at first. In about 1980, he attended an industry exhibition in Melbourne:

> Pretty big exhibition, as I recall. A lot of very excited people, buzzing around lots of machines that were working on their own computer-assisted NC machines. ... At the time, I had no idea what I was looking at. It all

looked a bit scary to me. I couldn't really see, then, how those particular machines were going to change what I was doing, but all the talk around the industry was that one day there would be machines that operated without a person at them. ... It didn't worry me at all. ... Even though I'd seen the machines, I couldn't see how those machines were going to replace the sort of work that I was doing by hand, you know, with my hand tools at my bench.[32]

After he completed his patternmaking apprenticeship, Williams' occupational pathway traversed a number of directions. This included working on a cray-fishing boat in Tasmania, building props and scenery for the Melbourne Opera, working in a variety of patternshops, including being the sole patternmaker at Doug Evans' foundry, in Wangaratta, Victoria. Williams said, "I spent a couple of years floating around in the wilderness here, where I took any kind of menial labour I could get. The next immediate thing was actually a milk delivery run." He worked in forestry, and in a pub, among other roles. Williams struggled with alcoholism, before later successfully committing to Alcoholics Anonymous. "I didn't know where I was going or what I was doing, and I knew I was in trouble." The need for steady work drew him back to patternmaking, and he was grateful for having a trade to fall back on. Williams worked at a patternmaking and modelmaking shop called Beza Patterns in south-eastern Melbourne, which did not have a CNC machine when he first started in the early 1990s.

About 18 months into his time at Beza, the business owner invested "I think a quarter of a million dollars in a three-axis CNC machine".[33] I will quote the following section at length because it does justice to the gravity of the experience for Williams' life and career:

We brought that machine into the workshop, set it up. ... We mounted a block of composite material, a material known as Ureol [modelling board]. ... The machine was programmed. The 'go' button was pushed, and away it went, and in the space of a couple of hours ... this machine cut out from that solid block a perfect mag wheel, a mag wheel for a car. ... With five spokes and holes and all these intricate ... beautiful-looking <slight laugh> contours and shapes in it. And it did it all to three decimal places, so it was accurate to a ten-thousandth of a millimetre. Yeah, there it was. And we stood there, ... we watched the machine work back and forth, up and down, changing its own speeds and doing all those sorts of things.

Suddenly it was very, *very* obvious that the writing was no longer on the wall; it was right there on the shopfloor, doing our work. I looked at that wheel and I thought, if you wanted me to make that wheel using traditional means, it would probably take me two to three weeks, working 40 hours a week, using conventional methods, and I would only be able to guarantee you that it was accurate to a tenth of a millimetre.

So, that was when I ... decided I did not want to be the person who was feeding data into a machine. I liked using my skills and my hand tools and all that stuff that I'd learned over the years. .,. That was when I knew I had to do something else.[34]

At first, like Murrells, Williams chased the manual work. He reflected "at first I found myself looking—actually, in a sense, going backwards. Looking for traditional pattern work." At this point, Williams ended up briefly working at the same patternshop as Murrells, John Williams Patterns: "We went there chasing the work that we knew we could do, that we were interested in doing."[35] Williams describes a sense—felt by almost all the patternmakers he knew—that the ground was shifting beneath their feet. Even though the patternmakers collectively shared this experience of technological redundancy and precarity, their next path was one that they each took individually. In this way, it fragmented them:

The challenge for us, at that time, all of us fellas on the shopfloor, was: which way are you going to go individually? How are you going to feed yourself? How are you going to stay in work?[36]

The transitional path Williams chose was into technical education—he began teaching patternmaking at the aforementioned George Thompson School (RMIT) in the mid-1990s.

Williams enjoyed the work: he was able to teach traditional patternmaking to apprentices, using the methods he had learned at the same facility when he was a teenager. But the timing was unfortunate. In the mid-1990s RMIT was in the process of 'rationalising' their manufacturing education offerings, and shifting from a technical institute towards more of a tertiary-level university organisation. Williams was into his second 12-month contract, when he and his colleagues were called into a meeting room and told that the Faculty would be cutting 32 jobs. He knew his days teaching patternmaking at RMIT were numbered, and unemployment was on the cards. It was 1995, and on his way home one night, Williams passed a bookshop with a Jeremy Rifkin book in the window, *The End of Work*.[37] Williams reflected,

I bought the book and immediately started to read it. I read it from front to back fairly quickly, because I could see—this fella was talking about the demise of manufacturing, among other things, and I could see that it was happening. ... I was a part of it. I had been a part of manufacturing, and now I was a part of the demise of it. ... It was as clear as day. I actually became quite depressed about it, because it was now clearly evident to me that everything I'd loved previously about my trade, and what I'd learned, the skills I'd developed, the kids that I'd taught, the facility that I was now working in as a teacher, wonderful facility that it was, I could see that it was all doomed.[38]

Here, Williams is undertaking a self-conscious process of placing himself *in history*, both through reading Rifkin and, later, through having the opportunity to tell this story in our oral history interview. I say this to show the extent to which Williams was aware of his place in the wider social and economic context, and of how industrial craftspeople no longer fitted the mould (no pun intended) in terms of the dominant global and national visions for the future.

The next few years for Williams featured a cluster of roles, including working as a workshop technician and managing a boat-building programme that supported teenagers with difficult lives. Ultimately, a few years later Williams opted to formally retrain, undertaking a teaching degree, which was no easy task while working full time. Williams found a position at Wodonga High School, regional Victoria, where he was able to undertake his Graduate Diploma of Technology Education while being paid on a low 'Instructor' rate, before he became a fully qualified teacher. Undertaking the teaching qualification was a major financial struggle, particularly when Williams' wife was not in paid work at the time (her work was caring for their two babies). Again, the retraining process—moving out of manufacturing and eventually into secondary school teaching—was not something that Williams was supported in undertaking; he was out on his own, and it was a significant financial and emotional strain, in order to survive.

Patternmaking with CNC: An Employee's Perspective

Tim Wighton

A currently practicing patternmaker, Wighton was the youngest interviewee in this project. He had the inauspicious fortune to be fully trained in manual patternmaking methods when he started his apprenticeship at a Victorian foundry in 2005. By this stage, an engineering patternmaking apprenticeship was so little-known and obscure in Australia, that when Wighton applied for a government apprentice subsidy of $800 towards buying hand tools, he was initially denied the payment. "The government sent [it] back, [saying] you know, 'Pull the other one, patternmakers don't exist'."[39] Wighton's experience is unusual for patternmakers of his generation. He said,

> I was quite lucky, actually looking back, the first three or four years of my apprenticeship there was no rapid prototyping or CNC, or anything like that. ... So everything was made by hand. The original pattern would be all ... hand-machine, hand-carved.[40]

His traditional training, however, did not match the technologies that had become dominant in the foundry sector by the time Wighton finished his apprenticeship. Furthermore, Wighton was not fully trained in CAD or CNC throughout his apprenticeship, and he had to seek out these training avenues himself, later on. Wighton explained that the much-loved patternmaking educator, Wally Gore,

> encouraged us to see what we were learning at trade school ... [as] a 'step', to try and actually go out and get the CAD side of things [ourselves] ... the CNC experience. ... Not to be afraid of that change ... it was more of an evolution of the training, than an actual end point. But it doesn't seem like that these days.[41]

Some years after his apprenticeship, Wighton moved to another Victorian foundry on the (unfulfilled) promise that this new employer would train him in CAD and CNC. Wighton said,

> Well, personally I want to get off the bench and get into the CNC, the CAD-design side if it, 'cos that's where it all *is* ... that's where it is *now*, and even five or six years ago.[42]

In the end, that retraining was not provided, and Wighton sought it out himself. At the time of writing, Wighton looks set to complete a Diploma of Mechanical Drafting (which includes CAD training), all of which he has completed in his own time, at his own expense (all while parenting three young children and working full time as a patternmaker).

Wighton's apprenticeship experience has meant that he appreciated the decisional autonomy that fully qualified patternmakers used to have, before CNC, in how patterns were produced:

> The methoder would not tell you how to make the pattern, he'd just tell you how he wanted the pattern, I s'pose. ... Whereas the actual construction considerations were wholly and solely yours.

This awareness of patternmakers' former autonomy, however, has produced frustration in his current working life (as also noted in Chap. 4). Now, in a CNC-based patternshop, Wighton sometimes feels that the patternmakers are not properly respected or listened to, by managers or by the tertiary educated engineers they work with. The patternmakers' technical and applied understandings of manufacturing processes had been essentially forgotten. Wighton described work in a CNC patternshop:

> [We aren't] really making anything anymore. [We are] sort of assembling what someone else had already had the fun of making. ... All the fun parts, I suppose, are taken out of it. Because you're no longer deciding anything, you're not really designing anything, you're just sticking things together. ... Becomes like a model kit, really.

The CNC machine in this patternshop was dubbed 'Woody' by the patternmakers (Fig. 5.1). If you did not know Woody was a machine, you might have thought that Woody was simply a greedy patternmaker who refused to share the good jobs, leaving everyone else work that was fit for 'cabinetmakers' (still a skilled trade—but one that patternmakers' see as substantially lesser than their own skills). Wighton said,

> So [the patterns are] cut on Woody, and they come out, and you're just painting, finishing and sanding them, maybe adding branding. ... By and large, all the hard work is done. ... It's cabinetmakers' work. ... It's not really patternmaking at the end of the day, you know, you're just assembling parts.[43]

5 'JUST FINISHING': FROM MANUAL PATTERNMAKING TO CNC MACHINE... 141

Here there is an implicit hierarchy of skill being referenced, across wood-working trades. Wighton had hoped he would have exposure to CAD and 3D printing, but instead much of his work revolved around basic tasks, hand-finishing the CNC patterns and 3D printed models. For someone highly trained in wood-carving, this poverty of material challenge was insulting and frustrating, and experienced as a form of deskilling.

When I first interviewed Wighton back in 2017, Woody had broken down and was awaiting repair. Strangely, instead of the managers and engineers being grateful that the patternmakers still possessed the manual skills to make patterns without Woody's help, the making of new patterns entirely stopped while Woody was out of action. Wighton reasoned that the managers and engineers were "so used to everything being made on CNC ... they don't really consider anyone in the shop capable to make patterns by hand anymore".[44] In other words, the new technology had not only changed the material relations of the shopfloor, it had also changed the way in which the managers and the engineers thought about skills and work processes.

The results of this type of technologically dependent thinking were both irrational and inefficient. As a result, the skilled staff were effectively 'dumbed down', even though they had the skills to complete the work without a CNC machine. Wighton said,

> The management then treat you like you're just sticking things together. You're just a labourer then, they don't want to listen to you, or talk to you, or hear your opinion.[45]

If managers had let the patternmakers return to handmaking patterns while Woody was out of action, work could have continued, but the managers and engineers would have *lost control* of the production workflow and craft knowledge, control that they had successfully wrestled from the skilled workers, and did not want to relinquish.

Over the years of this research project, Wighton sporadically emailed me, sharing updates about his experiences at work. Some years were more bleak than others. His emails often included lists of patternmakers who had retired or who had moved into other sectors. One "joins the Navy next week", while another "retires next year and counts the days each morning". Wighton is not 'anti' technology (although sometimes he wishes things were like the 'old days'). Rather, he is happy to work in digital fabrication, but finds these areas dominated by a white-collar, managerial class, who do not consider trade-qualified patternmakers suitable for the digital systems, and would rather hire engineers from overseas, even if those new employees have no steel foundry or casting experience. In Wighton's view, it suits management to keep him in 'high vis', on the shopfloor, hand-finishing CNC-milled patterns (and repairing damaged patterns that come back from the foundry, after being mis-handled by unqualified moulders). It is neither smart nor efficient, but it does not disturb the status quo.

This quandary recalls Marilyn Zapf's study of engineering craftspeople in Britain between 1960s and 1970s.[46] Zapf, following work by Bryn Jones,[47] noted that there is nothing particular to CNC that should result in wholesale 'deskilling' of craftspeople. Rather, it depends on the social relations of the shopfloor, as to how the technology is implemented and managed, and who has a say in how it is run. Zapf says the "process of alienation was not driven only by the machine or technology, but also by the social forces surrounding it".[48] Zapf cites examples of craftspeople who are happy to adapt to newer technologies when it makes a mundane job easier or eases physical discomfort.[49] But the important factor here is decisional autonomy and the opportunity to apply their expert knowledge in production processes.

In terms of retraining, Wighton has not been supported in any meaningful way by government or by his employers, to shift from manual patternmaking to CNC or CAD/CAM. Wighton has paid for all equipment and courses himself and taken unpaid time out of work to undertake his training. The challenge of retraining in this industry is made particularly clear when we compare it to another sector, historically. When Linotype operators in the printing industry (in the 1970s and 1980s) felt the pressure to retrain in computerised typesetting, many of them bought themselves a typewriter with a qwerty keyboard and re-learned to type at home.[50] At least in terms of a personal investment, this was not a big ask. But for Wighton, retraining in CNC and CAD has led to him buying computer parts and building computers at home, as well as purchasing a laser-cutter and other industrial equipment. Wighton now undertakes silicone moulding, resin casting and laser CNC engraving/cutting from his home workshop. It is a side-operation, supporting his hobby interest in tabletop gaming, but, importantly, it also provides experience for Wighton in CAD, programming and casting for industrial modelmaking.

Patternmaking with CNC: Small-Business Perspectives

Deborah and Greg Tyrrell: Kimbeny Pty. Ltd.

We now shift to the small-business perspective, to see how the economic and technological challenges—offshoring and automation—have been experienced by those with patternmaking businesses in Australia. Deborah Tyrrell and her patternmaker husband, Greg, have run a patternmaking business, Kimbeny, in Sydney's Northern Beaches since 1990 (see also Chap. 6). Their discrete specialisation within the wider field of pattern-making was vacuum forming for plastic tray manufacturing (e.g. the plastic trays that hold cosmetic bottles in retail displays). Initially, all the work was done manually, and the patterns were first made out of Jelutong timber, then made into resin tools for high production-run manufacturing. Today, Kimbeny have had to diversify their techniques, providing CNC machining, low-volume manufacturing, modelmaking, 3D printing, timber fabrication, polyurethane casting, in addition to vacuum forming.

Unusually, the Tyrrells were early adopters of automating technologies. They invested in 3D printing in 2006, before investing in a CNC machine in 2009. In their case, the delicate forms that can be produced through additive manufacturing with a filament (3D printing) were suitable for their specialist type of patternmaking. Deborah Tyrrell said,

> We bought a three-dimensional printer, which was probably a major significance in that it got us into CAD work; it got us into modelling software [SolidWorks]. … I'm probably the one that likes cutting-edge technology and new things, probably more than my husband, but he saw the value in this and the fact that it could create very intricate, fine patterns. … We were at the beginning of the technology.[51]

The Tyrrells have since sold their 3D printer, as 3D printing has become 'so common', and the machine had an expensive service contract, a technician based in another city and was swiftly becoming out of date. In 2009 the Tyrrells invested around $125,000 and bought their first CNC machine, a HAAS CNC Machining Centre[52] (Fig 5.3).

The Tyrrells' decision to purchase the Haas CNC Machining Centre was based on what they felt was an industry expectation:

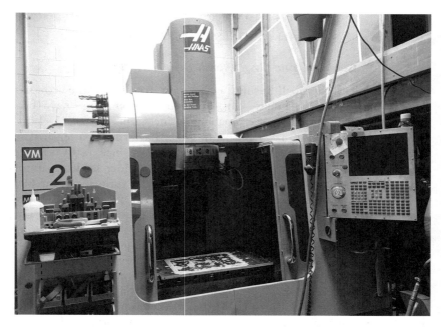

Fig. 5.3 Haas CNC machining centre, access granted by Deborah and Greg Tyrrell, Kimbeny Pty. Ltd., Sydney. (Photograph by the author, 2018)

> Literally, we were at a point [where] it was do or die. It was either move along in this direction … because the designers were designing using the CAD packages, and to machine what they wanted to machine, it needed CAD machining.[53]

Added to this was the increasing offshoring of manufacturing, away from Australia. In the early 2000s, the cosmetic companies that manufactured cosmetics trays gradually offshored their production, mainly to China, which had direct run-on impacts for the Tyrrell's business. She explained,

> Those companies, all in short succession, took all their display work that had been done in Australia offshore to China, and that hit us very badly, very quickly, and it took a long time to recover.[54]

In response, the Tyrrells shifted their patternmaking specialisation away from cosmetic trays to larger patterns:

5 'JUST FINISHING': FROM MANUAL PATTERNMAKING TO CNC MACHINE... 145

> We've gone from making cosmetic trays to doing [patterns for] pump housings, enclosures for forklifts that work in freezer units, fittings for caravans and mobile homes ... so, things that are too big, really, to bring in from overseas.[55]

With the investment in the Haas machine, the Tyrrells also had to purchase software to go with it, in this case Mastercam.

The division of labour at Kimbeny is notable. At the time I interviewed Deborah Tyrrell, Kimbeny consisted of Greg and Deborah, with no other employees. Greg—a trained patternmaker—sets up the timber or tooling board and undertakes the hand work. Deborah—originally focused on Kimbeny's business administration—has become the software expert, after they purchased their 3D printer and then the CNC machine:

> When it actually comes to working the software on the laptop or the desktop, that's where I come into it. So it was a very large learning curve, because I had to learn about feed rates ... how deep we can make the cut within the material ... the clients were giving us a CAD file if the actual part they wanted ... [but] from that file we had to create another CAD file which would create the tool. ... These were very stressful, difficult learning times. ... I have learnt SolidWorks and I have learnt Mastercam. I have not had any formal training either, so it's been a big learning curve.[56]

Here is a case where a technology is adopted not as a form of labour replacement but as a small-business attempt to survive, in a context where much larger and more powerful forces were demanding a particular way of doing things. Deborah admits that Greg probably finds the transition to CNC "a frustration":

> [E]very so often we get a pattern that he'll hand work, and he likes doing this. But it was a transition that we felt was necessary to keep the business going.[57]

Was it worth it in the end? Deborah concedes, "[Y]es, we can now make the machine sing".[58] However, at the time of interview, the Tyrrells were considering options to transition out of patternmaking, towards other forms of bespoke wood construction, potentially into furniture.

There was a sense of deflated frustration about the Tyrrells. They both had worked so hard, over decades, to keep their business going. But ultimately, no matter what they did, they found themselves in a

146   J. A. STEIN

manufacturing environment that was small and volatile, leaving them utterly vulnerable. The investment in CNC had certainly helped them survive the difficult years following the Global Financial Crisis, but with the technology came major challenges, expensive software and service contracts, and the increasing difficulty of finding a suitable industrial location to house their machines in Sydney (given the considerable power requirements of such machinery).

Added to the Tyrrells' woes is a broader problem in supposedly 'post-industrial' cities such as Sydney. Industrial-zoned areas are being regularly re-zoned into residential or retail zones, or ear-marked as 'creative industries' sites. This occurs despite the fact that a limited number of manufacturers are still working in those areas. As a result, industrial-zoned urban sites are increasingly rare, sought-after and expensive to buy or rent, in larger cities. As argued by Chris Gibson (et al.), "The creative industries/manufacturing interface requires access to affordable, and physically suitable, industrial land within proximity of major economic and cultural hubs."[59] The complete rezoning of industrial areas into residential zones, for example, does not allow for diversity and connectivity to occur across and between manufacturing and creative industries, and it can produce urban areas that are exclusive, expensive and hollow.

Peter Phipps: H.H. Phipps Pty. Ltd.

Peter Phipps is a third-generation patternmaker and director of H.H. Phipps Pty. Ltd. Here he describes the environment he grew up in and how that shaped his expectations of what the future would hold for patternmaking:

> I would have been an apprentice [in] '81, '82, '83, '84. Yeah, computers—didn't know what they were. … Everything was made by hand … or you're running a machine by hand. … In Sydney back then there would have been forty patternshops, at least thirty, and they all had staff of five, ten, fifteen people. That's just in Sydney. So then you copy that in Melbourne, in regional areas and so on, around the country. There was a lot of it, and a lot of foundries that they were servicing. … I was sure that I was going to stay in the industry for the rest of my life.[60]

In truth, Phipps has. However the patternmaking industry looks very different to how it did three or four decades ago. For Peter and his father

Bruce Phipps, it was the opening up of global trade from the mid-1980s onwards—not emerging technology—that spelled the real decline of their business. But for the decline of patternmaking as a *trade*, Peter blamed technology, as we shall see further on. Peter reflected on the impact of offshored manufacturing and global imports:

> As those tariffs slowly got taken away and we got more and more imports from overseas, well that really hit the industry hard. … Just to survive, you had to match what was coming in from overseas. … So you've got overseas workers that didn't have the same overheads and conditions that we had, and we had to compete with them. … It's that much harder for us to compete. … That's a challenge these days. … I've always enjoyed the job, but it's been degraded … because of globalisation. … [These days] you have to be a super-large company … to be able to compete successfully with overseas … small family businesses don't have the sort of money to do that, so they're all closing up. There isn't much of it left. It's a really diluted industry.[61]

Like other small-business patternmakers I met, Peter felt that they had been placed on an 'uneven playing field', against much larger, overseas companies with lower overheads and poorer conditions for their workers. Against the odds, however, the business is still running—albeit in a much smaller form than it was in the 1980s and even 1990s. The Phipps business found a niche by combining toolmaking and patternmaking skills. They specialised in 'gravity dies', often out of cast-iron, initially using a pantograph and Deckel machine. Their work includes patterns and dies for petroleum tanker parts and railway parts, among other industrial purposes.

Peter Phipps was first exposed to CNC machinery when he was working in Canada in the 1990s, where he had moved for a few years, to "get out of this bubble and live somewhere else for a while".[62] Overseas-trained patternmakers found finding jobs in Canada relatively easy, as there was a skills shortage and a lack of formalised training in this area. While in Canada, an English patternmaker friend had shown Peter how he was using Mastercam CAD software, simply to plot out 2D shapes. Peter saw how this method could be used in other applications, such as milling materials three-dimensionally. He concedes that patternmaking was much slower to take up CNC milling, compared to toolmaking:

The toolmakers were into that before the patternmakers, because they really needed it, because they're cutting steel ... so their labour and quality and everything was just so much improved by that.[63]

When he moved back to Australia from Canada, Peter Phipps convinced his father that the business needed to invest in CNC and computers. Bruce, who at the time was handing the business management over to his son, reluctantly agreed. Peter said,

Dad doesn't understand computers, really. He'll see it [and say], "Oh, look at that! ... How can we get into that?" So he was on board.[64]

I also asked Bruce Phipps about the introduction of CNC into their patternmaking business, and his response was a little different:

No. I wasn't happy about. I could see that patternmaking as it was, which was interested in—because it's all hands on—is not there anymore. I didn't like it, but I just had to go with it, or go broke. ... Peter's found it a lot harder [than I did]. And it's not his fault. It's just how it is.[65]

However this change was not as simple as buying one machine, as Peter explains:

Computers had to come into the picture, so with the older factory we couldn't put CNC machinery in it, so we had to knock down, build a large, modern facility, to house them, so we did. ... We invested a couple of hundred thousand in a CNC machine centre, plus the computers, plus the CAD software. All of that. It was quite an expense ... it was approximately $20,000 in 1999 to buy that CAD software.[66]

Peter saw CNC as "another big tool in your kit" and "a more efficient way to do something". But no sooner has one bought new software, then it is out of date. Peter spoke of having to invest thousands of dollars every few years, to keep the software up to date, until they got to a point where "we stopped on that version that we're at, and a lot of small businesses did". When compatibility becomes a problem, Peter searches online for converters and drivers, as well as asking clients for "an old-fashioned drawing", which they used to produce their own, in-house CAD files. "We'll just design it and draw it ourselves. ... Ultimately, we always create our own file, no matter what."[67]

During our interview, there were times when it seemed like Peter Phipps was so convinced that this particular technological path was inevitable, and he seemed very bound up with it. So it surprised me when I asked him about whether he missed manual woodwork, to which he replied enthusiastically:

> Yeah, yeah! You hit the nail on the head there. Really. I can honestly say I wish computers were never invented. Quality of life for everyone, I feel, was a lot better. I know they've got a lot of benefits. ... As far as our business goes, as a patternmaker, if computers were never invented, we would all be on double or triple our wage, because our skills were very much relied upon.[68]

Peter went on to describe the more widespread skill loss that has accompanied digital dependence. Patternmakers' ability to make three-dimensional forms from a two-dimensional drawing was something that has become "a bit of a lost art".[69] He identified these lost skills with frustration:

> You go to most, like, any tradesperson, you go to a building site and ask the guy who looks like the smartest person on the building site—don't let them have a computer—[and say] "I want you to make this shape." They'll look at you like you've got two heads. They'll have no idea how to do it ... because they have been taught *how to make things*. Really, our job comes down to making things. ... You have to be able to work inside out to achieve them. ... Before the world of computers, it was a real premium trade.[70]

The mood, whenever I spoke to the Phipps family, was of consistent frustration. They had thrown everything at a technological solution, but knew, ultimately, that their problems were tied to much larger political and economic issues. With Australian manufacturing receiving little meaningful government support or encouragement, and large global competitors offering far lower prices for manufacturing pre-production, even successful small patternmaking businesses like H.H. Phipps regularly faced worrying declines. In some cases, as we shall see below, it was better to emphasise one's manual skill, to make it a positive point of difference: to market one's self as an industrial craft specialist, as an inherent value.

150   J. A. STEIN

RESISTANT CONTINUITY OF CRAFT PRACTICES

Despite the current dominance of CNC in engineering patternmaking, there are still some Australian patternshops that continue to operate without CNC. These shops often specialise in particular kinds of patterns, or rush jobs, where the skills of the patternmaker are still more useful and adaptable, when compared with the logistical and financial challenges of using CNC equipment or ordering parts from overseas. On the Patternmakers' Facebook group (now a global group, but one that started in Australia) patternmakers often post a photograph of their recent work, boasting, "no CNC here, all done by hand" and "No CNC, all traditional patternmaking".[71] It is clearly a point of pride, to be able to still work manually in this trade, particularly now, in the third decade of the twenty-first century.

As noted earlier in this chapter, there are clear parallels that can be drawn here to surfboard shaping, where the industry is now dominated by machine-made boards, shaped by CNC. As observed by Warren and Gibson, a discrete group of surfboard makers nonetheless continue hand-shaping boards, for a specialist market made up of highly experienced surfers and professionals.[72] In part, this is because of a shared understanding of the cultural value of hand-shaping surfboards, and the sense that a hand-shaped board has an intrinsic value and integrity that cannot be produced through automated milling.[73] Of course, patternmakers do not make final products—such as surfboards—at least not in their work time (although several I interviewed are surfers, so there are crossovers here). But the *cultural* value of manual patternmaking methods is less of a force, as it does not impact on how people feel about the final product. However, in some cases manual patternmaking methods are still more effective and efficient, compared to CNC, as we shall see below.

W.G. Kay & Co. Pty Ltd

Small-business patternmaker Paul Kay (Fig. 5.4)—now a sole-operator—is an example of a patternmaker who now runs a non-CNC patternshop (although in the past he has used a CNC machine). Kay's discrete specialisation is confectionery patterns (for glucose jubes, also discussed in Chap. 7), which has meant that manual work remains an option, due to the small, organic forms he produces. Kay explains that his company

Fig. 5.4 Paul Kay in his home workshop, W.G. Kay & Co. (Photograph by the author, 2018)

> started making the confectionery products in 1985, and to give you an example … one of the more complicated pieces was a … baby with a head and body features. But it was only 23 mm long, and it had to be a certain volume. The customer said to me,
> 'Look do you think you could do this?' and I just looked at it, and I'd been doing some wood carving things through my own interest, and I [said],
> 'I think so, yeah.' And I think it was better than reasonably well [done]. And I think they were ecstatic with that, and I never looked back after that. From making this baby in 1985, we just kept going from there, and it was busy and never required any demand to have a CNC machine.[74]

At the time of interview, Kay saw himself as semi-retired, although he continues making work for two confectionery clients. Kay sold his factory building and shifted his workshop to the underneath area of his house in Sydney's Northern Beaches area, where he now works alone. It is curious how, through the diminution of patternmaking as an industry, Kay's

152   J. A. STEIN

situation almost echoes a pre-industrial 'putting out' system, or a cottage-industry domestic system. Here we have the skilled craftsperson, working from home, subcontracting out to larger manufacturers. This is not imagined as a long-term situation, however, but more as a phase in the lead-up to retirement. Kay concedes that many large confectionery clients today would expect CNC work: "They're using the latest technology, all CAD drawn, all CNC, I couldn't do it."

CONCLUSION

Patternmaker and TAFE Queensland educator Anthony Freemantle had a relatively positive attitude to digital fabrication technologies, viewing them as an evolution of his skilled craft. But his embrace of emerging technologies was not viewed favourably by other patternmakers:

> When I travel a lot of people said,
> "Ay it's a dying trade, why would you bother doing that? It's a dying trade."
> And a lot of people still tell me that, and I am constantly saying to them,
> "No, it's not dying, it's evolving. It's just changing."
> The tools we're using are changing … but one thing I've learnt—you've gotta go with change and pretty much just evolve with it. … Some of the older patternmakers, they weren't willing to make the change to CNC and all that. Some of them actually looked at me back then like I was actually betraying them, and shutting them out, crossing over to the CNC technology, and I kept telling them,
> "I'm not betraying you, I'm not selling out." We pretty much have to evolve with the technology otherwise the trade will die out.[75]

There are a number of different ways of viewing this position. On the one hand, it could be interpreted as a neoliberal ideological position on automation, containing an assumption that technological 'progress' is something that we must succumb to and adapt as we go. This view sees all technological changes as essentially the same, regardless of their outcome—with CNC being 'just another tool'.

On the other hand, we could more charitably view Freemantle's position as pragmatic. Given patternmaking's wholly contingent place in the manufacturing supply chain it could be argued that most patternmakers essentially had no choice. As we have seen, the small-business patternmakers here generally felt that they had to invest in digital technologies in order to compete in a highly competitive global market. In the end, the technologies did not 'save' them, but it perhaps meant they survived a little longer than they might have done. Should the patternmakers have banded together more collectively to resist the incursion of CNC and CAD/CAM into their skillset? Given the low rates of unionisation among patternmakers, and their generally low numbers nationally, it is unlikely this would ever have been feasible. It is worth noting that there *is* an active employers' association, the Master Patternmakers' Association of New South Wales, which has historically worked collectively to advocate for their small industry. Membership today is less than 10.

Recalling patternmaker Wighton's desire to be trained in the emerging technologies—but he wanted to use them *with agency*. Rather than merely 'manning the machines' and 'just finishing', Wighton wished for patternmakers in CNC patternshops to retain intellectual involvement in the pattern planning and methods, rather than these decisions being handed over to the engineers and management. Perhaps it is possible to imagine, then, a fair distribution of intellectual labour, and a productive fusion of newer and older technologies, used in a manner that respects patternmakers' traditional knowledge and skillsets. Some industrial patterns do make more sense as CNC jobs, while others remain more suited to the human arm and a chisel. Some patterns are made as one piece, while many are assembled from smaller pieces and glued together.

Tools and technologies can and should be used flexibly, interchangeably, as long as the knowledge and skills of industrial craftspeople are remembered, respected and importantly, passed on to younger generations.[76] This does not make all tools and technologies the same, however. Above all, humane experience at work needs to be at the forefront, not efficiency or profits. The same applies for those who wish to retrain into new sectors. If we are to be part of a society that continually introduces disruptive, displacing technologies, then that same society must take responsibility for supporting those who are impacted by the change, and retrain those who wish to transition.

NOTES

1. Peter Williams, interview with author, *Reshaping Australian Manufacturing*, 26 November 2017 (Canberra: NLA), https://nla.gov.au/nla.cat-vn7540153. Parts of this chapter originated from an invited conference paper at *Production of Information Technologies: Media Markets and Labour in the Twentieth Century*, funded by the Fritz Thyssen

Foundation and the German Research Foundation (DFG), at Hamburg Museum of Work, 2018.

2. Key works in this area include Harry Braverman, *Labor and Monopoly Capital* (New York: Monthly Review Press, 1977); David F. Noble, *Forces of Production: A Social History of Industrial Automation* (New York: Alfred A. Knopf, 1984); Andrew Zimbalist (ed), *Case Studies on the Labor Process* (New York: Monthly Review Press, 1979); Cynthia Cockburn, *Brothers: Male Dominance and Technological Change* (London: Pluto Press, 1983); Mike Cooley, *Architect or Bee? The Human Price of Technology* (Revised ed) (London: The Hogarth Press, 1987).

3. This prevailing view is challenged in Eugene Schofield-Georgeson, "Regulating the Automation of Employment through Redundancy Law: A Comparative Policy Approach", *Australian Journal of Labour Law* 32, no. 3 (2020): 263–89.

4. Disruptive innovation is a business concept that relies on constant and ruthless change to technologies and business models, without regard for the long-term consequences. See Benoît Godin, *Innovation Contested: The Idea of Innovation over the Centuries* (New York: Routledge, 2015); Jill Lepore, "The Disruption Machine: What the Gospel of Innovation gets Wrong", *The New Yorker* (23 June 2014), 23–45.

5. David F. Noble, "Social Choice in Machine Design: The Case of Automatically Controlled Machine Tools, and a Challenge for Labor", *Politics & Society* 8, no. 3–4 (1978): 313–47; Donald MacKenzie & Judy Wajcman (eds), *The Social Shaping of Technology* (2nd ed.) (Maidenhead and Philadelphia: Open University Press, 1999); Langdon Winner, *The Whale and the Reactor: A Search for Limits in an Age of High Technology* (Chicago & London: University of Chicago Press, 1986).

6. See Cockburn, *Brothers*; Zimbalist, *Case Studies*; Jesse Adams Stein, *Hot Metal: Material Culture & Tangible Labour* (Manchester: Manchester University Press, 2016).

7. Joseph G. Horner, *Pattern Making: A Practical Treatise Embracing the Main Types of Engineering Construction* (3rd ed.) (London: Crosby Lockwood and Son., 1902), 313–4. My emphasis.

8. Geoffrey R. Needham & Daryl Thomson, *Men of Metal: A Chronicle of the Metal Casting Industry in South Australia 1836–1998* (2nd ed.) (Adelaide: South Australian Centre for Manufacturing/EEASA Foundry Council/ Australian Foundry Institute, 1998), 116.

9. Needham & Thomson, *Men of Metal*, 116.

10. Needham & Thomson, *Men of Metal*, describing John Stapleton's paper at the 1986 National Patternmakers Convention, Albury, 116.

11. Noble, "Social Choice".

12. Noble, "Social Choice".

13. Noble, "Social Choice", 318.
14. John Charles Wren, *Skilled Trades' Work and Apprentice Training in the Manufacturing Industry with a Primary Focus on the Millwright Trade: An Inter-Generational Study*, PhD thesis (Toronto: University of Toronto, 2008). Here Wren's use of the term 'millwight' is the North American skilled trade, involving the maintenance, repair and movement of machinery on the manufacturing shopfloor, not the medieval millwright.
15. Wren, *Skilled Trades*, 64.
16. Wren, *Skilled Trades*, 63–4.
17. Wren, *Skilled Trades*, 64.
18. Andrew Warren & Chris Gibson, *Surfing Places, Surfboard Makers: Craft, Creativity and Cultural Heritage in Hawai'i, California, and Australia* (Honolulu: University of Hawai'i Press, 2014).
19. Warren & Gibson, *Surfing Places*.
20. Warren & Gibson, *Surfing Places*, 201.
21. Scott Murrells, interview with author, *Reshaping Australian Manufacturing*, 25 November 2017, (Canberra: National Library of Australia [NLA]), https://nla.gov.au/nla.cat-vn7540149.
22. Murrells, interview with author.
23. Murrells, interview with author.
24. Stein, *Hot Metal*.
25. Murrells, interview with author.
26. Murrells, interview with author.
27. Tom Barnes, et al., "Employment, Spillovers and 'Decent Work': Challenging the Productivity Commission's Auto Industry Narrative", *The Economic and Labour Relations Review* 27, no. 2 (2016): 215–30. See also Tanya Carney & Jim Stanford, *Advanced Skills for Advanced Manufacturing: Rebuilding Vocational Training in a Transforming Industry* (Canberra: Centre for Future Work, The Australia Institute, 2018).
28. Murrells, interview with author.
29. Murrells, interview with author.
30. Murrells, interview with author.
31. Murrells, interview with author.
32. Williams, interview with author.
33. Williams, interview with author.
34. Williams, interview with author.
35. Williams, interview with author.
36. Williams, interview with author.
37. Jeremy Rifkin, *The End of Work: The Decline of the Global Labor Force and the Dawn of the Post-market Era* (New York: Putnam Publishing, 1995).
38. Williams, interview with author.

156 J. A. STEIN

39. Tim Wighton, interview with author, *Reshaping Australian Manufacturing*, 27 November 2017 (Canberra: NLA), https://nla.gov.au/nla.cat-vn7540155.
40. Wighton, interview with author.
41. Wighton, interview with author.
42. Wighton, interview with author. Wighton's emphasis.
43. Wighton, interview with author.
44. Wighton, interview with author.
45. Wighton, interview with author.
46. Marilyn Zapf, *The Making of Industrial Artisans: Training Engineers in Britain, 1964–1979*, Master's thesis (London: RCA, 2012).
47. Bryn Jones, "Destruction or Redistribution of Engineering Skills? The Case of Numerical Control", in Stephen Wood (ed), *The Degradation of Work? Skill, Deskilling and the Labour Process* (London: Hutchinson, 1982), 179–200.
48. Zapf, *The Making of Industrial Artisans*, 94.
49. Zapf, *The Making of Industrial Artisans*, 94.
50. Stein, "'Going with the Technology': The Final Generation of Hot-Metal Compositors", in *Hot Metal*, 98–130.
51. Deborah Tyrrell, interview with author, *Reshaping Australian Manufacturing*, 19 October 2018 (Canberra: NLA), https://nla.gov.au/nla.cat-vn7861536.
52. A Machining Centre is an enclosed machine; it generally makes less mess than a CNC machine.
53. Tyrrell, interview with author.
54. Tyrrell, interview with author.
55. Tyrrell, interview with author.
56. Tyrrell, interview with author.
57. Tyrrell, interview with author.
58. Tyrrell, interview with author.
59. Chris Gibson, Carl Grodach, Craig Lyons, Alexandra Crosby & Chris Brennan-Horley, *Urban Cultural Policy and the Changing Dynamics of Cultural Production Made in Marrickville*, report, Produced for the Australian Research Council Discovery Project: "Urban Cultural Policy and the Changing Dynamics of Cultural Production" (Sydney: 2017).
60. Peter Phipps, interview with author, *Reshaping Australian Manufacturing*, 11 May 2018 (Canberra: NLA), https://nla.gov.au/nla.cat-vn7765727.
61. Peter Phipps, interview with author.
62. Peter Phipps, interview with author.
63. Peter Phipps, interview with author.
64. Peter Phipps, interview with author.

5 'JUST FINISHING': FROM MANUAL PATTERNMAKING TO CNC MACHINE... 157

65. Bruce Phipps, interview with author, *Reshaping Australian Manufacturing*, 31 May 2018 (Canberra: NLA), https://nla.gov.au/nla.cat-vn7765732.
66. Peter Phipps, interview with author.
67. Peter Phipps, interview with author.
68. Peter Phipps, interview with author.
69. Peter Phipps, interview with author.
70. Peter Phipps, interview with author.
71. 'Patternmakers', Facebook group, https://www.facebook.com/groups/502920693172756.
72. Warren & Gibson, *Surfing Places*.
73. Warren & Gibson, *Surfing Places*.
74. Paul Kay, interview with author, *Reshaping Australian Manufacturing*, 30 April 2018 (Canberra: NLA), https://nla.gov.au/nla.cat-vn7765725.
75. Anthony Freemantle, interview with author (telephone interview), 4 September 2018.
76. Warren & Gibson, *Surfing Places*.

CHAPTER 6

Not Fitting the Pattern: Women in Industrial Craft

Introduction

Engineering represents everything that is defined as manly—the propensity to control and manipulate nature; the celebration of muscle and machine in action upon raw materials ... if engineering occupations have developed as a heartland of male hegemony, it is hardly surprising that female incursions into this domain don't occur easily or painlessly.

—Cynthia Cockburn, 1983[1]

In my previous book, *Hot Metal*, I included a chapter on women in the printing industry, which engaged with the experiences of female print workers—a manager, a tradeswoman and a 'tablehand'.[2] The content was historical; I focused then from the 1960s to the 1980s. When I wrote that chapter I imagined, naively, erroneously, that I was writing about a discriminatory situation confined to history. As I write this today in 2021, it would be comforting to think that those well-worn gender-labour battles—over equal pay, sexual harassment and sex-discrimination at work (etc.)—would be partly resolved in the Global North, at the very least. Unfortunately, this is not the case, and in some respects things have not progressed a great deal since the 1980s. In sectors such as manufacturing and engineering, the provision of anti-discrimination law has done very little to transform entrenched cultures of gender-labour segregation,

© The Author(s), under exclusive license to Springer Nature Switzerland AG 2021
J. A. Stein, *Industrial Craft in Australia*, Palgrave Studies in Oral History, https://doi.org/10.1007/978-3-030-87243-4_6

159

which implicitly classify work on the basis of its appropriateness for two (supposedly) normative gender types.[3] While legal reforms in the 1970s and 1980s have to some extent benefited middle-class and upper middle-class women (increasing their numbers in managerial or professional roles, for instance), such reforms have made negligible difference for working-class women. In 2020, the gender-pay gap in Australia was 13.4 per cent, and women's representation in traditionally male-dominated occupations continues to be very low, particularly in higher-status industrial trades (more data will be provided further on).[4]

Today, reading back through material written by sociologist Cynthia Cockburn from the early 1980s (such as the quote above), it is striking just how relevant her work *continues* to be. Cockburn examined hyper-masculine occupations and workplaces—from printing to engineering—considering both the fragile nature of craft masculinity (as it was threatened by new technologies and women's presence on the shopfloor) and analysing women's experiences in male-dominated occupations.[5] Cockburn skilfully connected feminist and Marxist analyses, showing an understanding of how both the gendered division of labour and workplace sexism are continually being reconfigured in new ways throughout different historical periods. This allows us to see that although technologies may transform labour processes, and industries may restructure, systemic male-dominance has a way of weaving back into new ways of working, and it is reproduced through deeply embedded social conventions and beliefs. Cockburn argued in the early 1980s that only through equal gender distribution in all occupations would we see a real end to workplace gender-discrimination and gender-based labour segregation.[6] Likewise, sociologist Sally Hacker called for a cooperative situation—using the cooperative Mondragon Corporation as a case study—that could put forward a fairer and more equal distribution of work and technology, across the broad strata of an organisation.[7] At the time of writing, we remain a long way from such a situation.

Thus far in this book we have mostly examined the dominant group in engineering patternmaking, that is, men's experiences. Patternmaking is, after all, an utterly male-dominated industrial craft—more so than printing, or fitting-and-turning, or carpentry, for example. But there is nothing inherently 'natural' about the way in which society assumes industrial craftwork to be the exclusive domain of heteronormative men. There is nothing inherent to men's bodies or minds that mean that they are more capable of the skills required for engineering patternmaking (or any other industrial craft, for that matter). Throughout this book I have retained an awareness of the ways in which apprenticeship learning, tool use and machinery 'ownership' can be tied to particular forms of masculinity. Craft masculinity is an historically specific social construction, intertwined with the reproduction of industrial craft practices.[8] I have no intention of essentialising men's relationship to industrial craft. Rather, I support the view that the long history of male-domination in heavy industry ought to continually be 'made strange', by not accepting it as an inherently natural way of being.[9] I again revisit craft masculinity in Chap. 7, particularly through Peter Watts' story—revealing how such conventions served to limit and restrict men's own choices and career pathways.

As I discovered in my research, there *are* women in patternmaking, and their respective working experiences differ greatly from men's. This chapter focuses on the experiences of two women in engineering patternmaking, from the 1980s to the present: Debra Schuckar and Deborah Tyrrell. Schuckar's and Tyrrell's respective stories are personal and specific, but, as always, I situate their oral histories in a wider historical and political context so that we may take away broader social understandings from this chapter, beyond the anecdotal. As a fully qualified patternmaker, Schuckar's story is representative of the experience of tradeswomen in a non-traditional trade, while Tyrrell's experience is that of a small-business owner and wife of a tradesman. Tyrrell shifted from 'doing the books' into a full technical engagement with the digital aspects of contemporary patternmaking.

This chapter first provides some background context for understanding matters surrounding women in non-traditional trades. I also establish some ethical issues related to name disclosure, before engaging with Schuckar's and Tyrrell's respective lives, as shared through oral history. Finally, I consider how this project fits within existing analytical and methodological work on gender and oral history practice, particularly with reference to the gendered nature of oral history as a practice.

BACKGROUND: WOMEN IN MALE-DOMINATED TRADES

From the 1980s to the present, a great deal of research has been conducted on women in non-traditional trades, analysing the barriers to entry, women's experiences while in these roles and employers' attitudes.[10] Likewise, the vexed issue of skill and the gendered division of labour has received significant scholarly attention over the past three decades, particularly in the fields of sociology and labour history.[11] I will not revisit this material here in detail, but, again, it is striking how little the *content* of these studies has changed, from the 1980s to the present. There remain deeply embedded social biases concerning what supposedly constitutes 'women's work' and what work is suitable work for men, and this is particularly prevalent in industries such as manufacturing and engineering. As noted by sociologists Ann Game and Rosemary Pringle, artificial binaries exist in manufacturing labour: skilled/unskilled, dirty/clean, light/heavy, interesting/boring which then transfer on to rates of pay and social status.[12] These categories tend to dissolve into grey complexity when the actual content of the labour process is considered. Traditionally in manufacturing, women were not entirely excluded from the work, but their work was generally imagined to be 'unskilled', involving menial and repetitive tasks: simple machine operators, packers, 'tablehand' assistants, workers undertaking repetitive manual movements. The entrenched binaries of skilled/unskilled continue to exist in the social consciousness, and they are transmitted generationally, continuing to impact upon younger people's career choices.

As long as manufacturing labour continues to be gender-segregated, the question of 'skill' remains political and contested. On one level, skill and knowledge can be said to objectively exist (as a product of years of hands-on experience and training, and as transmitted through training or education processes). However, the social understanding of 'high skill' or 'low skill' continues to be attached to gendered work roles.[13] 'High skill' jobs—including industrial crafts such as patternmaking and toolmaking—are routinely understood to be 'men's work', while supposedly lower-skill jobs, such as cleaning or care-work, are often considered to be work suitable for women and are remunerated accordingly.[14] As technological change has altered the labour process in manufacturing, the work should, theoretically, have become more accessible to bodies that do not conform to that of 'strong men'. Digitised and automated work systems have made work tasks less physically onerous, and devices now exist that make heavy lifting almost a non-issue (theoretically, at least).

Technological change, however, has not produced any meaningful shift in industrial workplace gender diversity. As noted by Game and Pringle (in 1983, but it remains relevant today), automation and digitisation mean that there are fewer manufacturing jobs and that:

all jobs are becoming like women's jobs, as they have traditionally been defined ... Changes in the labour process have not led to changes in the sexual division of labour ... [In highly skilled manufacturing areas:] These are traditional male areas, and remain so. Overall numbers have reduced, and management are attempting to replace traditional specialists ... but in a situation of high unemployment the men want to hang on to the jobs.[15]

Men therefore operate defensively—doubling down to reemphasise the importance of craft masculinity and their masculine ownership of tools and technologies. I explored this issue extensively in *Hot Metal*, following on from Cockburn's analysis of how hand-compositors first claimed Linotype machines (and then computer typesetting machines) as their 'own', so as to defend what is left of their work from 'incursions' from non-tradespeople, including women.[16] Essentially what we see here is the way in which newer technologies—employed in the service of capital—operate to reduce craft's labour power.

Today, women working in non-traditional trades in the twenty-first century continue to face systemic disadvantage, as well as both institutionalised and overt sexism. This has occurred notwithstanding many decades of feminist advocacy, which led to the passing of anti-discrimination law and equal employment opportunity policies.[17] Relevant legislative changes in Australia included the NSW *Anti-Discrimination Act* in 1977, and the South Australian *Sex Discrimination Act* in 1976, and the Australian federal *Sex Discrimination Act* 1984. A similar pattern occurred internationally, such as the US *Civil Rights Act* 1964, the UK *Equal Pay Act* 1970 and the *Sex Discrimination Act* 1975; and the UN Treaty stemming from the *Convention on the Elimination of all Forms of Discrimination Against Women* in 1979.

In the Australian context, these legislative reforms coincided with specific efforts (particularly in the state and federal public service) to encourage women to undertake trade apprenticeships in non-traditional areas. The aim was to address skills shortages, improve women's upward mobility and shrink the gender-pay gap. However, these 'apprenticeships-for-girls' schemes have been criticised in the past for encouraging a small number of women into the 'deep end' in industrial workplaces, publicising their recruitment success, and then providing little support once these women commenced their training.[18]

Once 'in', female apprentices in non-traditional trades almost uniformly faced differential treatment, bullying, harassment and mistrust, including

164 J. A. STEIN

from management. Often they found few official avenues for support.[19] Even simple design features (such as the location and provision of women's toilets and changerooms, or the ill-fitting size of personal-protective equipment) conveyed messages to women that they were not welcome in industrial spaces.[20] To give a fuller picture, however, it is important to note that many female apprentices from this pioneering 'girls in trades' period in the 1970s and 1980s also spoke of positive experiences. They acknowledged that some peers were highly supportive, and they often reported feeling a strong dedication to their trade, and feeling pride and satisfaction at work.[21] Nonetheless, tradeswomen had those positive experiences *in spite of* a widespread culture that did not accept their presence, and doubted their capacity to 'do a man's job'. These elements commonly coexist in people's recollections.

A brief statistical picture of women's representation in industrial craft gives a clearer notion of the ongoing gender segregation of these work arenas. Cockburn shared data from the United Kingdom in 1980, where, at the time, 0.37 per cent of "engineering craftsmen" were female.[22] When we move forward into the present, some 30–40 years after pathbreaking programmes bringing women into non-traditional apprenticeships, industrial trades still rate extremely poorly when it comes to gender balance.[23] Today in Australia, the rates of women in male-dominated trades remain persistently low, generally hovering between 0.5 and 3 per cent, depending on the trade.[24] For example, in 2016 First Class Welders, metal fabricators and fitters and turners were all 1 per cent female.[25] In 2014, the percentage of female automotive and engineering trade workers in Australia was 0.6 per cent.[26]

What about female representation specifically in engineering patternmaking? The Australian Government's *Job Outlook* website uses the Australian Bureau of Statistics' Labour Force Survey data to provide public information on occupational trends. *Job Outlook* states that of the 270 engineering patternmakers recorded in 2016, 22 per cent of these were women.[27] And 22 per cent would be around 59 female patternmakers. Based on my research, I find this statistic to be highly unlikely. Labour Force Survey data uses samples to generate estimates, and such a small occupational group means that reliable estimates are unlikely. And 2014 Australian Bureau of Statistics Labour Force data indicates women made up only 0.6 per cent of *all* automotive and engineering trade workers (which would include patternmaking). A larger group of trades clustered together provides for more accurate estimates based on samples.[28]

6 NOT FITTING THE PATTERN: WOMEN IN INDUSTRIAL CRAFT   165

In six years of research into engineering patternmaking in Australia, I have only come across one fully qualified female engineering patternmaker. One female in 270 employees would be 0.37 per cent. The good news is that, at the time of writing, there is one female apprentice currently training to be a patternmaker in Victoria.

The ongoing gender segregation in industrial trades is a feature of other deindustrialising economies, although some argue that Australia remains the most sex-segregated of OECD nations.[29] In 2017, 4.5 per cent of skilled tradespeople in Canada were female.[30] The US Bureau of Labor statistics (2017) likewise reveals a consistent pattern where women are well represented in more lower-paid and lower-status manufacturing occupations (such as process workers, assemblers and machine operators, at around 20–40 per cent female).[31] But skilled manufacturing and construction trades (with higher status and remuneration) tend to have female participation rates of between 0 and 6 per cent, depending on the trade.[32] Likewise, in South Africa, men are four times more likely to be 'artisans or operators' (technical and trade-based roles) than women.[33] In the United Kingdom women make up around 10 per cent of 'skilled trades' (this figure does not distinguish between types of trades; the percentage could well be smaller if we looked more specifically at manufacturing and construction trades, for example).[34]

The reasons for this continued gender segregation in industrial contexts are not a mystery and relate to the aforementioned embedded cultural assumptions, implied binaries and economic structures. This results in women and girls being less exposed to particular ways of working and being, a process that starts in early childhood.[35] Girls may not be taught how to use machine tools by their families and in formal education, for instance. They may learn to hold their bodies in particular ways, ways that are seen as more traditionally feminine, rather than balancing their weight with widely spaced feet when using machinery, for example. Women and girls are more likely to think "I can't see myself doing that," "I don't know anything about that" or "I'm not good at heavy machinery". Other influential factors include employer attitudes, inflexible working hours, a lack of part-time options and a lack of affordable childcare (particularly relevant in a context where it is still assumed that women will be primary carers, regardless of employment status).[36]

Women have also made an understandable choice to avoid careers where they suspect they will be marginalised at work and subjected to a great deal of harassment and bullying. Tradeswomen often feel great pressure on their workplace performance, more so than their male peers. They feel the constant gaze of the men, sometimes objectifying them, but also a sense of constant scrutiny in their work. They speak of regularly hearing doubts about their capacities, from their male colleagues and managers. As a result, female apprentices report feeling pressure to make sure their work is 'perfect', so as to be *better than* the male apprentices in their cohort, in the search for acceptance and respect. Female apprentices also feel social pressure to assure other women that industrial trades are a good choice; they feel they have to make the way safe for others to follow in their footsteps. It is difficult to be honest about your experience at work when you might be discouraging other women from joining you. (We will return to these issues in the section on Debra Schuckar, further on.)

Some might question: why does this matter? If women do not want to undertake training in industrial trades, is the gender segregation in these areas really a problem? There are several arguments against this defeatist position. First, Australia is currently experiencing skills shortages in a number of industrial trades, including sheet metal trades workers, metal fitters and machinists, structural steel and welding trades workers.[37] Encouraging and supporting 50 per cent of a *potential* trainee population makes basic sense in terms of increasing numbers.[38] Secondly, it is widely recognised that worker diversity makes for a more positive, inclusive and ethical workplace, regardless of the industry. As observed by Karen Struthers and Glenda Strachan, a segregated labour market "contributes to labour market rigidity, suboptimal productivity and economic inefficiency" as well as aforementioned skills shortages.[39] Today, various organisations exist that provide support and advocacy for women in male-dominated trades, such as Tradeswomen Australia and the National Taskforce on Tradeswomen's Issues (the United States). The existence of such organisations is vital. As we shall see in the following section, Schuckar was alone in what she experienced as an apprentice and engineering patternmaker, and she credits her survival in the trade to family support, in the absence of other networks.

ETHICAL QUANDARIES: WHEN THERE'S ONLY ONE FEMALE PATTERNMAKER

It is common for oral history to retain participants' full names in publications: with an emphasis on individuals' life stories, the deidentification of quotations tends to occur only if the participant has specific concerns about what is being said. In the case of women in patternmaking, however, I had a problem. In my six-odd years of research into this trade, Debra Schuckar is the only fully qualified female engineering patternmaker I have come across in Australia. As mentioned, there is currently a female apprentice undertaking a patternmaking apprenticeship in Victoria, which is a statistically significant shift, given there are only six apprentices training in patternmaking across Australia. Nonetheless, Schuckar's situation is rare enough that it would be unhelpful to use a pseudonym, as she would likely remain identifiable if I included her trade and used female pronouns. Of course Schuckar would, first and foremost, prefer to be defined as a person—and a fully qualified patternmaker—rather than over-emphasising her gender. But to leave out the fact that she is (most likely) the only fully qualified female patternmaker in Australia would be to miss an important part of her experience.

Yet I knew that there were parts of Schuckar's story that she would not be comfortable with making public, if her real name was used. Schuckar and I discussed this problem extensively, and she decided she wanted her real name to be associated with my work. We ultimately came to an agreement about what could be shared and what could not. Correspondingly, this chapter shares some of Schuckar's experience, but it is by no means the 'full story' (arguably this is always the case in oral history, but here it has been negotiated very specifically). We are still working towards a society in which women can feel wholly comfortable coming forward about their experiences without fear of judgement or other downstream consequences.

DEBRA SCHUCKAR

Tradeswomen often come from families of tradespeople, as was the case with Debra Schuckar (Figs. 6.1 and 6.2). Schuckar's father Vern was a German émigré and bricklayer by trade, and her older brother worked at the Victorian State Electricity Commission (SEC), a government-run industrial enterprise. Her mother Margaret was also practical and more interested in outdoor tasks than domestic labour:

Fig. 6.1 Debra Schuckar as an apprentice patternmaker, 1982, State Electricity Commission of Victoria, Melbourne. (Courtesy of Debra Schuckar, reproduced with permission)

> Mum didn't like cooking … When Mum gave up cooking roast, that was my saddest memory. She said,
> "That's it. I'd rather work in the garden. No roast on Sunday. We're only having noodles and meat out of the can."[40]

Schuckar reflected:

> We were always working with Mum and Dad. Sometimes I'd be in with Dad in the workshop, and he'd give me a hammer and nail and a bit of wood. It wouldn't be making anything particular. Maybe just whacking nails in a piece of wood![41]

Schuckar described her own tendencies as creative and artistic, and she was originally planning to undertake an education degree and become an art

6 NOT FITTING THE PATTERN: WOMEN IN INDUSTRIAL CRAFT   169

Fig. 6.2 Debra Schuckar as an apprentice in the patternstore, 1982, State Electricity Commission of Victoria, Melbourne. (Courtesy of Debra Schuckar, reproduced with permission)

teacher. In the early 1980s, Margaret found a newspaper advertisement for apprenticeships at the SEC:

> My mum came in one day and she goes,
> "Debra, there's some jobs in the paper that the SEC are putting out. Painting and Decorating. Why don't you go for it?"
> So, I thought, "Oh, yeah, alright," … I read the description … and then I saw Patternmaking, and I thought,
> "What's Patternmaking?" … I'd never heard of that in my life. I read it up and it said, making things out of wood, plaster … and I thought,
> "Oh, this sounds more interesting than painting. I might just apply for that. Give that a go."[42]

SEC apprenticeships had a competitive entry process, and Schuckar's father ensured that his daughter learned more about the trade before undertaking the aptitude test and the admission interview. At this stage—to the family's credit—there was no doubt cast over Schuckar's appropriateness for the trade, on the basis of her gender. Vern introduced Schuckar to the Head of the Foundry department at the George Thompson School for Foundry Technology, at Royal Melbourne Institute of Technology (RMIT). By the time of her interview, Schuckar knew enough about patternmaking to impress the assessors. She was practical, detail-oriented, good at mathematics and interested in timber. Moreover, Schuckar had a clear capacity to visualise form: perfect potential for an apprentice patternmaker.

At this point it is worth introducing the significance of the SEC in the industrial training of generations of working-class and middle-class teenagers in Victoria. The SEC offered apprenticeships in electrical trades, but also fitting-and-turning, engineering patternmaking, moulding, among others. The Richmond workshops had their own foundry on-site, which made parts for electrical power plants across the state. As with other state-run industrial organisations in mid-twentieth-century Australia, the SEC held the farsighted understanding that a broad-ranging, high-quality trades education was a public responsibility. Other than providing electricity to the citizens of Victoria (albeit via fossil fuels), it also generated skilled tradespeople. In a pattern common in government apprenticeships, first-year apprentices at SEC underwent a programme where they were exposed to *all* trades on offer across the site, as well as health and safety training, before focusing in on their specific trade. Schuckar has very positive memories of her apprenticeship years at the SEC, largely due to the sense of community and friendship fostered by this public service organisation and due to her family's support. But these memories are also punctuated by regular experiences of harassment, differential treatment and bullying.

Schuckar always mixed positive and negative descriptions of her apprenticeship, emphasising her strong friendships at the SEC, as well as memories such as these:

> There were some lovely guys, but there were also ones that used to stir me up bad. Like, throw hot metal at you after they'd cut it, so you'd catch it and burn your hand
> … it was always talked about that, you know,
> "Oh, the only reason they're employing women is because they're trying to look good as a big company," and things like that … It was always a bit of a struggle … there was a lot of doubting going on, even from some of the

teachers, because I was female, that I wouldn't last, I wouldn't finish my apprenticeship ...
I remember this notebook I had, it used to say: "Women have to work twice as hard to be thought as good". I've never forgotten that line, because I felt that a lot when I was training.[43]

Schuckar's experiences are very similar to accounts provided by women in other non-traditional trades across Australia in the 1980s and 1990s.[44] The treatment of female apprentices is endemic to the system, not an isolated or individual experience of a few 'bad apples'.

Once settled in at the SEC, Schuckar also had to endure the experience of being the only female in her 'trade school' patternmaking cohort at the George Thompson School (the formalised teaching component of the apprenticeship) (Fig. 6.3). Schuckar recalled:

Fig. 6.3 Debra Schuckar's patternmaking class, George Thompson School of Foundry Technology, RMIT, Melbourne, c. early 1980s. (Courtesy of Debra Schuckar, reproduced with permission)

There was one guy who was quite nasty at the trades school, I remember. I said something about a maths thing … No-one knew the answer to this maths equation, and then I put my hand up … and said what it was, and some guy at the back said,

"You smartarse slut." You know? … I just felt that quite demeaning. Like, it didn't need to, I think the teachers handle it the best way they can, and say, "Enough of that," but nothing was ever really said to these people. [Later] that same person [who] said that was coming up to me … and I remember saying to him,

"Don't you ever talk to me like that ever again."

I said it very quietly, and he apologised on the spot, and never ever, never ever said one derogatory comment to me! [slight laugh] But I handled it in that way. I didn't handle it by being vocal … Diplomatic, and just teaching people to hold their tongue, and not be so frivolous with their words.[45]

I asked Schuckar how she dealt with the regular taunting and mistrust of her capacities, both at the SEC and in trade school. She conceded:

Well, first it was to give up! [laughs] Came home crying after two months. "Dad, I can't stand this! It's terrible!" And he said,

"Well, Deb, boys have only just graduated from kindergarten." … I think I debriefed a lot on him, and he would encourage me to go and how to handle situations, and I remember my brother's mates, they were all really good … they could give me tips on how to work around the guys. That's the only way I could really handle it … So no, there was no counselling. Come to think of it, it probably would have been a good thing, on how to manage it.[46]

With the lack of a formalised support network for female apprentices (at this stage in the early 1980s), family support was a lifeline. SEC management appear to have meant well, but their strategies sometimes made things worse: Schuckar was continually in the spotlight, featuring in SEC marketing and annual reports.[47] The publicity did allow Schuckar to include some excellent 'one-liners', useful for future female apprentices. One SEC article said:

Debbie Schuckar turned the tables on the boys who wanted to know why she wanted to be an apprentice. "I just asked them why they wanted to be apprentices."[48]

6 NOT FITTING THE PATTERN: WOMEN IN INDUSTRIAL CRAFT   173

Although the SEC was keen to publicise their shining example of equal employment opportunity, it is notable that they only implemented a policy on sexual harassment in 1984, two years after Schuckar had commenced her apprenticeship.[49] Added to this, the weight of expectation was heavy:

> I was the first in Victoria, so that was quite scary ... I felt a lot of pressure to succeed. ... You were on show. You were publicised a lot ... I didn't want to fail anybody because I was the first ... I did feel a responsibility to be successful so that other women could follow in their own way.[50]

But Schuckar was committed (this part seems to have been hard wired in her character): "You had to finish what you started. There's no such thing as dropping out because you didn't feel comfortable."[51]

Schuckar completed her apprenticeship, becoming a fully indentured engineering patternmaker in 1986. With this, she gained the full respect of her peers (as with her male colleagues):

> When you come out of your time, it's like,
> "Oh, I've got my ticket now!" And ... you're at the top of your game ... I know I was a good patternmaker then. I don't know how I am now. I'm a bit behind the times now! [laughs] But it was a good feeling, I guess, and the respect was there. It took a long time, but the respect was there that I *was* a tradesperson, and if the boss went away, I was the boss, so you had that rapport, because you worked amongst them and everyone had that respect for you.[52]

The years of making sure her work was *better than* the male apprentices had paid off: Schuckar was awarded an Honourable Mention for patternmaking craftsmanship and the CIBA-GEIGY Prize for plastics patternmaking. Schuckar stayed working as a patternmaker at the SEC in the years that followed, almost reaching her ten-year long service leave at the organisation. For some men in a similar position, they may have imagined that with becoming a tradesman they would have 'job for life'—they'd gained the skills of a highly prized trade, and they had steady employment in a government job.

As it happened, however, the political economy of the period came to be a decisive factor. In the early 1990s, the Victorian state government under Liberal premier Jeff Kennett was undergoing a neoliberal strategy of rapidly privatising government assets. The SEC was targeted. It was first disaggregated and then privatised. Voluntary redundancies were offered

174   J. A. STEIN

to staff in the early 1990s. At the time, Schuckar was pregnant with her first child. While on maternity leave, she was offered a redundancy package, which she accepted:

> Originally, I was going back to work to get my ten years' long service, but because they'd offered me the money, I just didn't go back, then.[53]

In some ways Schuckar was shielded from the blow, away from the low morale and shock of the restructuring and privatisation of the SEC.

> Everyone was pretty down in the mouth, I think. Figuring out what they're going to do, I suppose. I didn't really hear too much of what they were going to do, in the end, because I was off having a baby.[54]

Schuckar's absence meant she had little agency in how her situation was handled, although she did not express to me any concerns about this.

As parents know well, having a baby completely alters your professional outlook and self-definition, particularly for women. For Schuckar, as for so many other mothers, there was no prospect of returning to work 'as it had been before'. For tradesmen at the SEC, the question might have been 'where am I going to find another job in my trade?', but for Schuckar, the questions ran much deeper: not just 'where?', but also 'how?' and 'what?' Engineering patternmaking jobs were still available in small numbers, but automating technologies were on the horizon at this stage, so the outlook was increasingly grim (see Chap. 5). In the 1980s and 1990s, patternmaking positions were not generally offered on a part-time basis, and they rarely had hours that were family friendly. Added to this, Schuckar's first marriage split up, and she ended up raising her first child as a single mother, while juggling further study and precarious employment.

As I interviewed Schuckar, the gravity of these cumulative challenges really struck me. It seemed an impossibly difficult situation. Meanwhile, she breezily talked through this period in her life. Schuckar's life dramatically changed with the birth of her first child; her daily work was in the home, caring for her daughter and ensuring that everything was 'done':

> It's very vague, really, because I think you're tired all the time, and you're just *doing*. Sterilising bottles, cooking, sleeping, getting up doing the same thing. Maybe not even getting dressed all day! Washing nappies, because I used the cloth nappies … there was dinner on the table. The garden was

6 NOT FITTING THE PATTERN: WOMEN IN INDUSTRIAL CRAFT   175

weeded. I was always—everything had to be done, you know? That's just how I was. I'm a bit more relaxed now![55]

When her first daughter was around 18 months old, Schuckar enrolled in a degree at Victoria University, first in Graphic Arts, then shifting to Fine Arts (see Chap. 7). Schuckar supplemented government-provided study income by sewing costumes for her daughter's dance school. This is a whole world of complex craft-making that adds a dimension to Schuckar's story and her identity. "One year I made three hundred costumes," she said, adding that the costumes were complex, involving many separate parts and tiny details.[56]

Schuckar explained that woodwork was not a feasible activity at this stage in her life. By this time, she had remarried and had her second child:

> You can't have a baby out amongst saws and wood dust and everything, whereas you can sew with your children in the room and still be able to tend to them. So, I was being a bit practical … Not much sleep in those days. Lucky I was a night owl! So, there was no time for woodwork then. It was just costumes.[57]

Schuckar's work history then involved a variety of different jobs and positions, including book-keeping, hospitality work in a café and at a catering company, working in communications at a ventilator company, working in administration at a university and working for a plasterer. The jobs were sometimes casual and insecure, but Schuckar wanted to emphasise the positive when she spoke to me—she was open to developing new skills and unafraid to try something different. After her second marriage ended, Schuckar decided to gain a skill she had always wanted to hone: singing. At the same time as balancing parenting and precarious work, Schuckar took singing lessons. She ultimately formed a duo, *Debra SoulPlay*, performing at pubs, parties and corporate events.

In around 2016, Schuckar was able to return to patternmaking. A Melbourne patternshop was looking for a part-time patternmaker. The hours were suitable, and Schuckar knew some of the patternmakers working there. Moving back to patternmaking was somewhat daunting, however, as the industry had changed a great deal in 16 years. Schuckar described how it felt to return to patternmaking:

Scary. Daunting ... Not the confidence I had when I finished my trade. And it changed. ... I noticed the first time I went back ... we never carved anymore! We didn't do any carving! We were ... using a lot of filler, and sculpting that instead. And now ...we use other plastics to mould patterns ... So, it's pretty amazing, the changes ... But not a lot of carving, no. Lots of bog-squashing, they call it! Lots of bog-squash! ... It's faster, it's neater, instead of carving it.[58]

This patternshop is unusual, in that it remains a non-CNC (computer numerically controlled machines) patternshop, even today. This job should have been the absolute dream patternmaking job for Schuckar. Finally, she was able to return to patternmaking, work part-time and in a non-CNC shop. Perfect!

Unfortunately, over time, it became apparent to Schuckar that this return to patternmaking was far from ideal. After five years of working for this patternshop, Schuckar had well and truly adapted to the new methods. But she still found that management doubted her capacity as a patternmaker. Five years on, her tasks were generally confined to finishing the work done by other patternmakers. This is how Schuckar's experience is a different form of 'just finishing', compared to the 'just finishing' experienced by male patternmakers discussed in Chap. 5. The degradation of the labour process, for Schuckar, was a management decision, likely to be on the basis of gender (whether this was a result of conscious or unconscious bias, Schuckar was not sure). For five years, Schuckar was left in a casual position, rather than being put on a permanent part-time contract. She felt that her work was always doubted by the patternshop—not so much by her fellow patternmakers, but by the management. Schuckar said:

It's awful to go to work and no one has faith in what you're doing ... This is the worst I've dealt with, worse than at SEC. [*withheld*] always questioned what I was doing.[59]

Finally, in 2021, Schuckar decided she had had enough and resigned. "I'm too old to be fighting this fight," she said. "It saddens me that men have not moved far in 40 years. A percentage of them have had no mind-frame change." She is sad to leave patternmaking, "but I don't want to be treated like rubbish either".[60] Schuckar now works as a book-keeper at a Melbourne foundry and says there's still a chance she could make the odd pattern for the foundry, if needed.

6 NOT FITTING THE PATTERN: WOMEN IN INDUSTRIAL CRAFT   177

The last time we spoke, I reminded Schuckar that unlike the other patternmakers she had worked around, she was multi-skilled, having worked in such a broad variety of occupations, and having refined other skills throughout her working life: textiles, singing, cooking and single parenthood. Debra Schuckar is, I would argue, the most highly skilled interviewee I encountered during this project.

DEBORAH TYRRELL

Deborah Tyrrell's life history is an example of a relatively common trajectory for women in Australian manufacturing small businesses: the life of the tradesperson's spouse. Women in this role often conduct the bookkeeping and manage business administration. As the wife of an engineering patternmaker, Tyrrell became deeply enmeshed in the patternmaking industry, through her co-management of the business Kimbeny, which she runs with her husband Greg Tyrrell.

Deborah Tyrrell grew up in the 1960s in the northern Sydney suburb of Beacon Hill. Her background was essentially middle class, and, like Schuckar, her father was of German origin (although he grew up in China). Tyrrell's father was multi-lingual and an accountant, and he worked for a large packaging container firm (which, as it happened, hired patternmakers). Her mother had a passion for fossicking (searching for gemstones), and Tyrrell would join her mother on trips with a fossicking club. Tragically, Tyrrell's mother was killed in an accident when Tyrrell was 17, in her last year of high school. Like Schuckar, Tyrrell had originally planned to become a high school teacher:

> I had always planned on going on and becoming a home ec' [economics] teacher, which was more or less food sciences … When my Mum was killed in my HSC [Higher School Certificate] year, by the time we got through my HSC I decided I then couldn't turn around and face another three years, four years [of study] … so I joined the Commonwealth Bank instead.[61]

The Commonwealth Bank is a large Australian bank, and at the time Tyrrell worked there, it was a publicly owned entity.

Tyrrell's interview included descriptions of banking technologies from the early 1980s, with references to deposit books, punch cards and tape. She recalled that the computing roles in the Commonwealth Bank tended

178   J. A. STEIN

to be around "90 per cent male", but there were women working in support roles and in typing pools. Tyrrell recalled,

> I used to go to the IBM headquarters to pick up the punch tape-style things ... they were big reels, like old-style film reels ... Walking into this massive building, you could just see this room glassed off with these big, grey things which were computers. It was all very air-conditioned and climate controlled.[62]

Tyrrell met her husband Greg Tyrrell on a fossicking trip, "out the back of Nundle, we were looking for sapphires and fossilised dinosaur poo."[63] At the time, Greg was an apprentice engineering patternmaker, which is the first she had heard of the trade. Greg undertook his apprenticeship at a thermoforming company in Brookvale, which led to his specialisation in vacuum form patterns. They married when Deborah was 19 and Greg was 21.

Tyrrell worked at the Commonwealth Bank until 1986, when she left to have her first child. The transition was one that Tyrrell was happy to make, although it cannot have been easy, as there was no local family support, and she was the first among her friends to have children. Tyrrell had her second child in 1990. Domestic textiles work became a big focus. She had learned sewing from her mother and at high school.

> I made all the kids' clothes. I did ... bumper protectors for the cots ... made the kids all continental quilts for when they were bigger ... living on one income back then, money was tight.[64]

Tyrrell returned to part-time work when she could, working at Hanimex in photographic film processing.

The Tyrrells started their own patternmaking business in 1990, after the birth of their second child. They named the business 'Kimbeny', after their children Kimberley and Benjamin. Starting the business was a significant shift for Tyrrell, although she did not specifically articulate this in our interview. Her own career was not something to be eked out independently, and from then on, domestic labour had to be balanced with business administration. The shift towards the subject position of family business owner is reflected in the way that Tyrrell structures her speech in the interview. Everything, from then on, was 'we', as the Tyrrells worked towards making their business Kimbeny viable. To supplement their income, Tyrrell ran Tupperware parties. This lasted for around six years, until "the business got too busy. We couldn't do everything."[65]

As Tyrrell describes, the decision about *when* to start the business was very much about the availability of machinery and equipment:

> We were looking at starting the business, and in the trade that we're in, it's very much about the machinery, and there are certain items that we felt that unless you had [them], you couldn't start a business. And one of them is a large, 30" disc sander. We'd been looking for one for a while, and one came up on the market … We set up the business in our garage initially.[66]

Tyrrell explained her various roles in Kimbeny:

> When we established the business, my involvement was in bookwork [book-keeping] and administration, and helping Greg lift something if he needed a lift! [laughs] And sourcing materials that we used.[67]

Over time, this changed. As we have seen in Chap. 5, Tyrrell was instrumental in encouraging the business to take up 3D printing and CNC machining. Tyrrell recognises that the changes in her role came about partly due to the technological shifts happening to patternmaking but also because her children grew older and required less constant care:

> Where previously I was only involved in the bookwork side of the business, I'm now involved in all aspects of the business … I'm very hands-on in the business these days. As the business has evolved, I've become a lot more involved … As the kids have got older … I'd struggle to hold the role I hold now if the kids were young … But the business and patternmaking as a whole has evolved dramatically since the 1990s with CAD work and computerised controlled machines.[68]

This is a case in which technological change, in part, led to Tyrrell having more involvement in the production process, whereas, when the pattern-making work was more manual, Tyrrell's role was more distant.

With the Tyrrell's transition to 3D printing and then CNC machining, Tyrrell taught herself how to use the CAD/CAM (Computer Aided Drawing/Computer Aided Manufacturing) programmes SolidWorks and Mastercam and came to understand toolpathing, as it applied to CNC. It is worth pausing here for a moment to acknowledge that these are complex and technical software programmes, and mastering these programmes is a significant achievement, particularly inasmuch as it is highly contingent on specialised production processes. Tyrrell laughed, telling a story of how a software sales representative for Mastercam used to spruik the alleged ease of the CAD software by saying, "Well, I've trained a fifty-year-old housewife how to do it, so yeah, you can do it if you're determined enough."[69] Perhaps 'housewife' is not the term that immediately comes to mind when considering Tyrrell's extensive work for Kimbeny. This quote, however, is a useful illustration of how Tyrrell's presence may be interpreted very differently by those in highly male-dominated work contexts, such as manufacturing or engineering.

I asked Tyrrell if she had encountered any pushback or prejudice on the basis on her not being a qualified patternmaker and/or on the basis of her gender. Tyrrell replied:

> Yes. [laughs] I'll have to say not generally within the patternmakers themselves. When we started the business I did go out on the road and talk to a lot of people … I was trying to drum up work, I was doing a bit of a sales role. And yes, particularly some of the older men … [But] I've been involved in a patternshop for a long time. I'm pretty familiar with the processes.[70]

Tyrrell suggests here that her knowledge was usually what prevented sexism from becoming a problem for her: as long as she could demonstrate her technical familiarity with patternmaking, she was essentially accepted. She referred to one moment in a meeting of the Master Patternmakers' Association of NSW that demonstrates how attitudes to technological change, and to women working in industrial trades, are still understood by tradespeople as being intertwined, even in recent years. At the meeting, one patternmaker complained (he is quoted below, but this is in Tyrrell's retelling):

> "That's the problem with this. You get everybody who can now do the toolpathing, and they don't understand the manufacturing process, and it's devaluing what we're doing, because *anybody* can do it."
> More or less, he was referring to *me*. Or me and other people.[71]

The objection patternmakers may have here to 'anybody' doing their job is tied together with an understandable fear of redundancy due to technological change. But in this case, the fear is essentially unnecessary. Had the Tyrrells invested in automating technologies with the view to offloading a

6 NOT FITTING THE PATTERN: WOMEN IN INDUSTRIAL CRAFT

great deal of labour—sacking workers—then the objection would be well founded. Greg and Deborah Tyrrell invested in digital fabrication technologies so as to stay competitive as a small business, in a swiftly changing market, as discussed in Chap. 5.

Notes on Gender and Oral History Practice

Oral history theories and methods have come a long way since early attempts to 'tell women's stories'. It is no longer imagined that the oral history process is as simple as 'giving voice' to a marginalised group, and our work is done. Over several decades, the international oral history community has engaged in deep and critical discussion on the gendered nature of memory, and the role of gender in relation to oral history as a practice.[72] It is now widely understood that the oral history interview is a relational site of meaning-making, wherein the subject position of the interviewer and interviewee produces very particular, contingent outcomes. Gender is but one factor in that relational encounter. As noted by Joanna Bornat and Hanna Diamond, the connection between oral history and feminist perspectives has, over time, entailed a shift from 'women's history' and studies of the working class, towards examining oral history in relation to categories such as 'gender', 'identity' and individual subjectivity.[73]

The way we speak, converse and share memory is also a gendered phenomenon, which again influences how the oral history interview unfolds.[74] This issue was examined extensively by oral historian Daniel James in his detailed account of the life story and oral testimony of Argentinian union activist Doña María Roldán.[75] James locates Roldan's gendered position through specific relation to Peronist ideology and discourse, which came to set particularised roles for women, in relation to industrial work, political activism, domesticity and familial relationships. Roldán's personal narrative demonstrated a "lack of fit between conventionalised cultural forms and gendered experience", which resulted in dissonance between available gendered narratives and Roldán's own biography.[76]

The gendered nature of oral testimony was also discussed by oral historian Caroline Daley, who noted that we cannot simply recount "women's words as though the way they have presented themselves is unproblematic".[77] Daley urges us to consider the "silences and omissions, confront the contradictions and complexities" and "analyse the self-presentation" in the interview.[78] This recalls oral historian Luisa Passerini's call for attention to silences and consensus in normative, everyday life, as it is within

182   J. A. STEIN

these moments that resistance and acquiescence can be detected.[79] Likewise, Daley notes that "the same is true for men's accounts". Daley states:

> The ways men present themselves, the stories they tell, or don't tell, the ways they were shaped by the material conditions of their experiences, all need to be investigated.[80]

Reflecting on her own interviews, Daley said, "What struck me as I transcribed the tapes ... was how gendered the very form of oral history is."[81] Daley noted how the *content* of the interviews differed between the men and women she spoke to. The women "had stories to tell of home and family", while the men "were more likely to talk in long bursts", centring themselves as heroes of an exciting narrative.[82]

This to some extent accords with my own interviewing experience for *Reshaping Australian Manufacturing*. The majority of the male interviewees spoke with a sense of authority and in long stretches, needing little questioning or interruption from me. They were comfortable presenting themselves at the centre of the story, as flawed heroes. Several, such as Peter Williams, Bryan Poynton, Serge Haidutschyk and Peter Watts, might be described as 'born storytellers' and were very comfortable sharing their stories extensively. They seemed to feel no doubt about the relevance or interestingness of their stories (and nor should they). Patternmaking educator Jim Walker also approached his interview with no doubt as to his authority as narrator. This passage is one example where Walker comfortably intertwines his personal background with a broader political context and refers to having a family—notably briefly:

> I did join the Freemasons in the early, mid-fifties, I would think. I'm still a member, of course ... I'm not active now. Not many people are. It's sort of ... it's sort of lost its place in society. ... And there were factions. There was ... the Democratic Labour Party, who were very Catholic in their outlook, and they were always pushing for wage rises and that, but that passed. And then there was the AEU, which was the Amalgamated Engineering Union, which I joined after I finished my apprenticeship. ... Of course, all the while, I was married and having kids, and working our butts off, and my wife worked![83]

One of the few male interviewees who spoke with more caution and deference was Tim Wighton, who was younger than me. The issue there may

6 NOT FITTING THE PATTERN: WOMEN IN INDUSTRIAL CRAFT 183

have been one of (assumed) social status or perhaps it was more to do with his particular personality. Generally, the older men were quite comfortable presenting themselves as experts and craftsmen with long, authoritative stories to tell.

On the other hand, the two interviews I undertook with women—Schuckar and Tyrrell—were in some ways more difficult interactions, at least in terms of being oral history interviews. Both interviews tended to have much shorter statements and many more questions by me. Our interviews were more 'conversational', with more interactions back and forth, which may also indicate a gendered manner of interacting (although I am reluctant to essentialise here). The Schuckar interview was punctuated by moments of nervous laughter from us both. For instance, during the interview we were sitting in Schuckar's study, which was piled high with papers, craft projects and miscellaneous objects. There was a moment of silence in our interview, and we both watched a large pile of stuff slowly start to slide and then crash down to the floor, as if in slow motion. The loud crash made a mockery of my unnecessarily anxious attempts to ensure audio quality, and Schuckar and I both fell about laughing.

At times, it seemed as if Tyrrell and Schuckar were not quite sure how to authoritatively place themselves as the centre of the story, or did not quite see themselves as worthy of being included in 'history'. They also stepped back from particular topics. For instance, when discussing the offshoring of manufacturing, Schuckar said,

> Manufacturing costs, which have probably, are so high here, that they have to do it overseas. I don't know too much of the political side of things. I haven't kept up with that. That's what I hear.[84]

James' analysis of Roldán's story reminds us of the widespread ways in which "politics was considered to be an inherently masculine preserve for which women were ill-adapted".[85] Schuckar also distanced herself from a clear statement of feminist politics, even though her experiences and her views on women in trades would suggest a clear and understandable feminist perspective.[86] In discussing how female apprentices were given a hard time, when the male apprentices got away with all sorts of behaviours, she said:

> But what about boys? ... Why don't they get a bad rap? But then, that's political. I don't want to go into that political area.[87]

184 J. A. STEIN

Tyrrell was more assertive about her views on Australian manufacturing and the value of local vocational training. But one clear, notable element in her interview was the way in which her own personality, needs and identity receded in her story, as soon as the Tyrrells started their family business. This may well reflect Tyrrell's lived reality. When I asked her if she had any other interests or hobbies in her life, she explained:

> The trouble is, when we're busy, we're busy, and there's no time to do anything else ... Most of the friends that we still socialise with have been self-employed [so] they understand, "Yes, we *were* going to this party, but the machine has been playing up for the last five ours and this job's not run. It's got to be delivered Monday morning. ... We've got to stay here and get this machine running now" ... I don't even drive out to the other side of Sydney without my Surface [tablet] with me! [slight laugh] So, yes, always on, looking at emails, checking what's going on. Everything's on a very short timeline now.[88]

Tyrrell explained that "more often than not" she would work on weekends, although she and Greg were attempting to wind this back, when they could. The pressure of trying to run a successful manufacturing business in a disintegrating manufacturing sector is all-consuming.

CONCLUSION

This chapter has established how the experience of deindustrialisation is framed incredibly differently for women, particularly for mothers. It is probably fair to say that the attempt to change the gender-ratio of industrial trades in the 1970s and 1980s was almost a complete failure. Legislative change alone was not enough to transform deeply embedded social assumptions, behaviours and biases. We have seen how, for engineering patternmaker Schuckar, the notion of 'just finishing' holds a vastly different meaning, compared to the male patternmakers in Chap. 5. As described above, Tyrrell followed a different journey—from book-keeper and 'patternmaker's wife' to a self-trained CAD technician and business manager. The picture I have provided here is very localised and specific: the story of two very different women and their distinct journeys within the industrial craft of engineering patternmaking.

Despite their differences, however, it is possible to discern clear themes emerging from Schuckar's and Tyrrell's life histories. Evidently, these

6 NOT FITTING THE PATTERN: WOMEN IN INDUSTRIAL CRAFT

women do not fit a stereotype of the heroic-skilled craftsperson; they are not simply unsung female versions of this cliched identity. They are, in many ways, *more than* this identity. They are multi-skilled. Both women's lives are marked by a strong sense of precarious balance, and a determination to make things work, despite challenges and adversities. Furthermore, their stories speak to a great deal of unrecognised skill and hard work, occurring both at home and in the workplace. To speak only of their paid working lives—and leave out the immense labour of childcare—would be to excise a significant and important part of their experience. But until the stories of men are *also* narratives of childcaring and unpaid domestic labour, then we know there is still a long way to go, in terms of gender parity at work and in the home.

NOTES

1. Cynthia Cockburn, "Caught in the Wheels", *Marxism Today* 27 (November 1983), 18.
2. Jesse Adams Stein, "(Re)making Spaces and 'Working out Ways': Women in the Printing Industry", in *Hot Metal: Material Culture and Tangible Labour* (Manchester: Manchester University Press, 2016), 131–59.
3. One important acknowledgement that must be made here is that industrial arguments about 'women in non-traditional occupations' can risk setting up an artificial binary between two genders, 'women' and 'men'. Evidently, we now know that gender identity is by no means this simple. It is worth mentioning that mainstream, hegemonic Australian masculinity currently has *even more* difficulty accommodating queer and trans-identities in non-traditional occupations as it does with women, so there is much work to be done in redressing these broader imbalances and biases.
4. "Australia's Gender Pay Gap Statistics" (Sydney: Workplace Gender Equality Agency, 2020), online: https://www.wgea.gov.au/sites/default/files/documents/Gender_pay_gap_fact_sheet_Feb2020.pdf, accessed April 2021.
5. See, for example, Cynthia Cockburn, *Machinery of Dominance: Women, Men and Technical Know-how* (London, Sydney, Dover: Pluto Press, 1985); Cynthia Cockburn, *Brothers: Male Dominance and Technological Change* (London: Pluto Press, 1983); Cynthia Cockburn & Susan Ormrod, *Gender and Technology in the Making* (London & Thousand Oaks, California: Sage, 1993); Cockburn, "Caught in the Wheels".
6. Cockburn, "Caught in the Wheels".

186   J. A. STEIN

7. Sally Hacker, *Pleasure, Power and Technology: Some Tales of Gender, Engineering and the Cooperative Workplace* (London & New York, Routledge, 1989).
8. Ruth Oldenziel, "Boys and their Toys: The Fisher Body Craftsman's Guild, 1930–1968, and the Making of a Male Technical Domain", in R. Horowitz (ed.), *Boys and their Toys? Masculinity, Technology and Class in America* (New York and London: Routledge, 2001), 139–68; Andrew Warren, "Crafting Masculinities: Gender, Culture and Emotion at Work in the Surfboard Industry", *Gender, Place & Culture* 23, no. 1 (September 2015): 1–19; Steven Maynard, "Rough Work and Rugged Men: The Social Construction of Masculinity in Working Class History", *Labour / Le Travail* 23 (Spring 1989): 159–69.
9. Alice Kessler-Harris, "Treating the Male as 'Other': Redefining the Parameters of Labor History", *Labor History* 34 (2/3) (1993): 190–204; Ava Baron, "Masculinity, the Embodied Male Worker, and the Historian's Gaze", *International Labor and Working-Class History* 69 (Spring, 2006): 143–60; Nina Lerman, Arwen P. Mohun, & Ruth Oldenziel, "The Shoulders we Stand on / The View from Here: Historiography and Directions for Research", in Lerman, Oldenziel, & Mohun (eds), *Gender & Technology: A Reader* (Baltimore & London: The Johns Hopkins Press, 2003), 425–49; Lerman, Mohun & Oldenziel, "Versatile Tools: Gender Analysis and the History of Technology", *Technology & Culture* 38, no. 1 (1997): 1–8.
10. Sally L. Hacker, *Doing it the Hard Way: Investigations of Gender and Technology*, D. E. Smith & S. M. Turner (eds) (Boston: Unwin Hyman, 1990); Cockburn, "Caught in the Wheels"; Ann Game & Rosemary Pringle, *Gender at Work* (Sydney, London, Boston: George Allen & Unwin, 1983); Karen Struthers, & Glenda Strachan, "Attracting Women into Male-dominated Trades: Views of Young Women in Australia", *International Journal for Research in Vocational Education and Training* 6, no. 1 (2019): 1–19; Fiona Shewring, "The Female 'Tradie': Challenging Employment Perceptions in Non-Traditional Trades for Women", occasional paper (Adelaide: National Centre for Vocational Education Research [NCVER], 2009); Annette Bennett, " 'Doing a Man-sized Job': A Study of Women in Non-traditional Trades", *The Australian TAFE Teacher* (Winter 2006), 12–13.
11. See, for example, Raelene Frances, *The Politics of Work: Gender and Labour in Victoria 1880–1939* (Cambridge, New York & Melbourne: Cambridge University Press, 1993); Ava Baron, "Questions of Gender: Deskilling and Demasculinisation in the US Printing Industry 1830–1915", *Gender & History* 1, no. 2 (1989): 178–99; John Shields, "Deskilling Revisited: Continuity and Change in Craft Work and Apprenticeship in Late

6 NOT FITTING THE PATTERN: WOMEN IN INDUSTRIAL CRAFT   187

Nineteenth Century New South Wales", *Labour History* 68 (1995): 1–29; Laura Lee Downs, *Manufacturing Inequality: Gender Division in the French and British Metalworking Industries, 1914–1939* (Ithaca and London: Cornell University Press, 1995); Judy Wajcman, "Patriarchy, Technology and Conceptions of Skill", *Work and Occupations* 18, no. 1 (1991): 19–45; Judith Modell & John Hinshaw, "Male Work and Mill Work: Memory and Gender in Homestead, Pennsylvania", in Selma Leydesdorff, Luisa Passerini & Paul Thompson (eds), *Gender & Memory* (New Brunswick & London: Transaction Publishers, 2005) [First published in *International Yearbook of Oral History and Life Stories*, Vol. IV, (Oxford: Oxford University Press, 1996)].

12. Game & Pringle, *Gender at Work*, 28–31.
13. Rosslyn Reed, "Making Newspapers Pay: Employment of Women's Skills in Newspaper Production", *Journal of Industrial Relations* 29, no. 1 (1987): 25–40.
14. Rosemary Hunter & Clare Burton, *The Beauty Therapist, the Mechanic, the Geoscientist and the Librarian: Addressing Undervaluation of Women's Work* (Adelaide: Australian Technology Network, Women's Executive Development Program, 2000).
15. Game & Pringle, *Gender at Work*, 35.
16. Cockburn, *Brothers*; Stein, *Hot Metal*.
17. Rosslyn Reed, "Anti-discrimination Language and Discriminatory Outcomes: Employers' Discourse on Women in Printing and Allied Trades", *Labour & Industry* 6, no. 1 (1994): 89–106; Hacker, *Pleasure, Power and Technology*.
18. Reed, "Anti-discrimination Language"; Shewring, "The Female 'Tradie'".
19. Shewring, "The Female 'Tradie'".
20. Stein, *Hot Metal*.
21. Shewring, "The Female 'Tradie'".
22. Cockburn, "Caught in the Wheels", 16, citing the UK Engineering Industry Training Board data from 1980.
23. Bennett, "'Doing a Man-Sized Job'".
24. Struthers & Strachan, "Attracting Young Women into Male-Dominated Trades".
25. Statistics from the Australian Government *Job Outlook* website, which uses current Australian Bureau of Statistics data, see for example:
    'Welders – First Class, ANZSCO ID 322313', *Job Outlook*, Australian Government, online: https://joboutlook.gov.au/occupations/welders-first-class?occupationCode=322313, accessed 4 May 2021.
26. Struthers & Strachan, "Attracting Young Women into Male-Dominated Trades", using Australian Bureau of Statistics data.

188   J. A. STEIN

27. 'Engineering Patternmakers, ANZSCO ID 323411', *Job Outlook*, Australian Government, online: https://joboutlook.gov.au/occupations/engineering-patternmakers?occupationCode=323411 (accessed 23 April 2021).
28. Struthers & Strachan, "Attracting Young Women into Male-Dominated Trades", 8, using Australian Bureau of Statistics data.
29. Bennett, "'Doing a Man-Sized Job'".
30. Struthers & Strachan, "Attracting Young Women into Male-Dominated Trades".
31. "Women in the Labor Force: a Databook" (Washington D.C.: US Bureau of Labor Statistics, published 2018, using 3017 data), online: https://www.bls.gov/opub/reports/womens-databook/2018/pdf/home.pdf, 60–1, accessed 5 May 2021.
32. 'Women in the Labor Force: a Databook', 61.
33. "Gender Statistics, South Africa, 2011" (Cape Town: Statistics South Africa, 2011), online: http://www.statssa.gov.za/publications/Report-03-10-05/Report-03-10-052011.pdf, accessed 2 May 2021.
34. "Women in the Labour Market" (United Kingdom: Office for National Statistics, 2013), online: https://webarchive.nationalarchives.gov.uk/20160108012507/http://www.ons.gov.uk/ons/dcp171776_328352.pdf, accessed 24 April 2021.
35. Struthers & Strachan, "Attracting Young Women into Male-Dominated Trades".
36. Shewring, "The Female 'Tradie'".
37. Adele Cochrane, "Australia's Skills Shortages: How They Can Help You Find In-Demand Careers", Skills Shortages Australia (Department of Jobs and Small Business, 2018), online: www.training.com.au/ed/skills-shortages-australia, accessed 10 December 2021.
38. "Skill Shortfalls and Future Skills Need," *Bridging the Skills Divide*, inquiry report (Canberra: Australian Parliament, Education, Employment and Workplace Relations, 2002–2004), online: https://www.aph.gov.au/Parliamentary_Business/Committees/Senate/Education_Employment_and_Workplace_Relations/Completed_inquiries/2002-04/skills/report/c02, accessed 21 April 2021.
39. Struthers & Strachan, "Attracting Young Women into Male-Dominated Trades", 4.
40. Debra Schuckar, interview with author, *Reshaping Australian Manufacturing*, 23 February 2018 (Canberra: NLA), https://nla.gov.au/nla.cat-vn7580622.
41. Schuckar, interview with author.
42. Schuckar, interview with author.
43. Schuckar, interview with author.

6 NOT FITTING THE PATTERN: WOMEN IN INDUSTRIAL CRAFT 189

44. Game and Pringle, *Gender at Work*; Reed, "Anti-discrimination Language and Discriminatory Outcomes".
45. Schuckar, interview with author.
46. Schuckar, interview with author.
47. "Equality at the Workbench", *SEC News* 268 (March 1982): 6–7; "Pattern for Excellence", *SEC News* (1986).
48. "Equality at the Workbench", 6.
49. [50] *Annual Report* (Melbourne: State Electricity Commission, 1985).
50. Schuckar, interview with author.
51. Schuckar, interview with author.
52. Schuckar, interview with author.
53. Schuckar, interview with author.
54. Schuckar, interview with author.
55. Schuckar, interview with author. Speaker's emphasis.
56. Schuckar, interview with author.
57. Schuckar, interview with author.
58. Schuckar, interview with author.
59. Schuckar, personal communication with author, April 2021.
60. Schuckar, personal communication with author, April 2021.
61. Deborah Tyrrell, interview with author, *Reshaping Australian Manufacturing*, 19 October 2018 (Canberra: NLA), https://nla.gov.au/nla.cat-vn7861536.
62. Tyrrell, interview with author.
63. Tyrrell, interview with author.
64. Tyrrell, interview with author.
65. Tyrrell, interview with author.
66. Tyrrell, interview with author.
67. Tyrrell, interview with author.
68. Tyrrell, interview with author.
69. Tyrrell, interview with author.
70. Tyrrell, interview with author.
71. Tyrrell, interview with author.
72. See, for example, Leydesdorff, Passerini & Thompson (eds), *Gender & Memory*; Joan Sangster, "Telling our Stories: Feminist Debates and the Use of Oral History", *Women's History Review* 3 (1994): 5–28; Susan Geiger, "What's so Feminist about Women's Oral History?" *Journal of Women's History* 2, no. 1 (1990): 169–82; Caroline Daley, "'He Would Know, but I Just Have a Feeling': Gender and Oral History", *Women's History Review* 7, no. 3 (1998): 343–59; Joanna Bornat & Hanna Diamond, "Women's History and Oral History: Developments and Debates", *Women's History Review* 16, no. 1 (2007): 19–39; Susan H. Armitage with Patricia Heart & Karen Weatherman (eds), *Women's*

190   J. A. STEIN

Oral History: The 'Frontiers' Reader (Lincoln and London: University of Nebraska Press, 2002); Sherna B. Gluck & Daphne Patai, *Women's Words: The Feminist Practice of Oral History* (London: Routledge, 1991).

73. Bornat & Diamond, "Women's History and Oral History".
74. Richard Ely & Allyssa McCabe, "Gender Differences in Memories for Speech", in Leydesdorff, Passerini & Thompson (eds), *Gender & Memory* (Oxford: Oxford University Press, 1996), 17–30.
75. Daniel James, *Doña María's Story: Life History, Memory and Political Identity* (Durham & London, Duke University Press, 2000).
76. James, *Doña María's Story*, 226.
77. Daley, "'He Would Know, but I Just Have a Feeling'", 344.
78. Daley, "'He Would Know, but I Just Have a Feeling'", 344.
79. Luisa Passerini, "Work Ideology and Consensus under Italian Fascism", *History Workshop* 8 (1979), 82–108.
80. Daley, "'He Would Know, but I Just Have a Feeling'", 344.
81. Daley, "'He Would Know, but I Just Have a Feeling'", 345.
82. Daley, "'He Would Know, but I Just Have a Feeling'", 345.
83. Jim Walker, interview with author, *Reshaping Australian Manufacturing*, 7 December 2018 (Canberra: NLA), https://nla.gov.au/nla.cat-vn7889849.
84. Schuckar, interview with author.
85. James, *Doña María's Story*, 220.
86. For a useful analysis of the tensions that emerge when an interviewer holds an essentially feminist perspective, and the interviewee has an alternate position, see Katherine Borland, "'That's Not What I Said': Interpretive Conflict in Oral Narrative Research", in Robert Perks & Alistair Thomson (eds.), *The Oral History Reader* (London & New York: Routledge, 1998), 320–33.
87. Schuckar, interview with author.
88. Tyrrell, interview with author.

CHAPTER 7

Patternmaker-Artists: Creative Pathways for Industrial Craftspeople in the Context of Australian Deindustrialisation

Introduction

The patternmakers discussed in this chapter are not examined in relation to their paid labour.[1] Instead, I engage with the deindustrialised aftermath, when many patternmakers have moved out of the manufacturing industry and into more creative endeavours. This chapter reveals how, for some patternmakers, their art practice can be seen as an assertion of technical and craft-derived mastery, in a context that no longer values their trade skill. For others, moving from patternmaking to art fulfilled creative aspirations never provided by their paid employment. Deindustrialisation is a gradual process—not a sudden rupture—which can be detected in the present in a variety of unexpected ways, including cultural expression.[2] As this chapter will outline, the trajectories of patternmaker-artists have been shaped by social expectations and limitations associated with Australian understandings of social class and hegemonic masculinity. Here I focus on the experiences of patternmakers Paul Kay, Serge Haidutschyk, Bryan Poynton and Peter Watts, alongside more abridged material from patternmakers Tim Wighton and Debra Schuckar. These patternmakers traverse complex territory across and between class-stratification, through shifting landscapes of skill and job security, within and beyond their industrial employment.

In the last section of this chapter, the patternmakers' experiences are contrasted against that of the Australian sculptor Robert Klippel, notable

© The Author(s), under exclusive license to Springer Nature Switzerland AG 2021
J. A. Stein, *Industrial Craft in Australia*, Palgrave Studies in Oral History, https://doi.org/10.1007/978-3-030-87243-4_7

192   J. A. STEIN

for his modernist assemblages featuring 'readymade' industrial objects. Klippel's chosen industrial objects included discarded foundry patterns, assembled in balanced, abstract agglomerations, in artworks with their own particular dynamism and integrity. Klippel benefited from the decline of Australian heavy industry—in part through access to its discarded remnants—but he also emerged from that world. He was a trained industrial modelmaker. Klippel's initial training—prior to his formal fine arts education—had some similarities to the patternmakers featured here (albeit from an earlier generation).[3] This counter-example points towards undercurrent tensions between industrial craft, Australian manufacturing, social class and the art establishment.

The gradual degradation of patternmakers' labour—through both factory closures and technological change—was not simply felt as a matter of job losses. It shifted their class position, it undermined the skill that was core to their identity, and it did not produce many viable or meaningful labour alternatives. As we saw in Chap. 5, patternmakers responded to these challenges variously: many left patternmaking for other industries, while some retrained (as patternmakers) in CAD (Computer Aided Drawing/Computer Aided Manufacturing) and CNC (computer numerically controlled milling machines). Moving into teaching at TAFE (Australia's public Technical and Further Education system) was a common pathway. Another accessible sidestep for patternmakers was into carpentry and building construction. One path, however, is rarely acknowledged: some patternmakers developed an artistic practice.

In keeping with other studies of deindustrialisation in the Global North, my interviews revealed a now-familiar story of personal and community heartbreak.[4] But they also revealed other narratives: one emergent theme was the satisfaction patternmakers achieved through undertaking creative practice, using their trade skills, making things that are not patterns. I had not anticipated this outcome; it emerged as the interviews unfolded. In this way, this project began as a study of technological change in Australian manufacturing, but resulted in a collection of articulate voices of tradespeople asserting their creativity. At the time of interview, five patternmakers were still working in manufacturing; seven were practising artists (often in addition to other activities and employment) and two were too elderly to continue patternmaking and creative practice. Six had sought design and fine arts education at some point in their lives, and of these, two had completed degrees in fine arts, and two had undertaken qualifications in industrial design. At least three interviewees had exhibited

7 PATTERNMAKER-ARTISTS: CREATIVE PATHWAYS FOR INDUSTRIAL... 193

in Australian galleries and museums, across the craft and fine arts sectors. Importantly, the fact that several former patternmakers gained fine art qualifications precludes me from an amateur/professional or outsider/insider binary. Journeys of artistic training and creative practice are invariably messier than such a neat categorisation.

CRAFT/ART

The idea of craftsperson making things in their home workshop is unremarkable, in and of itself. But for this chapter I want to anchor us within a specific nexus between technological change, deindustrialisation and creative practice, emergent across different modes of cultural production. The specific artworks made by these patternmakers are not, for the most part, my focus here. Certainly, the works are diverse in terms of aesthetics, and some may perhaps be considered by the established art world as outsider or amateur art.[5] But, as observed by Julie Bryan-Wilson and Benjamin Piekut, "it is probably a mistake to think that there has ever been a strictly policed line between the 'amateur' and the 'advanced' within Western canons of modernism".[6]

Just as the industrial landscape has dramatically transformed in the twentieth century, so too has the world of sculpture. Western sculpture evidently experienced a dramatic shift, from figurative, monumental sculpture in the nineteenth century, through the masculine confidence of modernist abstraction in the early to mid-twentieth century, and then on to a more expansive set of three-dimensional material and conceptual possibilities. As outlined by Rosalind Krauss in her well-known 'expanded field' essay, by the 1960s and 1970s sculpture was better defined by what it was not.[7] Minimalism, conceptual art and land art pushed sculpture to a point beyond modernism, into an ontologically negative sphere.[8] And yet, even for the most radical sculptors, the crafted quality of the thing still mattered very much, even when this was not openly admitted. Donald Judd is a good example: in creating his hard-edged minimalist forms, Judd turned to professional makers and tradespeople—sheet metal workers and metal fabricators—to get his work *crafted* as perfectly as possible (and thereby removing Judd's own hand from the process).

Other sculptors retained their personal, physical connection to the making process. Design historian Gregory Votolato helps us contextualise this differentiation. In describing American modernism post-World War II, Votolato explains how there was an "increasingly fluid culture of art

194 J. A. STEIN

production", which "blurred the old distinctions" between sculpture, painting, performance and traditional craft (etc.). Votolato notes, "A new generation of post-war craftspeople worked in studios *and* workshops. They called themselves 'artist-craftspeople' or 'object-makers'."[9] The patternmakers-artists introduced in this chapter have sculptural tendencies that are certainly not at an 'avant-garde' end of an artistic spectrum, but sit more comfortably, perhaps, in the world of the 'artist-craftsperson'. For the artist-patternmakers, 'sculpture'—as a term and as a discipline—has retained its more traditional connection to the integrity of the 'monument'. When the patternmakers use the term 'sculpture', they are generally referring to a three-dimensional object that was *carved* and *shaped* from traditional materials: timber, metal, clay or stone.

Craft theorist Glenn Adamson explores this art/craft relationship. In exploring the tensions between craft and fine art, Adamson follows Theodor Adorno in dismissing the 'but is it art?' question as unhelpful.[10] Rather, Adamson argues that craft "might be more usefully conceived as a process ... not as a classification of objects, institutions or people".[11] By considering craft a verb, as a *way of doing*, Adamson opens our eyes to how craft comes into being, its organisation "around material experience" and the role of skill in the understanding of craft as an "active, relational concept rather than a fixed category".[12] This emphasis on relationality allows us to leverage craft's long-established status as something 'lesser than' fine art. But rather than asserting that craft should somehow be elevated in an artistic canon, Adamson asserts "craft's inferiority might be the most productive thing about it".[13] In that engagement with inferiority, status and social position, we can learn a great deal about our world and its creative practitioners.

Accordingly, in this chapter, I emphasise patternmakers' artistic practice in a manner that pays heed to the subjectivities of class, and the opportunities and restrictions offered by creative practice, as experienced from the social and economic margins. Consequently, I am not particularly concerned with assertions of artistic quality, nor about defining whether something is 'art' or 'craft'. Rather, my emphasis is on how patternmakers discuss their connection to art-making, to skill acquisition, to cultural boundaries, and how they articulate their creative motivations. What is revealed is a distinct relationship between technology, social class, creativity and manual skill. Likewise, in Klippel's own reflections, similar concerns arose: a concern for personal artistic integrity and for creative freedom. I will expand upon the distinctions between the patternmaker-artists and Klippel further on.

When patternmakers completed their apprenticeships, they were precision woodworkers, with sophisticated materials literacy. Some of them spoke to me of how this capacity made them feel as if they had 'magic' hands: they knew how to produce form precisely in three dimensions (and this capacity is increasingly rare, from the late twentieth century onwards). Furthermore, this degree of manual skill opened up possibilities: what else could these hands produce? The patternmakers' drive to demonstrate the full extent of their manual skill is furthered, in some cases, by a desire to be 'better than the machines' that partially replaced them (CNC machines). In other cases, some patternmakers' artistic motivations grew from a yearning for independent creativity, beyond the limitations of reproducing an engineer's design in three dimensions. In every case explored here, the skill of manually producing form remains deeply important, while the patternmakers' encounters with various art worlds have at times shown them that this level of technical skill is no longer valued (particularly beyond the 1960s).

Patternmaker-Artists

Paul Kay

When we eat squishy candies and sweets, such as jelly babies and jubes (Fig. 7.1), we are not accustomed to recognising that those lolly forms were originally hand-shaped by a skilled maker. But that is precisely what Paul Kay does for a living. Kay—who was at the time of his interview still a practicing patternmaker—specialises in making patterns and moulds required for jube manufacturing (Fig 7.2). These jube patterns and moulds are made from resin, wax or timber and are designed to have a precise mass, suitable for food production. For this, Kay does not use digital rendering (CAD), and he eschews 3D printing and CNC. Instead, he produces moulds and patterns through hand carving, and using manually controlled machine tools. A second-generation patternmaker, Kay joined his father's business (WG Kay & Co.), becoming director upon his father's retirement. Recent years have been challenging for Kay, due to a combination of factors: confectionery clients perceive Australia as a redundant manufacturing producer, and some of Kay's clients have selected more

Fig. 7.1 Glucose lollies such as Swedish Fish, Gummi Bears and Gummi Worms. (Courtesy of ChildofMidnight, Creative Commons licence)

high-technology options overseas. Kay is now close to retirement. His factory has closed, and his client base has significantly reduced in size. He now works alone, from a workshop he constructed underneath his house in Sydney's northern suburbs.

Although Kay's training is trade based (he was apprenticed as a patternmaker), in the 1990s he did attend art classes at Julian Ashton Art School in Sydney. Kay reflected:

> I do think there are times when that's helped me with my confectionery work. I did that for … three years. Then I met my wife … and things changed pretty dramatically after that. We decided to build this house and get married and have children so there was no returning to the art world.[14]

As it happened, there was a 'return to the art world'. In the second decade of the twenty-first century, Kay's business took a turn for the worse. Kay decided to aim for an ambitious creative project, to keep himself busy:

> I had periods when one of these confectionery manufacturers went broke … we just didn't see any work in that industry for about eight or nine months. It just came to a stop … So I had this idea, and then it went from an idea, to a full-blown art exhibition in Double Bay, which was incredible … All I

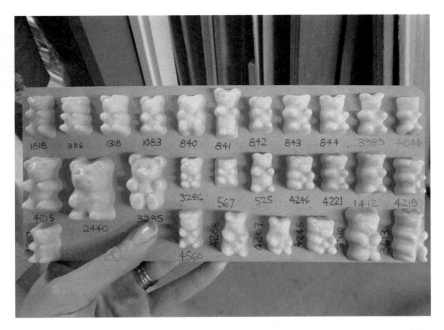

Fig. 7.2 Paul Kay's jube patterns for food manufacturing, 2018. (Photograph by the author)

was doing was, I guess, being creative and using my patternmaking skills as well, because I was making these sculptures out of wood.[15]

During this period, Kay created a series of small-scale timber sculptures that were eventually exhibited in a solo exhibition at Frances Keevil Gallery, Sydney, in 2017. (Eight of his eleven sculptures sold.) But Kay is realistic about whether this has become a career-changing move. Art-making, Kay says, has much "the same problems that patternmaking has—labour intensive, you're never going to make any money".[16] Nevertheless, Kay perseveres, and at the time of writing he is working towards another exhibition, in late 2021.

Kay's sculptures are stylistically resonant with postmodern eclecticism, with an additive visual schema. Not that this is something that Kay would have identified as a personal aesthetic: he nods to early modernism (potentially de Stijl or Constructivism) as an influence. His works are neither purely abstract nor completely figurative, but connect to both representative domains, depending on how Kay feels about each sculpture he plans. Like industrial patterns, the works begin as drawings, which Kay then uses to form up a shape from a single piece of wood. Using White Beech and Jelutong timbers, Kay sets himself constraints to guide consistency and test his skill:

> I guess the difficulty being that they were all being machined out of one piece of wood, there's nothing stuck onto them or built up, you really have to think about how you're going to achieve this sculpture out of one piece, and it's a mixture of machining and hand skills.[17]

The resulting forms are deliberately complex—with undercuts and meticulous geometric detail. This is deliberate—as forms they would be almost too complex for a CNC machine to produce, without breaking and splitting the timber:

> I go further in my sculptural designs creating internal corners that are tight and sharp, something a CNC machine cannot do in female form, as the machine is limited by the diameter of the cutter when machining, and how deep a programmer can allow a CNC machine with a small diameter cutter (say less than 2.5 mm diameter shank) for wood. Vibration starts to occur when using a long shank small diameter cutter leaving marks in the timber that I, the craftsman-artist would avoid at all costs. So all my tight, sharp, internal female corners are finished by hand, using flat chisels or gouge curved chisels to create this effect.[18]

CNC machines and CAD/CAM programmes, Kay explains, cannot understand wood grain.[19] Using a single piece of timber, Kay's carving method is also purely subtractive. This skill challenge is distinct from patternmaking: patternmakers are not purists about using a single piece of timber and will happily glue together pieces and build up surfaces with bog-filler, if it results in an accurate and effective pattern.

Kay's work might perhaps be dismissed by some art critics as amateurish, and his work does indicate some disconnection from formal art historical knowledge. But to emphasise this would be to miss the point. Kay's work is a response to the economic and technological conditions of his time, as well as a personal search for his own expressive aesthetic. This is no easy task, when one has worked exclusively in an industrial trade for their lifetime, particularly where the emphasis is on creating a three-dimensional copy of someone else's image. The titles of some of Kay's artworks are suggestive of his own precarious position, such as *Contemplation of an Uncertain Future* (Fig. 7.3). His work is an assertion of mastery, given its competitive relationship to automating machinery. It pits the human hand against CNC technologies, asserting the grace, comprehension and personalised technique of the former, against the dull consistency of the latter. We will see similar motivations in the following section on Serge Haidutschyk.

Fig. 7.3 Paul Kay, *Contemplation of an Uncertain Future*, 2017, Queensland White Beech, 37.5 cm × 37.5 cm × 5 cm. (Courtesy of the artist)

200   J. A. STEIN

Following studies of gendered technological practice in the printing industry by Cynthia Cockburn (among others),[20] it might be argued that the digitisation of patternmakers' tasks made their jobs less traditionally 'masculine', reducing their work to the 'feminised' activity of using a computer. The determination to continue to use their original manual skills— albeit in sculpture rather than industrial production—could perhaps be seen as an attempt by the patternmakers to retain their masculine sense of self. However, as is often the case, things are not that simple. CNC technologies can also become symbolically gendered—in this case as 'men's tools'—through social use. Likewise, artistic tendencies are sometimes, in the crudest iterations of mainstream Australian culture, belittled as the work of 'soft' men. All this is to say—it is unlikely that Kay wanted to restore his identity as a skilled *tradesman*, but rather, his artistic pursuits return a sense of self-respect, confirming his capacity to carve an object *better than a machine*.

Serge Haidutschyk

Serge Haidutschyk (Fig. 7.4), now retired, is a former engineering patternmaker based in Melbourne. The Australian-born son of Ukrainian refugees who escaped war-torn Europe in the 1940s, Haidutschyk is a passionate storyteller. In our interview he shifted with ease between detailed explanations of his family's hardship, his nationalistic passion for Australian native plants and his pride at acquiring patternmaking skills. These themes were interwoven with key moments in his life history: Haidutschyk was made redundant from his job three times, from his mid-career onwards. He was apprenticed in patternmaking at the Victorian Government's Newport Railways, where he worked between 1967 and 1992. In 1992 the Victorian state government (under Premier Jeff Kennett) closed down Newport Railways as part of a neoliberal economic programme of privatisation and funding cuts. After a period of unemployment, Haidutschyk worked at the foundry Graham Campbell Ferrum from 1995 to 2000, until this company also closed, unable to compete with overseas competition. Finally, Haidutschyk worked as a maintenance worker at an aged-care facility in Melbourne, for almost 13 years. He adored this position because it enabled him to talk to the residents. This too resulted in a redundancy, one year before his retirement age (65). Haidutschyk said:

Fig. 7.4 Serge Haidutschyk. (Photograph by the author, 2018)

> It was the best feel-good job I've ever had in my life. I'm sad that I was made redundant at the age of 64. I had twelve months to go before I retired I was made redundant by this company that I put my heart in ... And they put me on the scrapheap at the age of 64 ... I had to go and register with Centrelink. [Australia's welfare government agency] I felt embarrassed. Horrible. That was a dark age in my life, that 12 months.[21]

Haidutschyk followed this statement with a clarification; he did not want to dwell on negative times. "I'm comfortable now, doing my art work. Artisan," he corrected himself. He would not call himself an artist (he reserves "artist" for his wife Elizabeth, who paints).[22]

Notwithstanding his reticence in terms of terminology, much of Haidutschyk's work has such an intensity and incongruity to it that if exhibited in a more fashionable context, it might well be classified differently. For example, if he had formal art qualifications—if he spoke with ease about the relation of his oeuvre to Baudrillard's simulacra, for

202   J. A. STEIN

example—then Haidutschyk's work might easily be accepted as contemporary art, something not too far removed from the chillingly realistic but mono-material forms of Ricky Swallow's work in the early 2000s.[23]

Without it necessarily being his conscious intention, Haidutschyk's artwork speaks acutely of the human experience of deindustrialisation for skilled workers. One example is his life-size timber replica, *Makita 8" Circular Saw*, 1992–1994, (Fig. 7.5) a piece that has only been exhibited in craft contexts. It is a careful replica of Haidutschyk's own Makita electric saw from his workshop. Every part of the object is timber, including the intricately wrought electrical cable. The saw is produced from 13 different recycled Australian timbers, such as King Billy Pine, Red Gum, Huon Pine, Kauri and Blackwood. This piece was created during a period when Haidutschyk was between jobs, after his redundancy from the Newport Workshops. Haidutschyk explained:

> People say, "How can you work in one place for 25 years, at the same bench?" I could walk in there with my eyes closed. I loved it … It was my home. The environment, I loved my job. I loved working, what I was doing. When all that came to an end, I was actually quite depressed … I was told, "Wake up, grow up, be a man." That's what I was told by people outside. Anyway, it was difficult, it was very difficult, and I was very, very upset that I lost my job. I thought,
> "What am I going to do?" I was unemployed for two years … I was trying to get my head around things, and what am I going to do next in my phase of life? 42 years of age. I don't want to retire … I thought to myself,
> "I'm going to occupy myself, and make something completely different and unusual." I decided to make a model. I've got a Makita electric saw. It's an 8" diameter electric saw. I looked at that one day and I said to myself …
> "I'm going to make a model of my circular saw", which I started making in 1992. It took me three hundred hours to complete, and it took me two years.[24]

Haidutschyk entered the saw in the National Australian Woodwork Exhibition, Melbourne, in 1994 and was awarded first prize in the 'Decorative Woodwork Section'. This essentially sealed the work's place in the milieu of artisanal craft. Since then, he has made models of other industrial equipment and tools, including a model Stanley hand plane, which also won a prize at the Royal Melbourne Show. It is worth noting that Haidutschyk's industrial replicas are something of an anomaly in these woodwork shows. One might surmise that Haidutschyk wins prizes

Fig. 7.5 Serge Haidutschyk, Makita 8" Circular Saw, 1992–1994, 13 Australian recycled timbers. (Courtesy of Haidutschyk, reproduced with permission)

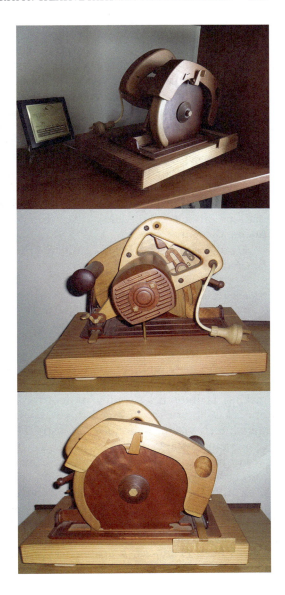

precisely because his works are so different from the usual bowls, furniture and other decorative pieces in this context.

Haidutschyk intentionally chose to replicate complex, industrial machinery and tools out of a soft, natural medium. Timber is notoriously fickle, especially when one chooses to combine 13 different types, each with their own grain, dimensional stability and density. The saw captures not only Haidutschyk's expertise as a woodworker but also his industrial experience as a tradesperson in manufacturing: it is *of his world* completely. Yet this object is not an industrial model, nor is it a pattern. It is a non-utilitarian thing, designed to impress, to be exhibited, to be seen. It was also generated—as with Kay's artwork—to keep Haidutschyk busy at a time of crisis. For Haidutschyk, the timber saw was produced as an affirmation of self-worth and as a distraction from the realities of unemployment.

Art historian Rachel Weiss considered the distinction between the replica and the original, noting,

> The replica is, in a way, the realm of pure craft. It is a vehicle par excellence for bravura displays of craftsmanship since, for one thing, its success is measured by the closeness of its resemblance.[25]

Certainly, in these terms, Haidutschyk is a craft artisan. But the saw is also *more than* a mere replica, by virtue of its material choices, which are both 'un-saw-like' and utterly impractical in the context of industrial model-making. Haitudschyk's combination of 13 timbers adds complexity to our understanding of the saw, and this was a very deliberate decision. If he were merely making a model for industry, Haidutschyk would have used a dimensionally stable timber, such as Sugar Pine or Jelutong. His emphasis would have been on the ability of the model to perfectly replicate the form, so as to facilitate mass-production, not for aesthetics or contemplation. Although 1992 predates the widescale uptake of digital fabrication (CNC) in Australian industry, Haidutschyk was nonetheless aware of this looming threat to patternmakers' skillset, developments in the United States and Japan certainly heralded what was soon to come in Australia. For its time, Haidutschyk deliberately produced an object that was near impossible to produce in timber through machine production, in a similar manner to Kay.

7 PATTERNMAKER-ARTISTS: CREATIVE PATHWAYS FOR INDUSTRIAL...

Bryan Poynton

Referring to the late Bryan Poynton as a 'patternmaker' would be reductive; it does not capture the breadth of his experience or creative practice.

> I could no more just be a violin maker, or just a furniture maker, or just a woodturner, because I'm interested in so many different aspects of [woodwork].[26]

Poynton undertook an apprenticeship in engineering patternmaking at the International Harvester Company in North Geelong in the 1950s. His life and career included patternmaking, but also fine woodwork, instrument-making, hand-built house construction, poetry, surfing and sculpture.

Even prior to his patternmaking apprenticeship, Poynton had a passion for woodwork and for making things. His memories of his childhood included this recollection of playing 'Cowboys and Indians' with the other boys, by making his own bows and arrows (including casting his own lead arrow-heads):

> Saturday afternoon, I'd sneak out to the Eastern Gardens, which were only about a mile away from our house, with a little saw of my father's, and I'd go around until I found a little cypress tree with nice, curved branches on it, and I'd make sure that the caretaker or the ranger wasn't around anywhere, and I'd saw off one of these little branches, and ... I'd use my father's meagre collection of tools—like a little plane and a spokeshave—and I'd shape these bows. Then I'd sneak around the back lanes and find any paling fences that were a bit loose, because in those days all the palings weren't sawn; they were split ... and I'd split them down again and make little squares, and then I'd plane them with a little plane and make round arrows. Then I would go to the local market where they sold chickens and pigs and turkeys ... and I'd pester the blokes to give me some turkey feathers, because I knew all about this 'Indian lore', you know? I thought I did. So I glued those on to the shafts.
>
> Then as a result of the War [WWII] and my uncles coming home, there were a few 303 bullets lying around so, probably very dangerously, I'd take the tops off those and get rid of the powder. I just had the pointy bit, and I'd shave down the end of the arrow and glue those on, so I had my bow and arrow. The ones that I'd made somehow used to fire a lot better and faster and longer shots than my other friends in the little gang that we had. They could afford to go and buy a bow and arrow from the sports store ...

206 J. A. STEIN

> When I ran out of those arrow heads, I contrived to get one of my father's soldering irons, and I'd poke it in the ground and leave a little hollow … and then I'd suspend … the arrow inside the hole with a couple of little nicks in it, and then I'd light a fire and melt some lead—I can't remember where I got the lead from, I probably pinched a few sinkers—and then I'd pour the lead around the arrow, and as soon as it set, I put it in water … So, I was under nine when I was doing that sort of thing.[27]

From an early age, Poynton had a commitment to precision and creativity in his woodwork. (See Chap. 3 for details about his toolbox and handmade tools.) As a patternmaker, Poynton excelled because of his commitment to precision, which was ideal for the trade. After his apprenticeship, Poynton worked at Des Renahans', a small patternshop in Melbourne, which included, among other things, making models for Ford Motor Company and other work for the plastics industry.

But patternmaking was never enough, for Poynton, to satisfy his creative energies. He said:

> Patternmaking is a wonderful trade and it gave me such a good grounding in skill that I've never regretted for one minute taking that as a trade, or working where I did, … in having to solve problems related to it … that part of it can be creative, but in an artistic or aesthetic sense, it didn't appeal to me because it was so restrictive: you had to work to somebody else's drawings and all their dimensions very accurately.[28]

Living in Melbourne, however, offered Poynton options in terms of creative practice and cultural exposure. He was able to attend concerts (early music was another passion of his), and he undertook art classes. While working as a patternmaker, Poynton arranged to have figurative woodcarving lessons from the sculptor Leopoldine Mimovich, in exchange for her having access to a bandsaw. Poynton said:

> I used to go around there at least one evening a week after work, and she'd provide dinner for me, and prior to dinner we'd go in the workshop for a while, and after dinner for another while. So, she taught me the fundamentals of carving faces and figures. That was off to the side of the patternmaking.[29]

Poynton also undertook night-classes in sculpture and drawing, at RMIT. He recalled being taught by sculptors Lenton Parr and Hermann

7 PATTERNMAKER-ARTISTS: CREATIVE PATHWAYS FOR INDUSTRIAL...

Hohaus (the latter of whom he had no respect for, after Hohaus was too interventionist with one of Poynton's sculptures, carving the pregnant stomach off a mother figure).

In 1967 Poynton chose to leave the full-time workforce, opting for a life where he was able to spend more time producing his own works and surfing. In the years following this, Poynton worked in hand-built house construction (producing houses in with no metal screws or metal beams, using precise joinery and adzing the timber by hand) and forestry. He made surfboards, ski-paddles, string instruments, furniture and a broad variety of other woodwork craft objects, and soon developed a reputation as one of Australia's finest woodworkers. In 1981, Poynton was commissioned to make a gift from the Australian Government for the wedding of Prince Charles and Diana: he made a strong Blackwood box with "secret mitre dovetails". A silversmith made 20 plates to go inside. It was a significant commission, although Poynton noted that this "big break" did not exactly result in a flood of further commissions or widespread public recognition.

Poynton's sculptural practice emerged alongside his other woodworking activities, and there is no neat dividing line between one practice or another. Indeed, the same could be said of Poynton's life generally. His *Self-portrait with Pigeon Hole* (Fig. 7.6) brings together different elements of Poynton's interests and influences. In the artwork caption, Poynton joked:

> The box/panel displaying symbols (symptoms!) should partially elucidate personal philosophies, lifestyle, history, values ... for the benefit of some psychologist who may wish to investigate 'woodies' as a potential risk to public stability.[30]

The work gestures towards Poynton's commitment to fine woodwork, his industrial training, his passion for the ocean and surfing, his interest in Japanese and Celtic aesthetics, his connection to spirituality and his identity with regard to some aspects of Australian culture.

During our interview Poynton explained his own personal aesthetic, which is grounded in his foundational skill as a patternmaker and woodworker:

> If I make something, a sculpture for instance, I have to do everything, you know I can't sort of farm bits out. I know sculptors who design things, and

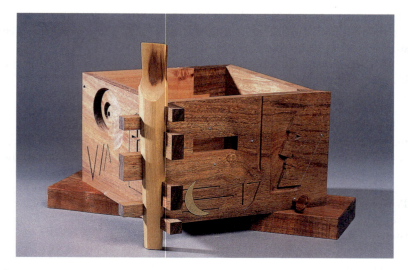

Fig. 7.6 Bryan Poynton, *Self-portrait with Pigeon Hole*, 2001, Blackwood, Myrtle, Huon Pine, Brass and Copper, created for 'Box Forms', an exhibition curated by the Victorian Woodworkers' Association. (Courtesy of the Poynton family, reproduced with permission)

> they have other people actually make it. Some of them don't even acknowledge that somebody else has made it … I could not do it that way … To me, sculpture has to really be saying something.[31]

While describing a 'renegade' sculpture he was making—to exhibit alongside, but not be an official part of the Lorne Sculpture Biennale in Victoria—Poynton made this distinction:

> Right at this moment I'm working on a renegade sculpture. Every two years there's—not a competition, but a sculpture show along the foreshore in Lorne, and the artists involved are usually—well … I think some of them, they already have a leg-in, I think, because of their qualifications in the art world, and, well, some people locally think—well, the likes of meself and a few others—should maybe be given an opportunity, perhaps, to be a 'wildcard' in one of these shows. But I don't have ten letters after my name, so nobody's approached me about it, and to be honest, I can't be bothered going through all the red tape and protocol that's necessary to try and worm my way into the list, so I don't really care.[32]

Here we can see that Poynton felt he had a particular 'outsider' status in relation to various art worlds—highlighting a keen divide between the Australian craft scene and fine art contexts. Poynton's viewpoint demonstrates a particular respect for craft labour and a world view that ties artistic integrity to the direct manual manipulation of materials.

Peter Watts

Peter Watts' life history covers quite different ground from the other patternmaker-artists so far described here. His journey shifts from the industrial factory floor at a large-scale Melbourne engineering works, to the alternative nightlife of the Melbourne art and theatre scenes in the 1970s and 1980s, to the fast-paced commercial world of special effects and film prop-making, and finally, to a quieter life of art-making and child-raising in regional Victoria. Of all my interviewees, Watts was most keenly aware of the structuring role that class, education and gender played in his life experience. Growing up in the 1960s in Doveton, a working-class suburb in Melbourne's south-east, Watts was from a migrant English family who clearly felt their difference from the white Australians in their neighbourhood. Watts described the local school culture as violent, and he retreated from that world by helping his father restore a 1928 Bentley car, accruing practical skills in the process.

Watts' grandfather was a toolmaker by trade. He noticed his grandson's inclinations and told him, as a child:

> "You know what Peter? When the time comes, I think you'll be a good patternmaker." Of course, I had no idea what a patternmaker was … but he said,
> "Peter, it's the cream of the trades."
> I said, "Well, it sounds pretty good."[33]

For Watts, this conversation was formative. The fact that Watts was also creative (and an avid reader) was not a consideration in the broad social configurations that shaped his initial vocational direction. No other pathway was presented as an option: an Australian working-class boy who was 'good with his hands' was, generally speaking, supposed to become a 'tradesman' and work in manufacturing or other heavy industries. Here, the expectations of gender and social class are tightly interconnected. For much of the twentieth century in Australia, apprenticeships in skilled trades offered boys from working-class and lower middle-class families a relatively secure path. It enabled ongoing employment on a breadwinner salary, and membership and social acceptance within the union associated with their trade. This pathway was widely understood to be socially responsible, practical and aligned with mainstream understandings of acceptable Australian masculinity.[34] So it was to be: in 1973 Watts began a patternmaking apprenticeship at Vickers Ruwolt's engineering works in Melbourne, where he was indentured for four years.

Vickers made large-scale timber patterns for casting in their foundry. Watts immersed himself in the factory environment: among toolmakers, moulders, fitters and turners, and other patternmakers. Watts effused:

> The first moment when I walked in the patternshop, on that first morning, and the thing that hit me was the smell of the Sugar Pine. Oh my god! The air was thick with it … It was intoxicating to me. Kind of ambrosia. I just loved it. I walked around the place and was introduced to the men, and I was terrified, but kind of secretly thrilled to bits.[35]

Watts soon developed into a highly competent patternmaker; his skill swiftly garnered respect. The patternshop was a zone in which a tradesman's sense of identity and masculinity was conjoined with the accrual of craft skill: these elements developed in tandem and were essential for acceptance into the group norms. But for Watts, acceptance into that world of craft masculinity also brought an awareness of that world's limitations. Watts explained:

> There was a sort of camaraderie amongst the men. I paused briefly there because you can't imagine how much hope I had pinned on this new life as a patternmaker, and the joy and how good it would be to be finally amongst adult men. And it became apparent after, I suppose about the first year, that in many respects it was not dissimilar to the playground that I'd experienced at school … The guys were very competitive … There was a kind of brutality to it, and for me, I had been raised … to accept that brutality as fairly normal, in the playgrounds of the schoolyard … There was also a, you know, a kind of extraordinary pecking order in there, from management down to the lowly apprentice, and if you didn't happen to fit in … it was really hard for men …
>
> As an apprentice, this is all a mystery unfolding, and I was as wide-eyed as any of them. But it became apparent to me pretty early on that people were watching me very carefully. Number one was that my hair was most of the way down my back … This set me apart from the crowd. It was fairly

7 PATTERNMAKER-ARTISTS: CREATIVE PATHWAYS FOR INDUSTRIAL... 211

clear to them that I was a hippie ... [But] if you were a skilled tradesman, or, as I like to think, an artisan ... you were highly respected ... People might overlook flaws of character ... It's hard to describe the little scraps of affection and tenderness ... the little things that gave men a sense of their own self-worth. They're pretty hard to find, and skill and ability was the main driver.[36]

As Watts' apprenticeship unfolded, he met other 'long haireds' who introduced him to Melbourne's theatre, music, art and university social scenes in the mid-1970s. His life soon became beset with tensions and conflicting priorities. On the one hand, Watts was a skilled patternmaking apprentice with a bright future; he won 'Apprentice of the Year' with the Apprentice Commission of Victoria. But in his spare time Watts read Bertrand Russell's *In Praise of Idleness* and socialised with creatives and university students in the 'world outside'.[37]

The world outside seemed so exciting, and I was getting glimpses of it in the evening, and despite the fact that I loved patternmaking and was enjoying working with these guys, I was finding the atmosphere in the patternshop ... pretty unpleasant ... This kind of gulf developed ... It began to dawn on me that this machinery we were making was the very machinery they were using to dig up, and, you know, destroy the Earth! ... I was getting to this kind of logjam.[38]

For Watts, something had to give. At the conclusion of his apprenticeship, Watts worked only briefly as a patternmaker. In 1978 he left the trade and enrolled in a Fine Arts Tertiary Orientation Program at RMIT, Melbourne. There, he built up a visual arts portfolio and then gained admission to a Fine Arts degree at the Victorian College of the Arts (VCA), Melbourne. Vickers Ruwolt had lost one of their most talented younger patternmakers (although the tradesmen were unsurprised, having sensed Watts' desire for a different life for some time). It is relevant to note that this was during the brief historical period in which university education in Australia was free, due to the Whitlam Government's policy change in 1974.

Watts' introduction to the world of fine arts education, however, was not smooth-sailing. It was the late 1970s and early 1980s, and it is relevant to point out that by this stage the Australian art world drew its influences primarily from the United States. Conceptual art, feminist art, installation, land art, minimalism and performance were increasingly in vogue. Watts conceded: "The art scene was rapidly changing, and I was

212   J. A. STEIN

still in a space where I imagined that Henry Moore … was the ultimate sort of sculptor, you know? Well, Henry … was pretty old hat."[39] Watts had by now developed highly refined technical skill in terms of shaping materials—wood, metals, wax and clay—and his initial artistic instincts were figurative. He swiftly discovered that he was just as much a 'fish out of water' at the VCA as he felt at Vickers Ruwolt. Watts had been enculturated into a factory environment, with its own particular idioms, group logic and culture of craft masculinity. Now, at art school, among largely middle-class students and university educators, Watts had to learn to shift his language and mannerisms. Moreover, his eyes were opened to feminist values and environmentalism: both were welcome surprises to be incorporated into Watts' world view.

It is worth mentioning, at this stage, that patternmaker Debra Schuckar also undertook a Fine Arts diploma (painting), approximately a decade after Watts. Unlike Watts, however, Schuckar did not speak to me about difficulties with identity or sociality. Her struggles related more to the challenge of attending university while parenting (and for some of that time as a single mother). Schuckar explained:

> I was always an artist when I was young, I've always been an artist. I felt the need that I wanted to study art and change my career, go down to a different path … I was living sort of an art-world life … But I realised after a while that freedom of thinking didn't pay the bills … Trying to bring up children—gotta have money to pay the bills.[40]

As discussed in the previous chapter, patternmaking at that time did not offer part-time work, which meant Schuckar could not stay employed in her original trade once she had children. The purpose of this brief aside is to emphasise that each interviewees' particular circumstances and subject position impact upon their educational and employment pathways considerably. Watts had the privilege of being white and male, which he only learned about during through encountering feminist art education at the VCA.

Nonetheless, Watts gradually realised that his identity—more specifically his background and skills as a patternmaker—was not at all valued by the art establishment:

> I kind of hit a crunch then because I began to realise that I was *so* skilled that it was actually working against me, and over several years I began to deskill

myself ... I was absolutely bewildered, really. Trying to plumb a new set of values that at that time were invisible to me ... I was utterly perplexed to try and find, what is this magic thing? ... How is it that art is created? That perplexed me for years ... and by the end of it, I was just making balls out of clay. I'd reduced myself to the simplest thing ... They were a little bit like Alexander Calder, except they were made out of wood ... There was a kind of elegance to them ... That was about as far as I was able to progress ... I'm on such a big learning curve with no prospect of any kind of employment. Conceptual art? God! I certainly didn't have the background of parents who even understood what I was doing, or could support me.[41]

By now the journey of this patternmaker-turned-artist may be looking as if it were heading for disaster, but it is to Watts' credit that he was able to adaptably carve a life from two such disparate contexts.

Space prevents me from providing extensive details about Watts' journey thereafter, but it included working in theatre and prop design, clay modelling for automotive design, special effects and prop design for TV and cinema, and teaching design and fine arts at RMIT. Watts loved teaching, but another seismic social and technological shift soon confronted him. By the 1990s, RMIT—like most tertiary institutions—was beginning to identify with a culture of specialised professionalism, and with that came an embrace of computing, for administrative, educational and creative work. Watts was not interested and avoided computers as much as he could. While his teaching work was not 'replaced' by digital technologies, he still had to contend with their influence. "The world of computers was kind of creeping in on to the field in a way that I ... was just so uncomfortable with."[42] Finally, Watts quit teaching and returned to art-making. He relocated to Castlemaine, in regional Victoria, with his wife. There, in addition to parenting, Watts finally had the space and time to create artworks without the approval or judgement of the art establishment. Watts asserts that he has now found his artistic 'voice':

> It is so far from the world of design, so far from the world of blueprints and drawings and timelines. It's so far outside of reason and logic ... You know, there's a sort of gossamer-light kind of impulse that passes through from time to time, and if one is responsive and ready, and receptive ... you can hear that voice ... I think they call it a 'moment of flow'. It's like you're not there ... It's like that with sculpture ... It's that quality of aliveness that, for me, is home.

Watts' potted biography holds wider lessons in terms of understanding the constraints the Australian masculinity placed upon men (and women) in terms of their careers and identities. As explored by Andrea Waling, the social construction of the Australian 'tradie' is of a relatively "rough working-class man", who is not expected to step beyond anything that is normatively gendered.[43] To put it simply, 'tradies' (in the Australian parlance) were (and are) not imagined to be 'creative' in a cultural sense. While the stereotype has shifted over time, it is still possible to make some generalisations: tradesmen were imagined to be unemotional, tough and heteronormative, and this perception was bolstered by homo-social banter that included the sexualisation of women, and the use of homophobic terminology to deride those perceived to be weak or somehow different.[44] 'Tradies' were expected to be strong and manually skilled, sometimes inventive and resourceful, but never 'intellectual'. They were not supposed to be philosophical, expressive, wistful or emotional. To that end, Watts did not fit the norm, and his awareness of this allowed him a sense of distance. This enabled Watts to reflect critically, during our interview, on the world in which he was first educated.

Watts' account also shows us that the middle-class 'cultured' art world was similarly beset by its own limitations. Generally speaking, a tradesperson's class position implicitly excluded them from full acceptance in the art world, except as a novelty or as a curiosity. Some tradespeople went to great lengths to conceal their industrial background, to avoid tarnishing their fine artisanal or artistic reputations.[45] For Watts, he now comfortably operates outside the demands of the art market and critical recognition. His work is now infused by the combined influences of his background—industrial, design-based and artistic. This emerges in works Watts now makes for himself and for his local community:

> I built a kind of water sculpture for the [Castlemaine] School ... It was all the old things I'd learned. A real hybrid mix, actually, of ... design, structural stuff, working with concrete, working with very beautiful, organic, circular forms. I brought everything to bear I had on doing that sculpture, and it took me quite a while.[46] (Fig. 7.7)

Over time, Watts has become cognisant of the contradictions at play in his own identity. These tensions were made particularly explicit upon encountering the work of Robert Klippel, as the following section describes.

Fig. 7.7 Peter Watts, *Creek Sculpture*, 2003, Castlemaine Steiner School, ferro cement, 12 m (length). (Courtesy of the artist)

On Encountering Robert Klippel

Deindustrialisation in Global North economies has evidently brought many profound (and often negative) changes to working life and job security for large groups of workers, but it also produced a wealth of redundant industrial *things*. For artists interested in readymades, found-objects and assemblage, this offered great opportunities. In Australia, as industrial establishments closed down from the 1960s onwards, factories auctioned off their equipment, including vast warehouses of wooden patterns. In some cases, artists simply 'scavenged' what they could find from abandoned industrial sites. In the 1960s Klippel, with the artist Colin Lanceley, discovered a trove of disused patterns from an industrial warehouse in the Sydney suburb of Balmain.[47] Lanceley used the patterns earlier, while Klippel kept them in storage, and it was not until the 1980s that he began using patterns in his assemblages[48] (Fig. 7.8).

During my interviews with patternmakers, the subject of Robert Klippel (and his use of patterns in his works) came up often. The general sentiment shared was of annoyance. For example, the large Klippel sculpture in

Fig. 7.8 Installation view of *Assembled: The Art of Robert Klippel*, TarraWarra Museum of Art, 2019–2020. (Courtesy of the Robert Klippel Estate, represented by Annette Larkin Fine Art, Sydney, and Galerie Gmurzynska, Zurich. Copyright Agency 2019. Photo: Andrew Curtis)

the foyer of the Art Gallery of New South Wales, Sydney, was experienced as an affront to patternmakers. For them, it felt as if Klippel was gaining recognition for *their* labour and skill. Klippel had not planned the pattern's layout, he was not the one who carefully sawed the timber, nor had he hand-carved the details and sanded the edges. Klippel had simply 'assembled' and was then acclaimed by critics such as Robert Hughes; his work celebrated as being of an international standard.[49]

Poynton remembered seeing his first Klippel assemblage:

> When I first saw his work I thought, "This bloke's a phoney!", you know? He's getting old foundry patterns and just sticking them together … The only creative part of that was perhaps in the assembly.

Poynton conceded, "at least I suppose they were saved," referring to discarded patterns from closed industrial enterprises. He recalled bleakly: "I was mortified to learn, later on, when [his first employer] the [International]

7 PATTERNMAKER-ARTISTS: CREATIVE PATHWAYS FOR INDUSTRIAL... 217

Harvester folded, all those beautiful patterns apparently went into the dump. I still have a little one out here. It's really nice."[50]

Watts, too, felt the discombobulating experience of encountering a Klippel assemblage, laden with industrial patterns:

> The very thing I'd been paid to make, he was now standing up, rearranging, maybe adding a bit of colour here and there ... and was showing them as art! Now, there's a great gulf there for tradesmen, whom I recall at the time showing them pictures of Robert's work, and they were really angry and upset that he seemed to be abusing or devaluing what they'd made. I, by contrast, thought he was adding value to it. But I could see where they were coming from. The kind of energy and expertise that created these things was almost being made a joke of. I don't think that's what he did, but it took me a long time to really see Robert Klippel's work and value it deeply ... There was a kind of expressive quality to [his sculptures which] transcended the origins or the skill of their making. They were no longer about the made product.[51]

Here we can see Watts wrestling with Klippel's work with a foot in each 'world'—industrial and artistic. The fact that Klippel was using these patterns *in the 1980s* is significant: while deindustrialisation was a feature of the Australian economy from the 1960s onwards, it was in the mid- to late 1980s that the 'crunch' really began. Manufacturing workers were particularly insecure and worried about their futures. It is possible to see how the use of industrial 'relics' appeared more of a statement about their own perceived societal redundancy in that period.

These patternmakers' responses to Klippel should not necessarily be seen as the uncovering of some kind of underlying 'truth', as revealed by an authentic set of workers' perspectives. To some extent, their reaction is unfair, in that it does not acknowledge the Duchampian legacy of the readymade in early twentieth-century modernist art. The patternmakers' view privileges both manual skill and the original industrial context, over other potential contexts for disused industrial discards. This tells us something of the patternmakers' own boundaries in their conceptions of Klippel's work: once they recognise particular parts as industrial patterns, they cannot un-see them, making it harder to appreciate Klippel's assemblages as unified aesthetic forms.

More interesting, however, is how the patternmakers' reaction focuses on the *labour* of artisanal craft production. This emphasis is important to note, given the patternmakers' subject position as (now) marginalised

218   J. A. STEIN

manufacturing workers. Patternmaker Tim Wighton, when discussing Klippel, described what he saw as an inequity of compensation:

> I think my reaction to Klippel's sculpture comes back to the artificial divide that's been put between art, design and industry. When used in an industrial way, the patterns a patternmaker produces brings him no credit and only an hourly wage. However, when they are used in an artistic way they are displayed in national gallery and the artist fairly well compensated.[52]

Implicitly, Wighton refers to the way in which class bestows cultural value (or otherwise). Wighton's statement should be understood in the context of his particular life experience. As a currently working patternmaker (in his mid-30s), Wighton's situation is more precarious than many of the retired patternmakers I spoke with. The matter of an 'hourly wage' is a genuine concern for a manufacturing worker with a young family, hoping to eventually own his own home.

Contrasting the patternmaker-artists' outsider status with the critical reception to modernist sculptors reveals how the art establishment prefers to frame industrial themes as aestheticised 'relics' of a distant past, rather than something that is still with us today, albeit in modified form. This speaks to a broader struggle between deindustrialising communities and elite, urban 'creative industries'.[53] Manufacturing communities feel forgotten, told that they need to 'move on' and 'get over' deindustrialisation (as Haidutschyk was). Remnant industrial areas are re-zoned as 'creative hubs', with little thought for the impacts on the remaining small manufacturing businesses (and their rental rates).[54]

The mild irony of this whole discussion is that Klippel himself trained in a trade and was a skilled craftsperson in his own right. Before the World War II, Klippel initially trained in wool-classing at East Sydney Technical College. He then served in the Royal Australian Navy during World War II, where he trained in industrial modelmaking at the Gunnery Instruction Centre, Sydney. In this capacity Klippel made models of ships and aeroplanes, which had been a childhood passion of his. During this immersion in modelmaking and war-time technology, Klippel was simultaneously attending art classes at night, taught by Lyndon Dadswell at East Sydney Technical College (an experience not unlike Poynton's, but around a decade earlier). Klippel was quickly immersed into art-making "because I had the craft behind me",[55] demonstrating the link between his industrial craft training and his ability to undertake artistic endeavours. It is relevant here to concede that a 1940s art-education environment would have been more receptive to Klippel's wood-carving skills than a late 1970s art-school environment was for Peter Watts' likely equivalent capacities.

In a 1965 oral history interview, Klippel explained the importance of his personal aesthetic concept. He also indicated that, for him, the *source* of his found-objects was insignificant:

> It's not good enough to just take bits of machinery and join them together. One must have some kind of concept, or some sort of philosophy, or something deeper … That's the nature of art, I think, is to give life to form … It doesn't seem to make any difference to me, you know, I don't see any meaning in where it has come from, or the sociological implications … I'm not trying to make any comment on our society as such … I'm more interested in a deeper, sort of, spiritual problem of our time.[56]

Curiously, this statement could almost have come out of the mouth of Poynton or Watts, discussing their personal views on sculpture. This is not to say that Klippel and the patternmakers should be conflated—their works, their skills and their journeys are obviously different. Nonetheless, it demonstrates that two diverse streams of creative practice may be more interconnected than might first appear.

Conclusion

The respective hegemonic cultures of modernist sculpture and twentieth-century manufacturing share a key feature: a cultural normativity that conjoins and celebrates skill and masculinity. This set of values admittedly excludes women and others who did not fit the norm, but perhaps provided an unexpected pathway between manufacturing trades and sculptural practice. Adamson alluded to this connection when examining a photograph of sculptor David Smith, posed with one of his wrought-iron pieces. Adamson notes:

> Here we have the craftsman as artist, or perhaps the artist as craftsman … Skill enters into the equation, to be sure, but that daring composition—a line drawing silhouetted against a broad sky—transcends its making and enters into the realm of pure, autonomous form.[57]

220   J. A. STEIN

Adamson's point is that "pure" art, and craft, in some kind of "unadulterated form", is impossible to pinpoint; human-made things—like sculptors—are inevitably a little bit of one and a little bit of another. It is the same for manufactured products: we tend to think of factory-produced plastic as 'machine-made', without realising that a patternmaker's (or a modelmaker's) hands made the original form, which was used to make the mass-produced object. This interconnection between machinery, organic form and human expression is threaded through the motivations of all these makers, whether they are defined as artisans, artists or patternmakers. Certainly, there are differences in terms of education, recognition, social class and understandings of culture and theory. But perhaps it is the similarities, not the distinctions, that bear remembering. Perhaps this is precisely the intersectional fusion and collective understanding that is required in our current time of damaging political divide between the left, the right and the angrily anti-political, as discussed in Chap. 2.[58]

Through their creative practice, these patternmaker-artists have broken through an invisible threshold between industrial production and fine art. Yet they think nothing of it. It feels like an appropriate extension of their abilities, demonstrating that the relationship between trade skill and creativity is ultimately generative. The patternmaker-artists seek quality in their sculptural work not in spite of their trades backgrounds, but because of it. Their industrial training steadies their hand and gives them the technical ability to confidently explore concepts and form without encountering practical barriers to realising their plans in three dimensions. Notably, this is the same dynamic in Klippel's work: his early technical training meant that his assemblages had the precise sculptural integrity he was seeking. Among other things, this also indicates the far-reaching value of trade apprenticeships as an institution, well beyond the direct industry application of the training. I make this point at a time when vocational education in Australia is facing the consequences of many years of funding cuts and educational strategies that encouraged students away from trades and into university study. Apprenticeship intakes are continuing to decline in many trades, and refined manual skills are increasingly in short supply.[59]

Trades devaluation and skills shortages are not merely a problem for 'industry'; they are also a cultural issue. Generations of Australians have internalised the notion that to undertake a 'trade' rather than university is to be on a 'lower' rung of social status. Moreover, the social framing of 'creativity' is also infused with particular conceptions about class and economic activity. Calls have been made to inject 'creativity' into Australian manufacturing, to make it more 'innovative', so that it may be able to withstand the challenges of the global capitalist market.[60] Usually these suggestions are aimed at bringing 'creativity' *into* industry, not at identifying creativity within the existing manufacturing workforce or within workplaces. This points to the notion that Australians not really accustomed to thinking about manufacturing workers as 'creative', nor as divergent thinkers in their own right.

The oral histories shared here do not uphold this mainstream construction of Australian 'tradie' masculinity. Instead, what has materialised is a plurality of identities both within manufacturing and emergent in its aftermath. It is imperative that we engage more closely with this cultural legacy of deindustrialisation, looking beyond the most obvious candidates. Doing so will help us gain a fuller picture of how creative practice manifests and will open our eyes to who else might be quietly practising on the cultural fringe.

NOTES

1. This chapter is a substantially revised and amended development upon the article: Jesse Adams Stein, "When Manufacturing Workers Make Sculpture: Creative Pathways in the Context of Australian Deindustrialisation," *Australian and New Zealand Journal of Art* 20, no. 2 (2020): 189–212.
2. Sherry Lee Linkon, *The Half-Life of Deindustrialization: Working-Class Writing about Economic Restructuring* (Ann Arbour: University of Michigan Press, 2018).
3. Klippel attended art classes at East Sydney Technical School and later studied at the Slade School of Fine Art.
4. See also Linkon, *The Half-Life*; Steven High, Lachlan MacKinnon & Andrew Perchard (eds), *The Deindustrialized World: Confronting Ruination in Postindustrial Places* (Vancouver & Toronto: UBC Press, 2007).
5. Julia Bryan-Wilson and Benjamin Piekut, 'Amateurism', *Third Text* 34, no. 1 (2019): 1–21.
6. Bryan-Wilson & Piekut, 12–13.
7. Rosalind Krauss, "Sculpture in the Expanded Field", *October* 8 (1979): 30–44.
8. Krauss, "Sculpture in the Expanded Field".
9. Gregory Votolato, *American Design in the Twentieth Century* (Manchester & New York: Manchester University Press, 1988), 169.

10. Glenn Adamson, *Thinking Through Craft* (London: Berg / Bloomsbury), 2–3; see also Theodor Adorno, *Aesthetic Theory* (London & New York: Bloomsbury, 1997 [1970]), 3.
11. Adamson, *Thinking Through Craft*, 3–4.
12. Adamson, *Thinking Through Craft*, 4.
13. Adamson, *Thinking Through Craft*.
14. Paul Kay, interview with author, *Reshaping Australian Manufacturing*, 30 April 2018 (Canberra: National Library of Australia [NLA]), https://nla.gov.au/nla.cat-vn7765725.
15. Kay, interview with author.
16. Kay, interview with author.
17. Kay, interview with author.
18. Personal communication with Paul Kay, 5 March 2021.
19. Kay, personal communication with author.
20. Cynthia Cockburn, *Brothers: Male Dominance & Technological Change* (London: Pluto Press, 1983).
21. Serge Haidutschyk, interview with author, *Reshaping Australian Manufacturing*, 4 December 2018 (Canberra: NLA), https://nla.gov.au/nla.cat-vn7889878.
22. Haidutschyk, interview with author.
23. Justin Paton, *Ricky Swallow: Field Recordings* (Melbourne: Craftsman House, 2004).
24. Haidutschyk, interview with author.
25. Rachel Weiss, "Between the Material World and the Ghost of Dreams: An Argument about Craft in *los Carpinteros*", *The Journal of Modern Craft* 1, no. 2 (2008): 34–6. See also Adamson, *The Invention of Craft*, 141.
26. Bryan Poynton, interview with author, *Reshaping Australian Manufacturing*, 22 February 2018 (Canberra: NLA), https://nla.gov.au/nla.cat-vn7580610.
27. Poynton, interview with author.
28. Poynton, interview with author.
29. Poynton, interview with author.
30. Poynton, artwork caption for *Self Portrait with Pigeon Hole*, 2001, created for 'Box Forms', an exhibition curated by the Victorian Woodworkers' Association.
31. Poynton, interview with author.
32. Poynton, interview with author.
33. Peter Watts interview with author, *Reshaping Australian Manufacturing*, 11 July 2019 (Canberra, NLA), https://nla.gov.au/nla.cat-vn8059117.
34. Andrea Waling, *White Masculinity in Contemporary Australia* (London: Routledge, 2020).
35. Watts, interview with author.

36. Watts, interview with author.
37. Bertrand Russell, *In Praise of Idleness* (London: Allen & Unwin, 1935).
38. Watts, interview with author.
39. Watts, interview with author.
40. Debra Schuckar, interview with author, *Reshaping Australian Manufacturing*, 23 February 2019 (Canberra: NLA), https://nla.gov.au/nla.cat-vn7580622.
41. Watts, interview with author.
42. Watts, interview with author.
43. Waling, *White Masculinity*, 161.
44. For parallels, see Andrew Warren, "Crafting Masculinities: Gender, Culture and Emotion at Work in the Surfboard Industry", *Gender, Place and Culture* 23, no. 1 (2016): 36–54.
45. Scarlett offers one such example of this, see Sarah Fayen Scarlett, "The Craft of Industrial Patternmaking", *Journal of Modern Craft* 4, no. 1 (2011): 27–48.
46. Watts, interview with author.
47. Brian Ladd, *The Sculptor's Studio: Robert Klippel*, exhibition catalogue (Sydney: Art Gallery of New South Wales, 1990), 5.
48. Fiona Gruber, "'He was a pure artist': Robert Klippel's Junkyard Sculptures Return to the Spotlight", *The Guardian* (12 December 2019), online: www.theguardian.com/artanddesign/2019/dec/12/he-was-a-pure-artist-robert-klippels-junkyard-sculptures-return-to-the-spotlight.
49. Robert Hughes, "Robert Klippel", *Art & Australia* 2, no. 1 (1964): 18–29.
50. Bryan Poynton, interview with author, *Reshaping Australian Manufacturing Oral History Project*, 22 February 2018 (Canberra: NLA), https://nla.gov.au/nla.cat-vn7580610.
51. Watts, interview with author.
52. Tim Wighton, interview with author, *Reshaping Australian Manufacturing*, 27 November 2017 (Canberra: NLA), https://nla.gov.au/nla.cat-vn7540155.
53. Linkon, op. cit.
54. See, for example, Chris Gibson, Carl Grodach, Craig Lyons, Alexandra Crosby and Chris Brennan-Horley, Urban Cultural Policy and the Changing Dynamics of Cultural Production Made in Marrickville, report, Produced for the Australian Research Council Discovery Project: Urban Cultural Policy and the Changing Dynamics of Cultural Production (QUT, University of Wollongong and Monash University: 2017), online: https://opus.lib.uts.edu.au/bitstream/10453/116643/1/Made_in_Marrickville_DP170104255-201702.pdf, accessed 9 September 2021.
55. Robert Klippel interview by Hazel de Berg, 17 May 1965 (Canberra, NLA), https://nla.gov.au/nla.cat-vn232877.

224   J. A. STEIN

56. Klippel, interview by Hazel de Berg.
57. Glenn Adamson, "Directions and Displacements in Modern Craft", *Australian and New Zealand Journal of Art* 10, no. 1 (2009): 23.
58. Michael Zweig, "Six Points on Class", *Monthly Review* 58, no. 3 (2006): 116–26.
59. Margo Couldrey & Phil Loveder, *The Future of Australian Apprenticeships* (Adelaide: National Centre for Vocational Education Research, 2017).
60. Sam Bucolo, *Design Led Innovation – Underpinning a Future Manufacturing Workforce*, Industry Skills Councils, *Manufacturing in 2030* Symposium Stimulus (2014).

CHAPTER 8

Conclusion: Industrial Craft and Alternative Futures for Australian Manufacturing

You can't keep digging stuff out of the ground forever. It amazes me that all the cars that are running on petrol all over the world. How do they get so much? I do think of these things, you know. I reckon Australia's going to turn upside down when they get all the minerals out!
—Former engineering patternmaking business owner, Bruce Phipps[1]

We should be looking at added value in Australia. Not taking our raw materials and sending them offshore, having them processed offshore, and then buying them back at astronomical prices … It's just madness … We have to become a smart country, and we have to concentrate on not losing all these skillsets [or] we will not be able to manufacture anything in Australia.
—Engineering patternmaking business owner Deborah Tyrrell[2]

I have shared here the perspectives of Deborah Tyrrell and Bruce Phipps not because their opinions are particularly unusual, they're not. But it is notable that these quotes are not from so-called latte-sipping lefties from the inner city, but are the views of a middle-aged small-business owner and a retiree small-business owner, both from greater Sydney. Australia has reached an impasse where even relatively conservative observers of politics and industry can identify the profound irrationality behind this country's continued commitment to expanding mining and carbon-based energy production. Conventionally, Australia's recent economic strengths were seen to be in minerals extraction and export, tourism and higher

© The Author(s), under exclusive license to Springer Nature Switzerland AG 2021
J. A. Stein, *Industrial Craft in Australia*, Palgrave Studies in Oral History, https://doi.org/10.1007/978-3-030-87243-4_8

225

education for international student markets, and certainly *not* manufacturing. However, since 2020 we have seen the economic and public health impacts of the Covid-19 pandemic, trade tensions with China, product shortages, and disastrous examples of climate change in Australia (such as bushfires of an exceptional ferocity and scale). All these issues have revealed clear weaknesses in Australia's economy, as well as exposing a fractured and unsustainable social fabric. Clearly, things cannot return to the 'status-quo' before 2020; we have to find alternative ways to think about jobs, production, sustainability and the environment.

While my observations in this chapter apply to the Australian context, similar points could well be made about other deindustrialising economies, such as Canada and the United Kingdom. Having said that, Australia is a particularly bad case, both in terms of governmental inattention to climate action and an entrenched political belief in the 'natural' decline of deindustrialising regions. With this context in mind, this concluding chapter considers alternative paths for sustaining and expanding Australian manufacturing, paths which could intelligently integrate industrial craft knowledge with appropriate emerging technologies.

Compared to the rhetoric we regularly hear from federal politicians, those directly experiencing the long-term impacts of deindustrialisation have very different perspectives on technology, employment and skills. Mainstream politics presents a vision of a globalised, 'high tech' future of services, finance and 'flexible work' (all the while relying heavily on carbon-based energy and raw minerals for export). And while those who support Australian manufacturing can at times strike an uncomfortably nationalistic chord, there is a great deal of common sense in value-adding to raw materials, and skilling the population in practical ways, rather than funnelling large numbers of school leavers into tertiary education. Manufacturing diversifies our social, economic and educational mix for the better. Investment in local manufacturing can also enhance national research and development capacity.[3] In addition, local manufacturing produces reasonably paid and desirable jobs: the work is frequently interesting and satisfying, paid at skilled award wage rates, and is supported by progressive unions such as the Australian Manufacturing Workers' Union (AMWU).

Industrial craft needs to be a core part of this equation. Without it, countries such as Australia will lack essential material literacies and wide-ranging production knowledge. A renewed emphasis on skills development in practical trades could combine both 'traditional' and emerging techniques and technologies. Over time, this could produce a deep cultural sensibility towards materials and how to handle them, which will extend well beyond the factory walls. This is something that Germany and Scandinavian countries have known for a long time: technical and craft skills ought to be built-in to our formal education systems. The Swedish craft education programme of *Slöjd* is a good example. It is no surprise that Sweden and Germany are globally recognised for high-quality design and manufacturing, as those nations provide the structural means for the population to gain the essential craft, design and production skills necessary to support this specialisation.

As we have seen in this book's Introduction, the recent history of Australian manufacturing is often presented as part of an inexorable global decline. We are familiar with similar narratives (albeit at a larger scale) in North America and Europe. And it *is* a story of decline. I do not mean to discount or avoid the reality of this decline, even though in this book I emphasise survival and potential future growth. The decline has been dramatic: in 1966 a quarter of Australian jobs were in the manufacturing sector, and by 2001 this had declined to under 12 per cent of total jobs.[4] By 2020 the percentage of manufacturing jobs had fallen to under 7 per cent of the total workforce.[5] None of this has been inevitable. Much of this decline has been the result of specific trade and industrial relations policies driven by successive Australian Liberal and Labor governments since the 1980s. Most particularly, the recent decline of local automotive manufacturing in Australia (and the lack of support for a potential electric car industry) is example of the close association between manufacturing and public policy.[6] It follows, then, that things need not be as they are and that there are concrete measures that can be taken—by government, educational institutions and the private sector—to shift this pattern. A meaningful, progressive and well-managed revitalisation of state involvement in manufacturing would provide a secure base from which to expand technical, skills and design capacity as a sovereign nation. Australia need not compete to mass-produce the same products that can be cheaply sourced elsewhere: the key will be to target support for discrete and specific high-quality products.[7]

For example, nations such as Australia could value-add to existing raw minerals extraction through production of high-quality, durable and sustainable products, produced with close attention to labour and training and to the downstream impacts of particular materials and processes. In this, manufacturing must be understood as operating within a generative landscape, combining older and newer skillsets and technologies, and encompassing small to medium size businesses (SMEs), not just large multi-national firms. Being able to use materials and technologies *well* means being willing to listen not just to engineers and project managers but also to skilled industrial craftspeople and makers, designers, other production employees and even those who work throughout the product cycle: repairers, waste sorters and recycling managers.

To make things more tangible I will provide a non-exhaustive list of suggestions. For instance, Australia's existing strengths in medical equipment manufacture could be expanded (this includes ventilators, but also smaller medical, surgical and personal-protective equipment). Likewise, Australia's local vaccine development capacity is another manufacturing area in need of substantial long-term investment; it was shown to be poorly lacking well into the second year of the Covid-19 pandemic. Australia could become a specialist in solar battery production, to complement the nation's enthusiastic embrace of domestic rooftop solar panels, and the local availability of minerals such as lithium. Targeted support could be given to sustainable construction materials manufacture, to support Australia's current building construction boom.[8] Recent research into bio-plastics, such as the possibilities of seaweed-based and algae-based polymers, has the future capacity for small- to medium-scale specialist manufacturing, among other applications.[9] Large-scale coral reef scaffolds can now be produced manually and with digital fabrication, which could be deployed to help renew large swathes of bleached coral along the Great Barrier Reef.[10] Recent research into the potential of e-waste as a productive input for new systems and recycled materials also has the capacity for niche manufacturing outputs.[11] As examined by Chris Gibson and Andrew Warren, Australia's production of sustainable-timber guitars is another example of bespoke manufacturing that capitalises on specialised craft skills and engages closely with local communities, places and the environment.[12]

Additionally, the emphasis need not always be on producing new things. This may go against the grain of conventional thinking about design and production, but given the significant problems of e-waste and landfill management, there are opportunities to look towards maintenance and repair as a key zone for employing and training current tradespeople and training future apprentices. As a relatively isolated nation, Australia is an appropriate venue for a strong national strategy for repairing and maintaining products and infrastructure. Presently, Australia lags far behind

Europe and the United States in terms of advocating for legally binding repair rights and in terms of the popularisation of community-led repair.[13] The on-shore production of spare-parts, and the local provision of skilled repairers, would each provide diverse and viable extensions of existing industrial craft skillsets.[14]

Sadly, in the current Australian political context, the idea of government taking a leading role in meaningfully funding and supporting manufacturing in Australia is sometimes dismissed as naively utopian or even dangerously 'socialist' in a pejorative sense. Yet, as the quotes at the beginning of this chapter indicate, these ideas are not 'fringe' or 'radical', but are increasingly seen as 'common sense' views, even held by voters living in conservative electorates. In an attitudinal study undertaken by the Australia Institute's Centre for Future Work in 2017, 71 per cent of respondents "totally agreed" that "it is better to add value to our natural resources through manufacturing, than to produce and export raw commodities", and 72 per cent agreed that global manufacturing companies should be required to establish production facilities in Australia if they want to sell their products without tariffs.[15] Too often, the concept of local manufacturing has been captured and mobilised by far-right and xenophobic political elements, but this should not mean that the idea of boosting domestic production is, in and of itself, toxic.

This requires a reframing of national manufacturing through a progressive sovereign effort. Speaking about sovereignty this way may have some concerned that this vision is a reactionary and exclusivist one. However, as argued by economist William Mitchell and author Thomas Fazi, emphasising sovereignty is not exclusively a right-wing concept:

> History attests to the fact that national sovereignty and national self-determination are not intrinsically reactionary or jingoistic concepts—in fact, they were the rallying cries of countless nineteenth- and twentieth-century socialist and left-wing liberation movements.[16]

In the twentieth century, a great deal has been achieved through the institution of the nation state, even though over the past 40 years neoliberal ideologues have done a great deal to curtail, roll back and destroy those achievements.

As noted earlier, since the 1980s there was an emerging (and erroneous) consensus that globalisation left the nation state powerless in the face of capitalist 'market forces', and national governments simply had no choice but to step back and give business the space to flourish, allegedly producing a 'trickle-down' effect. But, as explained by Mitchell and Fazi, things need not be this way. There remains the possibility for

> a progressive, emancipatory vision of national sovereignty that offers a radical alternative to both the right and the neoliberals—one based on popular sovereignty, democratic control over the economy, full employment, social justice, redistribution from the rich to the poor, inclusivity and the socioecological transformation of production and society.[17]

Mitchell and Fazi draw on Modern Monetary Theory (MMT) to explain how such a system could function, including how it would avoid hyperinflation. Given my book is about industrial craft, not economic theory, I will refrain from explaining the mechanism for this system in depth, but suffice to say that sovereign governments are capable of producing and funding systems of subsidised domestic production, at the same time as supporting welfare and full employment, because they issue their own currency by legislative fiat. Local production is key to making such a system effective.

It is evident by now that Australian manufacturing renewal cannot be left to the 'market' alone: industrial decline has gone on too long to hope that somehow business will just 'pick up' to meet particular demands. Australian manufacturing businesses in the current context understandably complain that, right now, the skillsets, industrial zones and supply chains are simply not available. It is clear that we need to think very differently about what to manufacture, and how, and this entails reframing our understanding about what is important. As noted above, the mechanisms to make these changes are available, over time, through national governmental means. Today, the changing climate, insecure work and practical skill loss are key considerations in how we might imagine an alternative future for Australian manufacturing, one that encompasses sustainability, genuine possibilities for employment, and the principles of care and intergenerational equity.

Things cannot sustainably continue as they are, on multiple counts: environmental, social and economic. It is imperative that we think differently about production, jobs, human skill and the life cycles of objects and materials. This means making the most of the resources we already have, and thinking well beyond the apparent 'logic' of the globalised capitalist market. If we think about climate change as something akin to a coming 'war', then it requires something that could resemble a state-led 'war effort' to tackle it. Although outside the scope of this particular book, it should almost go without saying that the global energy production mix needs to radically shift to renewable energy, in order to produce a meaningful and swift reduction in carbon emissions. Manufacturing should be part of this reformed picture, if nation states globally take a strong role in shaping which particular manufacturing industries, production methods and energy sources are used and meaningfully addressing how waste is handled.

SITUATING INDUSTRIAL CRAFT IN AUSTRALIA

Let us shift scale now, back to the patternmakers. Through focusing on the relatively unknown trade of engineering patternmaking, the chapters in this book have drawn us into a close encounter with the lived reality of life, skill, creativity and survival in deindustrialising Australia. As we saw in Chap. 2, those most affected by deindustrialisation have understandably grown to be highly suspicious of contemporary neoliberal ideologies and of the insecure work and disruptive technological systems that often accompany them. They have borne the brunt of the "scorched earth left behind by neoliberalism" (to borrow Mitchell and Fazi's term), and some are disgusted by the elites' excesses and corporate selfishness laid bare by the 2007–2008 Global Financial Crisis.[18] This has been made worse by decades of governmental austerity, resulting in the defunding, restructuring and closure of government services, educational institutions and state-run industrial establishments. As charted in Chap. 2, the ensuing sense of disaffection and anger has been leveraged by populist political opportunists, to the detriment of civil society. The influence of political populism is something that oral historians and social scientists will increasingly have to contend with, as we seek to speak with precarious workers from a number of sectors, manufacturing among them.

As explored in Chap. 3, in Australia the formal structure of apprenticeship has historically served working-class *men* fairly well. Traditionally, completion of an apprenticeship was seen to provide a secure 'job for life', and its rituals and culture served to embed industrial craft practices, skills, a particularised gender identity and collective social structures. Apprenticeship was evidently bound by hegemonic craft masculinity (which served to exclude women and others who did not fit the norm). But within this exclusive world, twentieth-century industrial craft culture allowed for apprentices and tradespeople to undertake creative and adaptive activities, furthering their material knowledge and deepening their connection to their trade. These activities built a particular sensibility—a craft ethic—and a broad material understanding, which has had far-reaching consequences, beyond the direct application of a particular trade to industry. This also speaks to the far-reaching value of Australia's threatened vocational training system (TAFE), which has a long history of enriching the nation's skill base and productive capacity, as well as contributing to material culture, repair and creative life in deindustrialising communities. The key, then, is to retain the most positive and effective elements of apprenticeship: that is, practical learning approaches, a sense of collectivity, the development of a craft ethic, paid employment, and the freedom to create and make mistakes.

All that being said, contemporary and future apprenticeships must be structured so as to distance themselves from the sexism, abuse and punitive hierarchical relationships that once characterised this educational framework. As we saw in Chap. 6, institutionalised and overt sexism in the Australian manufacturing sector is a key aspect that requires reform. The stark gender-divisions in industrial trades, and the almost complete absence of skilled tradeswomen in heavy industry, are a major missed opportunity for the manufacturing workforce, as well as being a fundamental example of ongoing historical inequity and patriarchy.

As we saw in Chaps. 3, 4 and 7, engineering patternmakers are first and foremost *makers*, and they apply their knowledge and creative tendencies to a wide range of practical and artistic pursuits. They have the capacity to produce complex and precise three-dimensional form, be it timber, resin, metal or plastic. This is a fundamental human skill, albeit refined for particular industrial purposes. As we have seen throughout this book, patternmakers are more than happy to apply their skills to things that are not, strictly speaking, patterns, as long as they are given the intellectual and physical freedom to make, think and be creative. More broadly, we should not underestimate the broader contribution of trade skills to Australian cultural and artistic life, to education, and to the creative industries.

Through rarely acknowledged as a form of 'design knowledge', we saw in Chap. 4 how patternmakers are an example of vital intermediaries in the production of manufactured things. A focus on patternmaking (among other industrial crafts) enables us to understand how embedded design knowledge exists in minds and practices well beyond the designer's studio. As observed by Glenn Adamson,

> knowledge of one craft or trade can inform an understanding of many others … It also cultivates curiosity about the material world in general, the habit of wondering how pencils or pillows were made, and by whom.[19]

This rich knowledge of processes and materials has an inherent value, which should not be casually discarded with the arrival of new technologies and software programmes, as I explore in Chap. 5. As this chapter established, different craftspeople have different relations to technology, and there is no 'one size fits all' approach when it comes to applying technologies to a particular task. Every industrial craftsperson will tell you there are a large number of variables that must be taken into consideration when deciding which technologies, tools, materials or techniques to use, and the answer will not always be the most 'high end' technological one.

The Current Status of Engineering Patternmaking: A Dying Trade in High Demand?

When I began researching engineering patternmakers, I did not initially understand that I would be analysing what is likely to be the smallest ongoing trade in Australia. As noted in the Introduction, at the time of writing (2021) there are six apprentices currently undertaking an engineering patternmaking apprenticeship (Certificate II in Engineering—Fabrication) in Australia. Other deindustrialising economies show a similar trend: in the United States in 2020, the occupational category of "Patternmakers (Wood)" was one of the smallest occupations in the country, with 190 employees. (See Chap. 1 for full details.) With figures such as these, surely I was examining the 'last gasp' of a trade that is about to disappear, soon to be relegated to the category of an entertainment stall at a 'Lost Trades' fair? Yet, the more I dug, the more significant and relevant the patternmakers' skillset was shown to be.

For example, employers within the Australian foundry sector kept telling me how much patternmakers were in demand, how busy the remaining foundry businesses were, and how hard it was to find skilled workers in the trades they needed. In 2018, the Secretary of the Australian Foundry Institute, Joe Vecchio, told me:

> Everyone keeps saying foundries are a dinosaur industry, they're dying. But every foundry is busy right now, and they want new apprentices.[20]

In 2019, the President of the Australia Foundry Institute (Victoria Division) Amber Maxwell explained:

> The current Australian foundry workers represent an ageing population; in Victoria alone, many foundry employees are more than 50 years old and without training of apprentices our industry will suffer permanently.[21]

Likewise, from an employee perspective, patternmaker Stuart McCorkelle summed it up well:

> Certainly still the demand there! We can barely keep up! As a relatively 'young' patternmaker at 33, I find it daunting thinking of [the] future and the lack of people being trained in the foundry industry. No foundry industry means no patternmaking for me, and I don't really want to do anything other than make patterns, as I really enjoy the work.[22]

For many years Australian foundries have experienced difficulty finding fully qualified tradespeople and apprentices in engineering patternmaking and moulding.[23] One of the reasons for this is the fact that Australia only has two TAFE institutions offering patternmaking apprenticeships across the country, TAFE Queensland (Acacia Ridge) in Brisbane, and Goulburn Ovens TAFE (GOTAFE) in Victoria. To formalise their training, patternmaking apprentices often have to travel long distances and find accommodation for 'block-training'. The costs of this are often prohibitive for small- to medium-sized foundries and patternshops. Added to this is the fact that apprentices are often teenagers, with the unique challenges that this entails. In 2020 and 2021, Australian state-border travel restrictions resulting from the Covid-19 pandemic have further exacerbated these problems. Some businesses have resorted to using unskilled or semi-skilled labour and providing in-house training. Generally speaking, informal training has its limits and does not produce the depth and breadth of knowledge that is needed. What foundry employers seek is not just the patternmakers' skilled manual labour at the patternshop bench, but their specialist knowledge: their in-depth and practiced understanding of manufacturing processes, metallurgy, design form, materials and surface.

The fundamental basis of this knowledge need not be made redundant by technological change, but can in fact complement it, if technologies are employed in a way that respects existing craft knowledge and human dignity in labour. As noted by patternmaker Debra Schuckar, digital technologies alone are useless:

> I'm concerned that people will not learn to make things ... I understand we have computers, but computers are just a tool. If the person behind the computer doesn't know what they're putting in, because they don't have a practical feel of what they're doing, it's going to waste a lot of time ... I guess trades are there for a reason.[24]

This sentiment was echoed regularly by the tradespeople I spoke to, and it is by now a familiar one: without skilled, knowledgeable practitioners, digital technologies merely reproduce human mistakes perfectly.

We have seen how engineering patternmakers have complex understandings of manufacturing processes, materials, craft, fabrication and design. What would happen if we treated this knowledge and creativity as a resource, rather than a burden? In the second decade of the twenty-first century, we are now at risk of losing such skills and knowledge entirely, as patternmakers—among other skilled industrial craftspeople—shift industries or retire, with very few apprentices being trained in their wake. If something does not change, the end-result will be a profound knowledge-loss about how to make things as a sovereign nation. The engineering patternmaking example shows us that the decline of industrial trades is not a 'natural' result of market economics or automation. As we have seen in industries such as the foundry sector, the market demand for skilled workers is there. It was a political choice to ignore these industrial craft skills, and it can be a political choice to revive them and diversify their application.

Evidently, a healthy industrial craft sector can contribute to the growth of a quality, niche, local manufacturing sector. But there is something deeper at stake here. Industrial craft—residing as it does at the intersection of manual work and mechanical industry—humanises our relation to technology and mass-production, and keeps us in closer touch with the fundamentals of the material world. We cannot solely rely on digital solutions to the impending problems of the future. Without industrial craft, we would be far less capable and more superficial as human beings attempting to survive in this fragile world.

236   J. A. STEIN

NOTES

1. Bruce Phipps, interview with author, *Reshaping Australian Manufacturing*, 31 May 2018 (Canberra: National Library of Australia [NLA]), https://nla.gov.au/nla.cat-vn7765732.
2. Deborah Tyrrell, interview with author, *Reshaping Australian Manufacturing*, 19 October 2018 (Canberra: NLA), https://nla.gov.au/nla.cat-vn7861536.
3. Jim Stanford & Tom Swann, *Manufacturing: A Moment of Opportunity* (Canberra: Centre for Future Work, 2017).
4. Productivity Commission, *Trends in Australian Manufacturing* (Canberra: Productivity Commission, Australian Government, 2003).
5. "Manufacturing", *Labour Market Information Portal* (Canberra: Australian Government, April 2021), online: https://lmip.gov.au/default.aspx?LMIP/GainInsights/IndustryInformation/Manufacturing, accessed 14 June 2021.
6. Jenny Stewart, "Path Dependence, Policy Learning and Australian Manufacturing Since the 1970s", *Australian Journal of Political Science* 51, no. 4 (2016): 652–66.
7. Chris Gibson, Chantel Carr & Andrew Warren, "A Country that Makes Things?", *Australian Geographer* 43, no. 2 (2012): 109–13.
8. Thanks to Cameron Tonkinwise for this suggestion.
9. An example of a science/design collaboration in this arena is the University of Technology Sydney's (UTS) Material Ecologies Design Lab (MEDL), investigating possibilities for algae-based polymers (2021).
10. See, for example, James Gardiner's 3D printed reef scaffolds, in Museum of Applied Arts and Sciences, and Matthew Connell, *Out of Hand: Materialising the Digital* (Sydney: Museum of Applied Arts & Sciences, 2013).
11. For example, research led by UNSW academic Professor Veena Sahajwalla at the Centre for Sustainable Materials Research & Technology.
12. Chris Gibson & Andrew Warren, *The Guitar: Tracing the Grain Back to the Tree* (Chicago: University of Chicago Press, 2021).
13. There has been some recent progress, with the Australian Government's Productivity Commission's recent Right to Repair Inquiry recommending a suite of repair-related reforms. But there is a long way to go, see: Leanne Wiseman and Kanchana Kariyawasam, "US and EU Laws show Australia's Right to Repair Moment is Well Overdue", *The Conversation* (3 February 2020), online: https://theconversation.com/us-and-eu-laws-show-australias-right-to-repair-moment-is-well-overdue-127323, accessed 21 May 2021.
14. Ignaz Strebel, Alain Bovet & Phillipe Sormani (eds), *Repair Work Ethnographies: Revisiting Breakdown, Relocating Materiality* (Singapore: Palgrave Macmillan, 2019).

8 CONCLUSION: INDUSTRIAL CRAFT AND ALTERNATIVE FUTURES... 237

15. Stanford & Swann, *Manufacturing: A Moment of Opportunity*, 25–30.
16. William Mitchell & Thomas Fazi, *Reclaiming the State* (London: Pluto Press, 2017).
17. Mitchell & Fazi, *Reclaiming the State*, 12.
18. Mitchell & Fazi, *Reclaiming the State*, 1.
19. Glenn Adamson, "Material Intelligence", *Aeon* (28 November 2018), online: https://aeon.co/essays/do-you-know-your-stuff-the-ethics-of-the-material-world, accessed 3 June 2021.
20. Joe Vecchio, personal communication with author, December 2018. See also J.A. Stein, "Don't be too quick to dismiss 'dying trades', those skills are still in demand", *The Conversation* (6 December 2018), online: https://theconversation.com/dont-be-too-quick-to-dismiss-dying-trades-those-skills-are-still-in-demand-107894, accessed 1 June 2021.
21. Benalla Ensign, "Exciting Study Options", *Shepparton News* (1 February 2019), online: www.sheppnews.com.au/2019/02/01/420055/exciting-study-options?amp=1, accessed 3 June 2021.
22. Stuart McCorkelle, quotation from Patternmakers' Facebook group, online: www.facebook.com/groups/502920693172756/search/?q=stuart%20mccorkelle, accessed 1 March 2021.
23. Larissa Romensky, "Hard, Dirty Foundry Work Copes with Digital Disruption and Lack of Apprenticeship Courses", *ABC News* (Victoria), (30 September 2018), online: https://www.abc.net.au/news/2018-09-30/hard-dirty-foundry-work-coping-with-digital-disruption/10303254, accessed 2 June 2021.
24. Debra Schuckar, interview with author, *Reshaping Australian Manufacturing*, 23 February 2018 (Canberra: NLA), https://nla.gov.au/nla.cat-vn7580622.

Glossary

3D printing See *Additive manufacturing*.

5S A workplace management theory that emerged in Japan, which focuses on neatness, standardisation and optimal efficiency.

ACTU Australian Council of Trade Unions.

Additive manufacturing Also known as 3D printing, the production of form by depositing material in an additive, layering technique, through the use of a computer-controlled process.

AEU Amalgamated Engineering Union.

AMWU Australian Manufacturing Workers' Union.

Bog/Bog-filler Also known as 'Builder's Bog', bog is trade-quality polyester repair filler that mimics the behaviour of wood.

CAD/CAM Computer Aided Design and Computer Aided Manufacturing. CAD software is used to generate technical, two- and three-dimensional drawings and plans for the purposes of digital fabrication. CAM software controls the direction and function of digital fabrication machinery, such as CNC machines (see also *Toolpathing*).

Circular saw A manually controlled machine tool that cuts material (typically timber) through a rotating blade. First invented in the late eighteenth century and in widespread use by the mid-nineteenth century.

Clay modelling Used in this text to refer to the clay modelling of automotive prototypes. It refers to the hand-modelling in plasticine clay of a half-car prototype through a collaborative process between industrial designers, engineers and clay modellers (the latter are often pattern-

© The Author(s), under exclusive license to Springer Nature Switzerland AG 2021

J. A. Stein, *Industrial Craft in Australia*, Palgrave Studies in Oral History, https://doi.org/10.1007/978-3-030-87243-4

240 GLOSSARY

makers or industrial modelmakers). Typically undertaken on a half-car model, it is then digitally replicated for the other side. While this technique dates back to the 1930s, some automotive designers still employ this method in their design stages as it can be quicker to make changes than through digital fabrication.

CNC machines Computer numerically controlled machines use a robotic arm with a tool attached and are controlled through computer software programs. CNC milling, for instance, subtractively mills material from a solid form. CNC machines are wide-ranging and can be used for milling, drilling, cutting, laser cutting and so on, and can be used on a wide range of materials, including timber, plastic, metal and glass. CNC differs from other standard workshop machinery, such as mechanical saws, electric drills and electric lathes, in that CNC is controlled by a computer program, while the others are manually controlled machine tools. See Chap. 5.

Contraction rule Also known as a 'shrink rule', contraction rules are a measurement tool that enables the calculation of the shrinkage of metal when it cools. They are material-specific, with rules for steel, iron, bronze, aluminium and so on.

Contraction See Shrinkage (metal casting).

Coreboxes Sometimes used in sand-casting, coreboxes are the box in which the core is made.

Cores Cores are used most commonly in the sand-casting process, but also in die casting, vacuum forming and injection moulding. They are forms that are used to produce internal cavities in a form.

Die casting A form of metal casting using high pressure in a moulding cavity, using steel dies.

Foreigners Also known as *foreign orders*, foreigners are an Australian colloquial term for objects made by workers at work, in work time, that are not part of the productive business of the enterprise. Also known as *homers*, side productions and *la perruque*, among other geographically specific terms. See Chap. 3.

GDP Gross Domestic Product.

Gravity dies A form of die casting for metals, particularly light alloys, using the force of gravity for accurately dimensioned and sharply defined form.

'High-Vis' Fluorescent high-visibility safety clothing, now ubiquitous and often mandatory in industrial and construction worksites.

GLOSSARY 241

Jobbing shop Also known as *job shop*, jobbing shops are typically small-to medium-size businesses that have no particular specialisation in their trade, but take on a wide variety of jobs, often producing small quantities and bespoke products.

Lathe A manually controlled machine tool that rotates a workpiece in an axis of rotation, producing a variety of effects, including cutting, drilling, smoothing, turning and facing.

Layout A traditional pattern planning drawing in the patternmaking process.

Leading hand A leadership role within a workshop or factory environment, usually in charge of a number of tradespeople and apprentices.

Mastercam A proprietary CAD/CAM software program.

Methoding Foundry terminology for manufacturing methods planning involving patterns, moulding and casting.

Millwright A modern millwright is a skilled industrial craftsperson who installs, maintains, repairs and moves machinery in industrial contexts. The mediaeval usage of the term 'millwright' was much broader, pertaining to the specialised knowledge, machine production and manual work conducted at mediaeval mills.

Moulder A qualified tradesperson with a specialisation in the industrial craft of pouring of molten metal into moulds, particularly pertaining to metal casting but the skills can be more broadly applied.

NLA National Library of Australia, Canberra.

OH&S Occupational Health & Safety (Australia).

Pattern A three-dimensional original, a positive form, which is used to generate a mould, for processes including but not limited to metal casting, die casting and injection moulding. Historically, patterns tended to be made out of timber, but can also be made from plaster, fibreglass, plastic modelling board, resin and metal.

Patternmaker A qualified tradesperson with a specialisation in planning and producing patterns, cores, coreboxes (and other collateral materials), for production processes involving moulding and casting. In Australia they are officially known as *Engineering Patternmakers*. A more extensive definition is provided in Chap. 1, and their processes and techniques are outlined in detail in Chaps. 4 and 5.

Patternshop The workshop in which patterns were produced by patternmakers.

RMIT Royal Melbourne Institute of Technology (RMIT).

242 GLOSSARY

Sand-casting The casting of molten metal in sand moulds, typically undertaken in metal foundries.

Shrink rule See *Contraction rule.*

Shrinkage The way in which metal contracts as it cools, in the casting process.

SolidWorks A proprietary CAD design software program.

TAFE Technical and Further Education. Australia's publicly funded vocational education training system.

Taper Taper is a gentle angle on a pattern that allows a pattern to be effectively removed from a mould, without damaging the mould. It is best demonstrated through close examination of a child's plastic sand bucket and wet sand. The bucket can be removed from the sandcastle underneath, because of its taper.

Toolmaker A qualified tradesperson who makes and repair tools, dies, jigs, fixtures and other precision parts to fine tolerances, for machine tools and other production machinery.

Toolpathing The direction and pathway of a drill bit through material in the CNC process.

UPMA United Patternmakers' Association.

Vacuum forming An industrial process whereby a sheet of plastic is heated to a forming temperature and stretched onto a mould by a vacuum. Vacuum forming produces products such as plastic fruit trays and plastic display trays for cosmetics and grocery items.

Vernier callipers A precision measurement tool.

INDEX

NUMBERS AND SYMBOLS
3D Printing, *see* Additive manufacturing
5S, 86–88, 239

A
Adamson, Glenn, 3, 4, 99, 100, 194, 219, 220, 233
Additive manufacturing, 5, 13, 23, 114, 115, 126, 141, 143, 179, 195, 239
 3D sand printing, 13
Adorno, Theodor, 194
Adzing, 207
Ageing workforce, 14, 131
Alcohol
 alcoholism, 136
 in Australian culture, 207
Alienation (of labour), 129
Amalgamated Engineering Union (AEU), 53, 182, 239
Amateur craft, 66, 193

Amateur design, *see* Design
Ansett Airways, 11
Anti-discrimination law, 159, 163
Apprentice Commission of Victoria, 211
Apprenticeship
 Australian apprenticeship, 65, 67, 68
 block training, 234
 child abuse, 68
 initiation/hazing, 68
 learning by doing, 66
 patternmaking apprentices, 24, 48, 49, 64, 66, 67, 69, 74, 78, 79, 85, 90n7, 104, 132, 135, 136, 139, 167, 205, 210, 211, 233, 234
 pedagogical approach, 66–70, 72, 77–80, 89
 technical colleges, 68
 trade educators, 44
 trade school, 68
 underfunding, 5, 13, 231

© The Author(s), under exclusive license to Springer Nature Switzerland AG 2021
J. A. Stein, *Industrial Craft in Australia*, Palgrave Studies in Oral History, https://doi.org/10.1007/978-3-030-87243-4

244 INDEX

Aristocracy of labour, 44, 47, 50
Art critics, 198
Art Gallery of New South Wales, 216
Artists
    art education, 212, 219
    artist-craftspeople, 194
    patternmakers as, 191–221
Arts & Craft Movement, 99
Ash Wednesday (Bushfires), 63,
        78, 79, 226
Assemblages (sculpture), 192,
        215–217, 220
Austerity, 231
Australian Council of Trade Unions
        (ACTU), 13, 239
Australian Foundry Institute, 233
Australian Manufacturing Workers'
        Union (AMWU), 53, 55,
        226, 239
Australian nationalism, 55
Australian Society of Engineers, 54
Automation, 122, 124, 125, 143, 152,
        162, 235
Automotive manufacturing, see Car
        manufacturing
Axe-making
    axe-sharpening, 35, 36
    competition axes, 35, 36

B
'Battler' identity (Australia), 41
Baudrillard's simulacra, 201
Bell Aircraft, 130
Bendigo Community Radio, 22
Beza Patterns, 136
Bio-plastics, 228
Blacksmith, 53
Boat-building, 138
Boilermaking, 4
Bolsonaro, Jair, 39, 42
Book-keeping, 175, 177, 179

Breadwinner, 26, 210
Bricklayer, 121, 167
Bushfires, 63, 79, 226

C
Cabinetmakers/cabinetmaking, 8, 46,
        108, 131, 140
Calder, Alexander, 213
Canada, 23, 59n16, 61n39, 147, 148,
        165, 226
Capitalism, 37, 38, 41, 52, 53, 82
Car manufacturing, 13, 133, 134
    Australian car manufacturing, 10
    closure of (in Australia), 13
    flow-on industries, 10, 13, 51
Carpenters, 8, 108
Casting (metal)
    aluminium casting, 11, 107, 240
    cast metal machine parts, 9, 35
    Chinese metal casting, 7
    history of, 6
    Mesopotamia, 7
    steel casting, 12, 35
Centrelink, 201
Childcare, 4, 21, 57, 165, 185
China, 7, 14, 144, 177, 226
    Australian diplomatic tensions, 14
Circular saw, 77, 108, 202, 203, 239
Class
    contradictory class position, 33, 50
    middle class, 41, 42, 70, 160, 170,
        177, 209, 212, 214
    and power, 40, 41
    professional class, 39, 134
    as relational, 40
    tension, 43, 134
    use of the term, 39–41
    war, 39
    white working class, 39, 41
    working class (Australia), 41, 46,
        47, 209, 231

INDEX   245

working class (United States),
  18, 41, 100
Clay Modelling (automotive
  design), 213
Climate change
  carbon emissions, 231
  fossil fuels, 225
  renewable energy, 231
Cockatoo Island, 54
Collectivity, 33, 124, 232
Commonwealth Bank (Australia),
  177, 178
Compositors, 123
Computer Aided Design (CAD), 5, 8,
  13, 25, 49, 89, 113, 114, 123,
  124, 126, 128–131, 139–145,
  148, 152, 153, 179, 180, 184,
  195, 198, 239, 241, 242
Computer Aided Manufacturing
  (CAM), 5, 8, 13, 25, 114, 123,
  124, 126, 128, 130, 131, 142,
  153, 179, 192, 198, 239, 241
Computer numerically controlled
  machines (CNC)
  CNC machine centre, 148
  CNC milling machines, 5, 13, 123,
    126, 130
  laser CNC cutter, 142
  NC machinery, 124, 130
Conceptual art, 193, 211, 213
Confectionery jubes, 6
Conservatism (United Kingdom), 43
Constructivism, 197
Cosmetics (plastic displays), 143, 242
Cottage-industry, 152
Covid-19 pandemic, 14, 226,
  228, 234
Craft masculinity, *see* Gender
Creative industries, 146, 218, 232
Creativity, 72, 106, 115, 134, 192,
  194, 195, 206, 220, 221,
  231, 235

creative practice, 3, 4, 19, 24, 26,
  57, 192–194, 205,
  206, 219–221
Cross, Nigel, 25, 96–98,
  104–106, 110
Culture industries, 18

D

Dadswell, Lyndon, 218
De Certeau, Michel, 70
De Stijl, 197
Decent work, 134
Deckel machine, 147
Deindustrialisation
  in Australia, 6, 12–14, 42,
    58, 191–221
  'half life' of, 18
Deindustrialization and the Politics of
  Our Time (DéPOT), 18, 60n16
Democratic Labor Party
  (Australia), 14
Democratic Party (United
  States), 39, 40
Deplorables, 41
Des Renahans' Patternshop, 206
Design, 95
  amateur design/non-professional
    design, 95, 101
  design thinking, 35, 106, 114
  history, 6, 16, 17, 24, 30n29, 95,
    97–101, 114
  industrial designer, 96, 104,
    112–115, 239
  intermediaries of, 95–115
  processes, 104
  star-designer, 100
  teaching design, 213
Design knowledge, 25,
  95–115, 232–233
  contestation of, 97
Deskilling, 115, 141, 142

246   INDEX

Die-casting, 8
Digital fabrication technologies, 4, 5,
    13, 67, 98, 115, 125, 152, 181
Digital labour, 5
Domestic labour, 167, 178, 185
Doug Evans' Foundry, 136
Drawing
    design & engineering drawings, 103
    technical drawing, 9, 66, 69, 103
Duterte, Rodrigo, 39

E
East Sydney Technical College, 218
Electricity generation, 11
Engineering patternmaking
    as a black art, 1
    engineering patternmakers, 1–27,
        33, 34, 37, 44–50, 53, 61n38,
        63, 64, 69, 96, 123, 134,
        164–167, 173, 177, 178, 184,
        200, 232, 233, 235, 241
    as an identity, 34, 66, 67, 88
    and metallurgy, 9, 10
    and moulding, 6, 8, 9, 11, 12, 50,
        69, 170, 234, 241
    patterns, 3, 6–9, 11–16, 23, 27, 47,
        50, 53, 78, 80, 82, 83, 89,
        100, 102, 103, 105–112,
        122–125, 127–130, 132–134,
        137, 139–145, 147, 150, 153,
        170, 176, 178, 192, 195, 197,
        198, 204, 210, 215, 218, 232,
        234, 241
    as a process, 6–8, 12, 14, 24, 34,
        38, 69, 96, 97, 101–104, 106,
        107, 109–114, 124, 127–129,
        135, 140–142, 176, 179, 180,
        234, 235, 241
    rarity of, 15–16, 52, 233
    and recognition, 67

and technological change, 8, 11–13,
    25–27, 123, 124
traditional forms of, 6, 8,
    101–106, 127–129
and wood-carving, 206
Engineers, 45, 48, 104, 105,
    107, 111–114, 123, 128–130,
    134, 135, 140–142, 153,
    228, 239
Ephemera – in oral history
    interviews, 23
Equal employment opportunity, 26,
    163, 173
E-waste, 228
Exhibitions, 135, 196, 197, 202,
    208, 222n30

F
Facebook, 15, 23, 37, 150
    Patternmakers' Facebook
        Group, 15, 150
Fascism, 39, 41–42
Factory closures, 192
    See also Plant Closures
Family business, 51, 147, 178, 184
Far-right extremists, 39
Fazi, Thomas, 60n29, 229–231
Female apprentices, see Women
    in trades
Feminism, 38
Feminist art, 211, 212
Fine arts (education)
    art school environment, 219
    teaching fine arts, 213
Finishing (manufacturing process)
    hand-finishing, 2
    sanding, 123, 140
Fitting and turning, 4, 53, 160, 164,
    170, 210
Ford, 134

Foreigners (colloquial term), 25, 70, 79, 240
Forestry industry, 11, 35
Fossicking, 177, 178
Foundry, 5, 11, 15, 23, 34–37, 49, 53, 55, 66, 69, 79, 80, 83, 84, 86, 87, 105, 111, 112, 114, 123, 125, 126, 128, 139, 142, 170, 176, 192, 200, 210, 216, 233–235, 241
  Australian foundry sector, 5, 233
Frances Keevil Gallery, 197
Freemantle, Anthony, 23, 69, 74, 85, 108, 118n42, 152, 157n75
Freemasons, 182

G

Gender, 27, 35, 44–46, 76, 122, 160, 161, 163, 185n3, 191, 210, 212, 214, 219, 221, 231
  craft masculinity, 76, 231
  division of labour, 160, 161
  gendered identities, 185n3, 231
  gendered memories, 19, 181
  gender-labour segregation, 26, 159
  gender-pay gap, 160
  masculinity (Australia), 185n3
  in oral history, 4, 26, 56, 161, 181–184
  patriarchal rituals, 68
  social construction of, 214
General Motors Holden, 134
Gentrification, 18
George Thompson School of Foundry Technology, 69, 132, 171
Global Financial Crisis (2007-08), 13, 39, 127, 231
Globalisation, 4, 55, 123, 147, 229
  global trade, 147
Gore, Wally, 139
Graham Campbell Ferrum, 200
Gravity dies, 147, 240

H

Haidutschyk, Serge, 9, 49, 50, 54, 55, 77, 78, 81, 82, 88, 95, 182, 191, 199–204, 218
Hand Tool Preservation Association of Australia, 23
Hand tools, 9, 23, 35, 46, 53, 65, 66, 79–83, 89, 123, 128, 136, 137, 139
Hanson, Pauline, 39
Heritage
  industrial heritage, 1
  living heritage, 2
H. H. Phipps Pty. Ltd., 146–149
High, Steven, 4, 24, 28n6, 40
High-vis, 14, 34, 43, 240
Hohaus, Hermann, 206–207
Homers, *see* Foreigners
Horner, Joseph, 125
Howard, John, 41
Hughes, Robert, 216
Huon Pine, 11, 202, 208

I

IBM, 178
Identity politics, 37, 41, 60n29
Industrial craft
  and academic recognition, 3–4, 16
  as bygone, 37
  defined, 57
  and knowledge, 14, 95–115, 124, 226, 233
  and manufacturing, 2, 6, 27, 235
Industrial modelmakers/industrial modelmaking, 8, 10, 142, 192, 204, 218, 220, 240
Industrial revolution, 3, 7, 99, 115
Industrial zoning, 146, 218
Innovation, 5, 35, 114, 122
  disruptive innovation, 122, 154n4
International Harvester Company, 48, 64, 205

248 INDEX

J

Jacquard loom, 130
Japan, 14, 130, 204, 239
Jobbing shops, 11, 12, 23, 241
John Williams Patterns, 132, 137
Judd, Donald, 193
Julian Ashton Art School, 196

K

Kay, Paul, 51, 52, 55, 75, 85, 88, 109,
    110, 124, 150–152,
    191, 195–214
Kimbeny Pty. Ltd, 143–146
Klippel, Robert, 27, 191, 192, 194,
    195, 214–220, 221n3

L

La perruque, *see* Foreigners
Labor Party (Australian) (ALP), 14
Labour histories, 5, 17, 71, 162
Labour market, 3, 166
Lanceley, Colin, 215
Land art, 193, 211
Lathe, 67, 82–85, 108, 240, 241
Left politics, 38–39, 41–42, 55, 60
Leslie, Edward, 47
Liberalism (Australia), 40
Liberal-National Coalition
    (Australian), 13
Life history form (oral history),
    19, 56
Lifting (heavy industrial), 162
Linkon, Sherry Lee, 18, 19, 28n6
Linotype machines, 163
Looker, John, 74, 76, 83, 84, 112
Lorne Sculpture Biennale, 208
Lost Trades fairs, 2, 233
Lula (Lula da Silva, Luiz Inácio), 42
Luthier, 46

M

Machine tools (manually controlled),
    49, 66, 82, 108, 123, 128, 165,
    195, 239–241
Maintenance, 27, 88, 89, 129,
    155n14, 228
  workers, 54, 200
Manual Production
  hand-built house construction, 205
  making patterns by hand, 6, 49, 86,
    127–128, 139
Manufacturing
  in Asia, 34, 127
  in China, 144
  employment in, 3, 40
  employment in Australia, 13, 227
  lean manufacturing, 80, 85
  local manufacturing industry
    (Australia), 13–14,
    35, 227–229
  local manufacturing industry
    (United States), 29–40, 67
  management of/managers, 67,
    135, 140
  National self-sufficiency, 14
  'offshoring' of, 127, 144, 183
  specialist/niche production, 5, 8,
    228, 235
  state involvement in, 27, 227
  workers in, 24
Masculinity, *see* Gender
Mass-production, 2, 6, 48, 50,
    204, 235
Master Patternmakers' Association of
    New South Wales, 153
Material knowledge, 3, 232
Maternity leave, 174
Maxwell, Amber, 234
McCorkelle, Stuart, 11, 12, 234
Men's Sheds, 2
Metallurgy, 9, 10, 83, 234

INDEX 249

Midland Railway Workshops (Western Australia), 72
Migrants, 37, 38, 41, 42, 55, 57, 209
Millwright, 16, 47, 131, 155n14, 241
Mimovich, Leopoldine, 206
Minimalism art, 193, 211
Mining/Minerals extraction, 9, 13, 14, 35, 69, 112, 225, 227
MIT, 130
Mitchell, William, 60n29, 229–231
Modelmakers, *see* Industrial modelmakers
Modern Monetary Theory (MMT), 230
Mondragon Corporation, 160
Moore, Henry, 212
Moulders, 7, 10, 47, 104, 107, 128, 142, 210, 241
Moulding (in metal casting), 6, 8, 9, 11, 12, 69, 240, 241
Murrells, Scott, 1, 28n2, 88, 105, 108, 112, 113, 118n43, 124, 132–135, 137, 155n21
Museums Victoria, 65, 79

N

Nationalism, 55, 60n29, 231
in Australia, 231
National Library of Australia (NLA)
Audio Management and Delivery System, 23
digital audio, 23
sound quality, 22
timed summaries, 23
National Taskforce on Tradeswomen's Issues (USA), 166
New Zealand, 23, 73, 77, 91n32
Noble, David F., 130, 131
Noke, John, 84
Nostalgia, 2
for traditional 'craftsmen,' 2, 17

O

Oral history
as a co-production of meaning, 19, 21, 43
and deindustrialisation, 6, 18, 24
and feminism, 38
and gender in, 4, 181
interviewing, 21
listening to, 23
and social class, 24, 27, 38, 40
sound quality, 22
and tradespeople, 17, 21, 33
and women's stories, 181

P

Palmer, Clive, 39
Pantographic machine, 11
Paperboy, 46
Parenting, 140, 175, 212
Parr, Lenton, 206
Part-time work, 212
Pattern planning methods
digital methods planning, 123
layout, 241
methoding/methoder, 123
Patternshops, 8, 10–12, 23, 47, 50, 51, 54, 55, 66, 68, 72, 74, 78–80, 86, 87, 99, 101, 111, 124–134, 136, 137, 140, 146, 150, 153, 175, 176, 180, 206, 210, 211, 234, 241
Phipps, Bruce, 54, 73, 74, 78, 80, 106, 111, 124, 147, 148, 225
Phipps, Peter, 48, 51, 54, 74, 79, 81, 88, 89, 111, 112, 146–149
Plant closures, 17
Plastics production, 8
plastic injection moulding, 6, 8
plastics industry, 8, 206
vacuum forming, 143, 242

250 INDEX

Political populism, 231
Polyurethane board (modelling
board), 127, 129
Poynton, Bryan, 11, 48, 49, 63–65,
73, 78–80, 86, 103, 108, 109,
182, 191, 205–209, 216, 218,
219, 222n29
Precarious work, 88, 175
Precision, 7, 8, 47, 48, 77, 108, 115,
124, 128, 130, 195, 206, 242
dimensional accuracy, 8
Pre-production (manufacturing
process), 2, 7, 11, 50, 97, 149
Printing industry
computerisation of, 123
computerised typesetting, 142
Privatisation (of government assets), 200
Production line, 2, 7, 50, 99
Prop-making, 209
Prototypes, 3, 100, 239
Public education, 68
Putting out system, 152

Q
Quarry workers, 19
Qwerty keyboard, 142

R
Racism, 40, 41, 70
Readymades (sculpture), 192
Repair
community-led repair, 229
repair rights, 229
repair skills/skilled repairers, 229
Retirement, 16, 66, 83–85, 152, 195,
196, 200
Retraining, 4, 25, 26, 129, 130, 132,
135, 138, 140, 142
Rifkin, Jeremy, 137, 138
Robotics, 2, 115, 126, 128, 240
factories, 99

Rohlfs, Charles, 100, 115
Roldán, Doña María, 181, 183
Royal Australian Navy, 218
Royal Melbourne Institute
of Technology (RMIT),
69, 137, 170, 171, 206, 211,
213, 241
Royal Melbourne Show, 202
Rubinich, Jon-Michael, 74
Ruskin, John, 99
Russell, Bertrand, 211
Rust belt (United States), 39, 40

S
Schuckar, Debra, 76, 77, 88, 103,
104, 161, 166–177, 183, 184,
191, 212, 235
Scientific management, 85–86
Sculpture
attitudes to, 212–213, 215–218
modernist sculpture, 219
sculptural practice, 207, 219
Service economy, 2, 55
Sewing, 175, 178
Sex-discrimination, 159
Sexism, 160, 163, 180, 232
Sexual harassment, 159, 173
Ship-building, 54
shipyards, 11 (*see also*
Cockatoo Island)
Shopfloor, 67, 73, 86, 114, 123,
124, 129, 136, 137, 141, 142,
155n14, 160
Shrinkage (cooling metal), 107, 108,
127, 128
Single parenthood, 177
single mother, 174, 212
Skilled manufacturing workers, 2, 4,
95, 99, 226, 233–235
Skill loss/knowledge loss, 14, 131,
135, 149, 230, 235
Skills shortages, 147, 163, 166, 220

INDEX 251

Slöjd, 227
Small businesses, 10, 24, 33, 34, 40, 41,
  44, 50–52, 123, 124, 127, 129,
  143–150, 152, 161, 177, 181, 225
  owners, 24, 40, 52, 127, 161, 225
Smith, David, 219
Smith, Stephen (patternmaker),
  71, 72, 77
The Socialist, 12, 53
Software
  mastercam, 147, 180
  SolidWorks, 143, 145, 179
Sole-trader/entrepreneur, 37, 40
South Africa, 165
South African Railways, 74
Sovereignty, 229, 230
Standardisation, 25, 72, 85–88
Steel production, *see* Foundry
Supply chains, 2, 7, 8, 14, 16,
  152, 230
Surfboard-making, 131

T
Tablehands, 159, 162
TAFE
  GO TAFE Victoria, 16, 234
  TAFE Queensland, 16, 23, 69, 85,
    152, 234
Tariffs (Australian manufacturing), 13,
  127, 147, 229
Teaching
  qualifications for, 138
  secondary education, 45
Technical High Schools, 45
Technological change
  boredom at work, 133
  embrace of, 115, 152
  labour replacement, 145
  technological determinism, 130
  time-lag in technological uptake, 6
  See also Retraining
Teenagers, 137, 138, 170, 234

Textiles manufacturing, 46
Timber craftsmanship, 8, 46, 73, 79,
  82, 141, 207
  craft mastery of, 8
  decorative woodwork, 202
  difficulty of, 77, 198
  woodworking, 46, 66
Timbers
  Australian timbers, 78, 202
  dimensionally stable timber, 9, 11,
    128, 204
Tool allowance, 66, 79
Toolboxes
  handmade, 6, 8, 66, 67, 81, 85–88,
    108, 206
  mass-produced metal toolboxes, 85
  toolmakers toolboxes, 73
Tool designer, 135
Tooling, 4, 6, 12, 51, 105, 110,
  113, 145
Toolmaking/toolmakers, 4, 8, 11, 48,
  53, 73, 74, 104, 131, 148,
  209, 210
Toolpathing (CNC), 128, 179, 180
Trades
  Australian industrial trades, 4, 166
  Camaraderie, 210
  educators, 44, 83–85
  job for life, 173
  school, 68, 69, 84, 139, 171, 172
  tradesmen, 21, 26, 46, 54, 174,
    211, 214, 217
  tradesperson, 4, 7, 44, 66, 149,
    173, 177, 204, 214, 241
  tradeswomen (*see* Women in trades)
Transcripts (oral history), 4, 6, 17–26,
  33–58, 58n5, 67, 89, 98, 101,
  138, 161, 167, 181–184,
  219, 221
Trump, Donald, 24, 36, 39, 40
Tupperware
  making of, 8
  parties, 179

252 INDEX

Tyrrell, Deborah, 51, 61n38, 113, 114, 143–146, 156n51, 161, 177–181, 183, 184, 225, 236n2
Tyrrell, Greg, 124, 143–146, 178–181

U

Unemployment/underemployment, 5, 35, 129, 137, 163, 200, 204
Unions
  amalgamation, 53
  closed shop, 54
  craft control, 44
  membership, 50, 54, 55, 210
  non-unionised workers, 24
  unionised patternmakers, 34, 52, 53
  unionised workers, 24
United Kingdom (UK) / Britain, 23, 26, 43, 53, 59n16, 61n39, 67, 70, 91n32, 112, 142, 163–165, 226
United Patternmakers' Association (UPMA) (United Kingdom), 53
United States (US), 14, 15, 23, 39, 41, 70, 130, 131, 163, 166, 204, 211, 229, 233

V

Vacuum moulding, *see* Plastics production
Vecchio, Joe, 233
Vickers Ruwolt, 210–212
Victorian College of the Arts (VCA), 211, 212
Victorian Railways' Newport Workshops, 49
Victorian State Electricity Commission (SEC), 76, 167, 169–174, 176

W

Wages, 13, 46, 51, 53, 55, 82, 149, 182, 218, 226
Walker, Jim, 84, 182
Watts, Peter, 57, 161, 182, 191, 209–214, 217, 219
Wedgwood, 100
Welders, 53, 131
W. G. Kay & Co. Pty. Ltd., 51, 150–152
White nationalism, 39, 41
Whitlam Government (Australia), 211
Wighton, Tim, 7, 22, 48, 49, 55, 56, 80, 86–88, 102, 104, 105, 111, 113, 114, 124, 139–142, 153, 182, 191, 218
Williams, Peter, 6, 45, 46, 69, 101, 104, 107, 109, 122, 124, 125, 132, 135–138, 182
Women in trades, 164–167, 171, 172, 183
  Tradeswomen Australia (Organisation), 166
Woodchopping (competition), 35, 36
Woodworking, *see* Timber craftsmanship
Workbench, 75, 86, 87
World War II
  reconstruction, 16
  refugees/post-war migrants, 55
Wright, Erik Olin, 52

X

Xenophobia, 40

Z

Zweig, Michael, 24, 34, 40, 41

Printed in the United States
by Baker & Taylor Publisher Services